Conducting Psychological Research

Developing Skills for Career Success and Social Impact

Danijela Serbic

Victoria Bourne

OXFORD
UNIVERSITY PRESS

Great Clarendon Street, Oxford, OX2 6DP,
United Kingdom

Oxford University Press is a department of the University of Oxford.
It furthers the University's objective of excellence in research, scholarship,
and education by publishing worldwide. Oxford is a registered trade mark of
Oxford University Press in the UK and in certain other countries

© Oxford University Press 2025

The moral rights of the authors have been asserted.

All rights reserved. No part of this publication may be reproduced, stored in a retrieval system, transmitted, used for text and data mining, or used for training artificial intelligence, in any form or by any means, without the prior permission in writing of Oxford University Press, or as expressly permitted by law, by licence or under terms agreed with the appropriate reprographics rights organization. Enquiries concerning reproduction outside the scope of the above should be sent to the Rights Department, Oxford University Press, at the address above.

You must not circulate this work in any other form
and you must impose this same condition on any acquirer.

Published in the United States of America by Oxford University Press
198 Madison Avenue, New York, NY 10016, United States of America

British Library Cataloguing in Publication Data

Data available

Library of Congress Control Number: 2025932094

ISBN 978-0-19-885065-6

Printed in the UK by
Bell & Bain Ltd., Glasgow

The manufacturer's authorised representative in the EU for product safety is Oxford University Press España S.A. of El Parque Empresarial San Fernando de Henares, Avenida de Castilla, 2 - 28830 Madrid (www.oup.es/en or product.safety@oup.com). OUP España S.A. also acts as importer into Spain of products made by the manufacturer.

Links to third party websites are provided by Oxford in good faith and
for information only. Oxford disclaims any responsibility for the materials
contained in any third party website referenced in this work.

Danijela Serbic: For my kids and my husband.

Victoria Bourne: For my family, yet again!

Meet the Authors

Danijela Serbic (Department of Psychology, Royal Holloway, University of London)
Danijela is a Professor (Education Focused) and the Director of Undergraduate Programmes in the Department of Psychology at Royal Holloway, University of London. She coordinates the Final Year Research Project module in the department, and has developed the module to embed employability and open science practice throughout. Additionally, she is a Chartered Psychologist, a member of the British Psychological Society Undergraduate Education Committee, and a Senior Fellow of the Higher Education Academy. Her contributions to teaching have been recognized through several awards, including the prestigious Higher Education Psychology Teacher of the Year 2023 from the British Psychological Society.

Victoria Bourne (Department of Psychology, Royal Holloway, University of London)
Victoria is a Professor (Education Focused) at Royal Holloway, University of London. She has taught research methodology and statistical analysis at all levels from first-year undergraduate students through to advanced postdoctoral researchers. At Royal Holloway, she is Deputy Head (Education) of the Department of Psychology, where she coordinates and teaches on the first- and second-year undergraduate research modules. Professor Bourne is the author of *Starting Out in Methods and Statistics for Psychology* and of *Understanding Quantitative and Qualitative Research in Psychology: A Practical Guide to Methods, Statistics, and Analysis*, both published by Oxford University Press.

Preface

For most psychology students, the final year research project is the pinnacle of their degree. However, few textbooks exist that aim to support students through the entire process beyond simply designing a study and analysing data. For us, three elements have often seemed to be lacking in this vital step in the student journey: enhancing employability, working with open science principles, and thinking more broadly about our social responsibility as psychologists.

Learning to become a researcher is an aspect of the psychology curriculum that many students feel apprehensive about. However, it offers many opportunities for you to develop a wide range of skills that will benefit you (and others) as you progress through your career. Throughout this book, we encourage you to recognize the skills that you are developing through your research project and to then think through how these can help you in succeeding in your career.

One of the exciting things about being a psychological researcher is that our understanding of how people think, feel, and behave is constantly developing, as are the methods that we use. In this book, we have tried to reflect this, partly by discussing open science principles throughout but also through chapters that support you in understanding, developing, and running more complex pieces of psychological research.

Finally, we passionately believe that education is for everybody, but at times research can feel a little sterile and exclusive. We aim to empower students to follow their passion and to develop the skills and confidence to become independent researchers who can make a difference in the world. This comes not only from the research skills that you will inevitably develop through this process but also from working with others in a range of ways.

We hope that this book will help you to develop the skills and confidence you need to build the career and life that you want and deserve.

Danijela Serbic
Victoria Bourne

Acknowledgements

We are both passionate about supporting students in their academic journeys, and this book is the product of many years spent teaching, supervising, and chatting with students. Thank you to all our students who have helped shape our ideas and the way we approach developing your education. Particular thanks must go to Holly Lawrence and Nusayba Saeed, who spent many hours reading through and commenting on draft chapters from this book, giving us a vital insight into how students will use the book and making many helpful suggestions that have greatly improved it.

In our department, we are lucky to be around a large number of education-focused academics who are passionate about enhancing psychology education in a wide range of ways. Working in an environment where pedagogy is valued, discussed, and created has enabled us to develop the ideas in this book, and we are incredibly grateful for this – in particular, the people in the THESIS group (https://thesis.psychologyresearch.co.uk), which has been so supportive and inspirational as it has grown over the past few years.

Many people at Oxford University Press have helped us to turn some ideas into a book, but Martha Bailes was particularly supportive in the very early stages of working out what the book would be about and how to embed our values within it. Thank you also to the anonymous reviewers who gave incredibly helpful feedback on the book. Finally, thank you to the employers and students who anonymously contributed their experiences and advice, and allowed us to develop these into the hints and tips that you see throughout the book.

Danijela

I would like to express my deepest gratitude to my husband, Sinisa, and our children, Jelena and Stefan, for their magnificent support throughout this journey. Your love, encouragement, and interest in my work have meant the world to me and I dedicate this book to you. I am especially grateful to my daughter Jelena for her kind and meticulous proofreading of several chapters.

I am also thankful to my former colleagues and dear friends, Inês Mendes and Alana James, whose dedication to inclusive education and boundless kindness have been invaluable. Lastly, my professional journey has been greatly impacted and shaped by my co-author, Victoria Bourne. Her passion for education and unwavering support have been constant sources of inspiration to me.

I am truly fortunate to have such amazing people in my life. Thank you all for being there for me.

Victoria

I am lucky enough to work in a department that is filled with talented academics who are kind, funny, and supportive. They also put up with listening to me chatting away about the joys of teaching statistics and various pedagogic endeavours. So, a thank you for putting up with me to my wonderful former colleagues, Inês Mendes and Alana James, and to those (in no particular order) who still put up with my popping by their office to disrupt their day: Jessie Ricketts, Luke Kendrick, Sam Fairlamb, James Ravenhill, Gemma Northam, and Narender Ramnani. Of course, extra special thanks as always to my wonderful friend Dawn Watling, the other half of my brain and the keeper of my chocolate supplies. Finally, a massive thank you to my co-author Danijela Serbic. This is absolutely your book and your passion for education shines through. Thank you for asking me to join you on this journey.

As ever, my wonderful family are the people who are always there to support me and to distract me from work. My mum and dad are just the best, and I am so grateful for all that they do. My husband, Mat, is beyond patient and supportive. Thank you for always being there for me and for not laughing when I bring up the possibility of writing another book!

Finally, it has to be my wonderful daughter Elizabeth. As I write this, she will soon turn ten years old and I have no idea where the time has gone. But she is just the best kid ever: funny, smart, and she bakes the best cakes going. I feel so lucky to have her in my life.

Outline Contents

Dedication v
Meet the Authors vi
Preface vii
Acknowledgements viii

Section 1: **Planning psychological research**

1	**The transition from learning about research to the workplace**	1
2	**Different ways of developing research projects**	12
3	**Working with a supervisor**	22
4	**Managing yourself and your time**	32

Section 2: **Doing psychological research**

5	**The current state of psychological research**	44
6	**Doing an experimental research project**	54
7	**Doing a correlational research project**	85
8	**Doing a qualitative research project**	114
9	**Doing a systematic review**	139

Section 3: **Applying psychological research**

10	**Presenting your research**	168
11	**Publishing your research**	182
12	**Using your research project to benefit your career and beyond**	194

References 207
Index 209

Detailed Contents

Dedication		v
Meet the Authors		vi
Preface		vii
Acknowledgements		viii

1 The transition from learning about research to the workplace 1
    1.1 What are the career paths for psychology graduates? 3
    1.2 Key skills and attributes gained through doing research 5
    1.3 Summary: Making the most of your research experience 9

2 Different ways of developing research projects 12
    2.1 How are student research projects usually organized? 12
    2.2 Independence and supervision in a research project 14
    2.3 What research experience do you already have? 16
    2.4 How might your personal situation influence your decisions? 16
    2.5 How might your academic strengths and interests influence your decisions? 18
    2.6 What transferable skills do you already have, and which do you want to develop? 18
    2.7 Summary: The key factors influencing your decision-making about the research project 19

3 Working with a supervisor 22
    3.1 Different ways that supervisors are allocated 22
    3.2 Understanding the student–supervisor relationship 23
    3.3 Setting up ground rules and managing expectations 24
    3.4 Being in the driving seat 25
    3.5 Consider your strengths and weaknesses 26
    3.6 What to do if things do not go according to plan 27
    3.7 What about group projects? 30
    3.8 Summary: Having a good working relationship with your supervisor 30

4 Managing yourself and your time 32
    4.1 The importance of having an in-depth understanding of your project before you start planning 32
    4.2 Thinking about your research project over time: timelines and Gantt charts 33
    4.3 Managing your research project time and tasks effectively 35
    4.4 Considering your stakeholders and setting for ethical research 38
    4.5 Dealing with challenges 39
    4.6 Working as an individual or within a group 41
    4.7 Summary: Managing your research project effectively 42

5 The current state of psychological research — 44
- 5.1 The replication crisis and open science — 44
- 5.2 The problems leading to the replication crisis — 46
- 5.3 The solutions open science offers — 48
- 5.4 Open science practices and developing transferable skills — 51
- 5.5 Summary: Reflecting on open science and research — 52

6 Doing an experimental research project — 54
- 6.1 Skills required to be a good experimental researcher — 54
- 6.2 A quick revision of the basics — 55
- 6.3 Designing an experimental study — 57
- 6.4 Running an experimental study — 69
- 6.5 Analysing experimental data — 72
- 6.6 Writing up an experimental study — 79
- 6.7 Building transferable skills through experimental methodology — 83

7 Doing a correlational research project — 85
- 7.1 Skills required to be a good correlational researcher — 85
- 7.2 A quick revision of the basics — 86
- 7.3 Designing an advanced correlational study – regression — 88
- 7.4 Designing a robust correlational study — 97
- 7.5 Ethics for a correlational study — 102
- 7.6 Running a correlational study — 102
- 7.7 Analysing correlational data — 104
- 7.8 Writing up a correlational study — 109
- 7.9 Building transferable skills through correlational methodology — 112

8 Doing a qualitative research project — 114
- 8.1 Positioning qualitative research within psychology — 114
- 8.2 Skills required to be a good qualitative researcher — 115
- 8.3 Key characteristics of reflexive thematic analysis — 115
- 8.4 Designing a reflexive thematic analysis study — 123
- 8.5 Running a qualitative study — 128
- 8.6 Analysing qualitative data — 130
- 8.7 Writing up a qualitative study — 133
- 8.8 Building transferable skills through qualitative methodology — 137

9 Doing a systematic review — 139
- 9.1 What are systematic reviews and why do we need them? — 139
- 9.2 Skills required to be a good systematic reviewer — 142
- 9.3 Designing a systematic review — 144
- 9.4 Conducting a systematic review — 158

	9.5 Synthesizing systematic review data	162
	9.6 Writing up a systematic review	163
	9.7 Building transferable skills through systematic review methodology	167
10	**Presenting your research**	**168**
	10.1 Developing research skills through presenting your project	169
	10.2 Research articles	169
	10.3 Presentations	169
	10.4 Sharing your research	180
11	**Publishing your research**	**182**
	11.1 Pre-registration and Registered Reports	182
	11.2 Where should you submit your paper to?	184
	11.3 Preparing your paper for submission to a journal	186
	11.4 The review process	188
	11.5 What happens after your paper is accepted for publication?	192
12	**Using your research project to benefit your career and beyond**	**194**
	12.1 Understanding the skills you have developed	194
	12.2 Skills developed through becoming a researcher	199
	12.3 Where to get advice for your career development	203
	12.4 Increasing your chances of success in employment	204

References 207

Index 209

The transition from learning about research to the workplace

 In this chapter you will learn . . .

- the importance of learning how to become a psychological researcher;
- why developing strong research skills makes graduates desirable to employers; and
- the key skills acquired through doing research, and how these relate to career development.

One of the most exciting aspects about doing psychological research is that the knowledge and skills we gain through being researchers are always developing and strengthening. Being a researcher means that we are continually learning and improving in a dynamic research environment. This is true at any stage of your career, from your first days as a student learning about research through to being an experienced, professional researcher. If you are reading this book, you are probably a psychology student who is about to embark on a research project. Therefore, you may already have some core knowledge about conducting research, and you will be familiar with the research process that is outlined in Figure 1.1. The aim of this book is to help you make the step up to becoming a more independent and confident researcher, and to support you in working alongside a supervisor and other researchers. Importantly, we will also emphasize the research skills that you will acquire and that will be instrumental in your future career plans. Moreover, throughout this book, we will also highlight how being involved in psychological research can provide opportunities for using your skills in inclusive and socially responsible ways that can benefit others.

Throughout this book, we will be emphasizing the links between your research project and your employability, with every chapter including a focus on how to use your research experience to maximize your chances of success after graduating. The book itself is split into three sections, which you can see in Figure 1.2. It starts with broad advice on how to get started with a research project, then specific research designs are discussed in detail (both qualitative and quantitative approaches). Finally, we will think about how to present your research and how to use your research experience to put you in the strongest possible position to achieve your career goals. As we work through different research designs in Section 2 of the book, we will give you lots of hints and tips to help you develop your research project and to highlight key ethical issues for you to consider, covering both ethical research design and ethical professional practice (e.g. treatment of data and the General Data Protection Regulations).

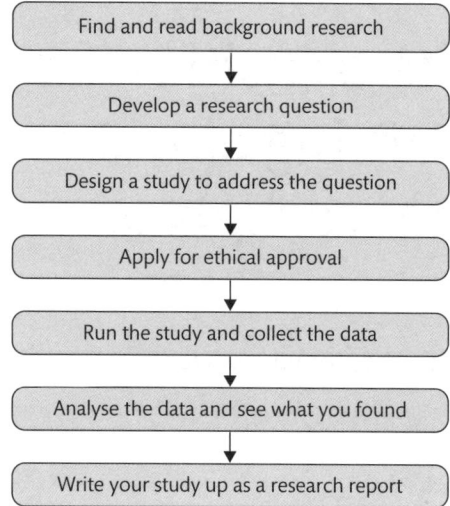

Figure 1.1 An overview of the research process

Throughout this book, we will be asking you to fully engage in making links between your research experience and your future career plans, focusing on the *three Rs (3Rs)*: *recognizing* the skills you have gained; *reflecting* on your experience, your strengths and your weaknesses; and *relating* your educational research experiences to the next steps in your career. You can

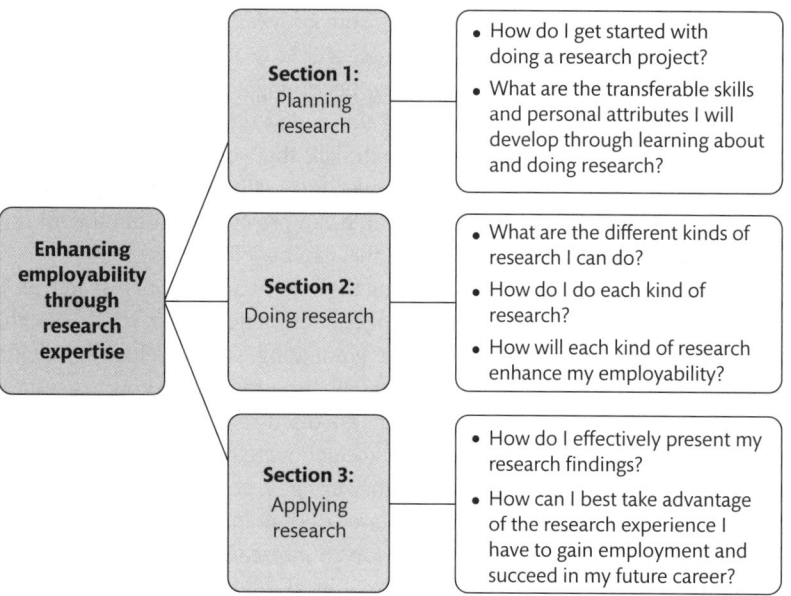

Figure 1.2 An overview of the three sections of this book, and how each will help you to develop as a researcher and achieve your career aims

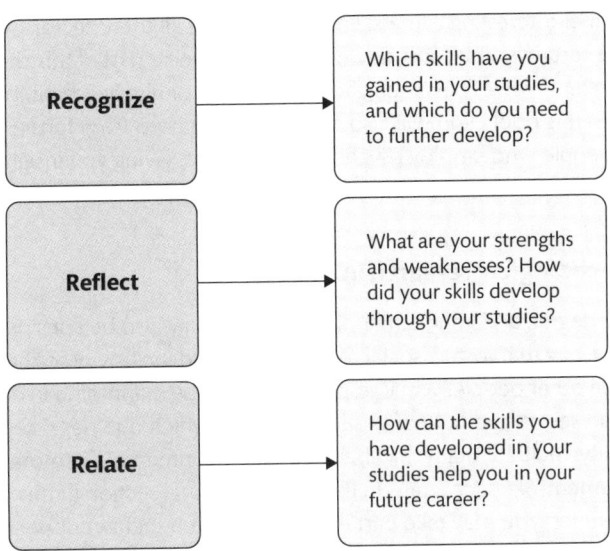

Figure 1.3 The *three Rs* help you to link your education experiences with your career development

see these in Figure 1.3 and we will be returning to them in various ways in each chapter of this book to help you apply the skills we are talking about to your own career development.

1.1 What are the career paths for psychology graduates?

Following graduation, about one-third of UK students continue in education and around two-thirds enter employment. However, it is important to acknowledge that an undergraduate degree is often only the first step on the career ladder, and many graduates will not go directly into their dream job. Some graduates will spend time in voluntary or assistant positions (e.g. teaching assistant, mental health support worker) to gain the kinds of experience that can be essential to being accepted onto doctoral programmes that allow you to pursue some careers such as clinical, forensic, or educational psychology. So, when you are planning your career, you may need to think a few steps ahead. Also, some graduates may choose to pursue careers outside psychology, such as in market research or human resources. So, there are lots of options for you to consider!

For those entering postgraduate education, a common route is via a Master's programme, either further specializing to extend one's psychological knowledge or diversifying into a different field of study. Some students do move directly from an undergraduate degree into a PhD programme, but many will complete a Master's degree before pursuing a PhD. If you are interested in continuing your education, most postgraduate programmes will have a large research component. Consequently, if you can become a highly skilled and confident undergraduate researcher, then you will be in a strong position to complete postgraduate studies.

For those who go into employment, there are a wide range of career paths that psychology graduates pursue, including those in mental health, education, research (academia), going into a business or human resources (HR) environment, working in marketing/advertising, and a whole range of other interesting careers. Employers across all these sectors seek out potential employees with a certain skill set and, as we will see in the next part of this chapter, learning to become a researcher involves developing a diverse range of highly desirable skills. At the end of each chapter in this book, you will also see some reflections from former psychology students and from people who employ psychology graduates, giving you insights into how your research work will be relevant even after you have submitted your research project.

The role of psychological research in society

Throughout your degree and your career planning, you may also be considering how best to use your skills in a way that fosters social responsibility and inclusivity so that you can have a positive impact on other people. Social responsibility can be manifested in different ways and situations. You can see an example of this in Figure 1.4, which outlines 4 key components of social responsibility: multicultural, ethical, civic, and environmental (for more information, see the Pearson document, *Skills for Today*, in the 'Wider reading' section of this chapter).

During your studies, you may take part in activities that benefit your peers or others from outside your university: for example, by becoming involved with societies, mentoring, volunteering, or being a student representative. In addition to helping you to build your CV and enhance your employability, such activities will help to ensure that your educational experience has benefits beyond yourself. You may also find that the ability to help others and to be socially responsible may shape your career and life choices once you have finished your studies. It is also important to ensure that the way you plan, design, and conduct psychological research protects and benefits others, so throughout this book we will be highlighting instances where you could (or should) be thinking about those aspects. In fact, many of the skills that we will be discussing in this book are about working with and benefiting others – for example, leadership, teamwork, and communication skills.

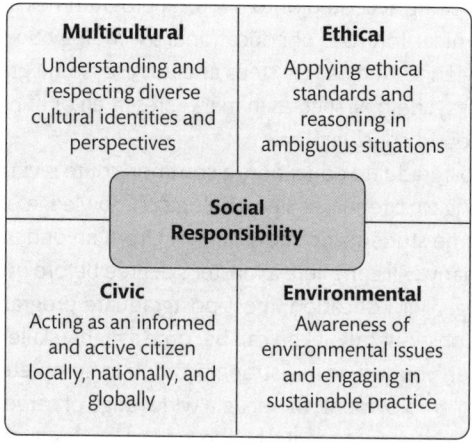

Figure 1.4 Different components of social responsibility

1.2 Key skills and attributes gained through doing research

Learning how to become a researcher equips you with a wide range of skills and helps you to develop your own personal attributes. Many of these are specific research skills, such as developing hypotheses, creating materials, or analysing data. However, when you learn how to do research, you will be further exposed to a broad range of experiences that will help you in gaining and succeeding in employment. The skills you develop are often called 'transferable', 'employability', 'generic' or 'soft' skills. Throughout this book, we will use the term 'transferable skills'. You will also be developing and enhancing your own personal attributes, such as how assertive, adaptable, or resilient you are as a person.

It is important to recognize that everyone has both strengths and weaknesses. It is not realistic to expect to be fantastic at absolutely everything. and understanding yourself and your potential is an important part of developing your transferable skills. If you are aware of your weaknesses, you can develop strategies that will allow you to still achieve what you want to achieve. Also, if you have a good understanding of your strengths, then you can pick careers and opportunities to make the most of these. So do take the time to fully reflect on your own strengths and weaknesses as you progress through your studies and your career.

As you develop as a researcher, it is really helpful to think about the broad range of skills and attributes that you are developing, and how these might map onto your career plans, whether that is going into further studies or seeking employment. We have identified 12 key transferable skills and attributes that you are likely to develop in conducting a research project, and which may be beneficial for you after graduation and beyond. You can see these in Figure 1.5. Now we will explain each of these skills and attributes, when you may develop them within a research project, and how you can use this book to help you enhance your own skills and

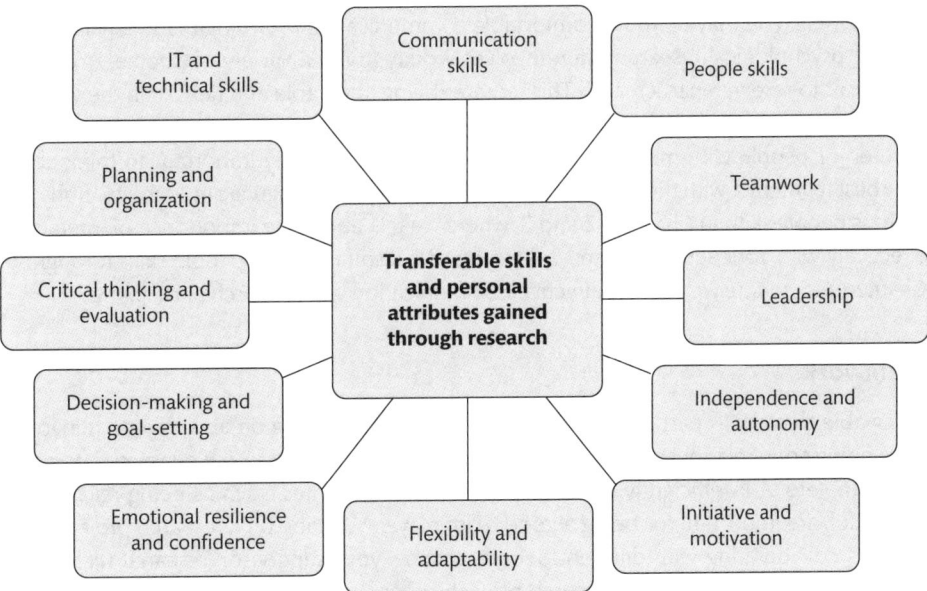

Figure 1.5 The 12 key transferable skills and personal attributes gained through learning to become a researcher

attributes to benefit your career ambitions. Use these 12 skills and attributes to broadly guide you through thinking about your research experience and note that there can be some overlap between the skills. For example, if you encounter a difficult situation when collecting data, you might need to show initiative to come up with a solution, decision-making to plan out the solution, and people skills to get the rest of the team on board to implement your solution.

Communication skills

In any situation, it is important to communicate clearly with other people, meaning that we provide accurate information in an appropriate way. This might be in written form or through speaking to others. When you work on a research project, whether you are working entirely independently or as part of a team, you will need to demonstrate a wide range of communication skills – for example, discussing initial research ideas and plans with your supervisor, recruiting and working with participants, and presenting your findings, either in a written report or as a spoken presentation. In this book, we will be giving you hints and tips about how to communicate efficiently throughout the research process, and, in the final section of the book, Chapter 10 is about Presenting your research, such as through oral presentations or posters at conferences, while Chapter 11 is about publishing research projects.

People skills

Having good people skills means that we are able to interact with others in an appropriate manner. This can include verbal and non-verbal interactions. Being able to relate to others, showing respect, empathy, and a genuine interest in them, are examples of people skills that employers look for. Working with others is a skill that may be challenging for some, but, again, try to think about strategies and approaches that may help you to make the most of the skills you have (e.g. you may be more comfortable communicating in writing than verbally). Conducting psychological research often involves working with a variety of people, from your supervisor to research participants. This requires being adaptable and flexible in the way you interact with them. For example, when working with vulnerable participants, such as young children or people with mental health conditions, it is extremely important to think about how best to interact with them, and to be mindful of our body language in such situations. We address people skills in Chapters 2 and 3, where we talk about the importance of interacting effectively with your supervisor and colleagues. We also talk about people skills throughout Chapters 6–9, where we address effective communication with research participants.

Teamwork

Being able to work as part of a team is important when working on any project. It involves developing good relationships with other team members in order to achieve a common goal and complete tasks efficiently and on time. Personal attributes, such as being reliable and respectful, are important for being a good team player. Working on a research project often involves collaborating with different people, such as your supervisor, research technicians and, if you are part of a group research project, other students. Academic research is often complex and requires a broad range of expertise and skills. Being able to work collaboratively with other team members by respecting their ideas, valuing their input, and complementing their strengths and weaknesses is extremely important for the success of a research project. Teamwork provides numerous opportunities to develop and practise social responsibility by ensuring that your behaviour and actions benefit your team members and beyond. Teamwork skills will be addressed primarily in Chapters 2 and 3 of the book, where we discuss how to collaborate effectively with your supervisor and other members of your project group.

Leadership

You do not need to lead a team of people to be able to demonstrate your leadership skills. Working with a team of people often requires all team members to be leaders some of the time. Passion, enthusiasm, trustworthiness, authenticity, and positivity are some personal attributes that can make a good leader. Good leaders are also able to delegate, listen, and solve problems effectively. Working on a research project is rarely an individual endeavour – it usually involves working through a maze of tasks with a team of people. In this situation, being able to motivate and influence other group members to do their tasks to the best of their abilities is an example of how you can demonstrate your leadership skills. We talk about leadership skills in Chapter 3 where we discuss different ways of doing research and how you can demonstrate your leadership skills in a variety of situations. Furthermore, we talk about leadership skills in Section 3, Chapters 10–12, where we discuss how you can use your research to enhance your employability prospects.

Independence and autonomy

To be able to think and work independently is an important employability skill. Some examples of independent and autonomous working are being able to complete tasks without your work managers or colleagues having constantly to check them, having confidence in your ideas, taking responsibility for your actions, and meeting your deadlines. To succeed at independent working, you also need to take responsibility for being highly organized, disciplined, and able to multitask. Doing research is usually a complex endeavour that involves working on a variety of tasks simultaneously, and, although you will have a research supervisor, learning to work without constant supervision will contribute to developing your independence and autonomy. We discuss this in more detail in Chapter 3 and also Chapters 10–12 of the book.

Initiative and motivation

Taking initiative means being motivated and able to decide and do things without being asked. It often involves showing enthusiasm and passion for your job, and it may sometimes involve going beyond your usual job responsibilities. So, being motivated and self-driven are personal attributes necessary to demonstrate initiative. Doing research is a highly creative enterprise and, as such, it offers numerous opportunities to show your ability to take initiative. Examples of how you can develop or improve this expertise while conducting your research project include proposing changes to the way your supervisor or your research team work, being able to recognize what needs to be done, and coming up with solutions. Chapters 3 and 4 discuss the importance of taking initiative when doing research in more detail.

Flexibility and adaptability

Being flexible means that you are able to manage change and think creatively about how to adapt your plans if any problems arise. No matter how skilled you are as a researcher, or how well-planned a project is, being flexible and adaptable can be highly beneficial at any stage of the research process. For example, research is often conducted within a team, which can require some compromise and flexibility. Once a project is up and running, no matter how well planned, it is always possible that problems may occur and it is important to be able to be responsive and adaptable in order to resolve any issues that may arise. We talk more about how to work with a supervisor or in research teams in Chapters 2 and 3.

Emotional resilience and confidence

Emotional resilience is important to allow you to push ahead through challenging times, giving you the confidence to tackle any difficult situations that may arise. Sometimes doing research can be tough and, whatever career path you follow, you are likely to encounter challenges that may feel insurmountable. For example, losing a full dataset because of IT issues, or having difficulties working with someone on your team, can be stressful. But learning to manage and deal with these kinds of stressors will put you in a stronger position in your studies, your career, and even in your personal life! In Chapters 2-4, we will offer various hints and tips to help you manage some of the more frequent challenges that can occur during a research project.

Decision-making and goal-setting

Being able to plan any piece of work requires you to set the various goals that need to be achieved at each stage of the process, and to make well-informed and clearly thought-out decisions. When you do research, there will be many decisions that you need to make, from initially devising your research question, through developing materials, to analysing data, and, finally, presenting your findings. In Section 2 of this book (Chapters 6-9), we talk through 4 different research approaches, and how to efficiently plan these different styles of research project.

Critical thinking and evaluation

Critical thinking can be defined as the ability to engage in reflective and analytical thinking. It requires you to be an active rather than a passive learner, and to think independently. Critical thinking and evaluation are at the heart of research because doing research is all about understanding the existing theories and methodologies, and then challenging them. Moreover, you will be expected to develop your own ideas, find the best ways of testing them, and analyse them systematically. Finally, being able to reflect on your ideas and research practices is an essential component of being a researcher. We cover critical thinking and evaluation in Chapter 5, where we describe the current state of psychological research, as well as in Chapters 10 and 11 where we discuss presenting research.

Planning and organization

Having good planning and organizing skills is a basic yet crucial employability skill that is required in almost any job. Some examples of these are being able to plan and manage your time, your tasks and your schedule, and to meet deadlines. In order to be able to plan and organize your tasks, it is also necessary to possess good problem-solving skills. Conducting research provides plenty of opportunities to develop planning skills, from initial planning through to fully designing your research and working out how to conduct it. Your organizing skills will be showcased throughout – for example, by managing your time efficiently and ensuring that all project deadlines are met. We discuss the planning and organizing of your project first in Chapter 4 and then in Chapters 5–9 (Section 2) of the book.

IT and technical skills

IT and technical skills refer to the ability to use technology in your daily job, from simple tasks such as using a photocopier or a computer for sending emails to using specialized software and programs. Depending on the nature of the job, this usually requires constantly learning and keeping up with new knowledge via training. Apart from having good basic IT and technical skills, conducting research usually requires the knowledge and use of highly specialized technology, such as research programming software and statistical packages for data analysis. You will be gaining these skills via your regular training, but it is also good to try to find out what technology is needed in the job you want and to engage in extra opportunities to learn it. Section 2 (Chapters 6–9) covers various ways of doing research and provides many examples of the IT and technical skills that you will be developing while working on your research project.

1.3 Summary: Making the most of your research experience

Conducting a large piece of research, such as a final year research project, can take quite a few months, have multiple stages, and require you to accomplish many different tasks. It can be easy to focus on the research findings and report write-up, but try to think about your skill development and your achievements during the research process. Throughout the project, we strongly recommend that you keep a record of examples of where you have demonstrated each of the 12 transferable skills and personal attributes, your strengths, and your opportunities for improvement. We have included an example of how this can be done as a self-reflective log in Box 1.1 and, if you go to the online resources for this book (in 'Wider reading' below Box 1.2), you will find a full self-reflective workbook to help you keep track of all your experiences.

Doing a research project is an incredible opportunity that allows you to develop and demonstrate a wide range of skills. However, it is important to *recognize* that you are developing these skills; to *reflect* on your skill development, strengths, and weaknesses; and to be able to *relate* your experiences to other situations – for example, in an interview setting. Very often, students underestimate, or perhaps do not even realize, the importance of the wide range of skills that they acquire when learning to do research. Throughout this book, we will be referring back to these *3Rs*: reminding you to *recognize* and *reflect* on all these skills, and prompting you to *relate* your experiences to other situations.

> **BOX 1.1 A case study showing reflection on the flexible and adaptable skills developed when conducting psychological research**
>
> **Reflecting on your transferable skills and personal attributes**
> An example – being flexible and adaptable
>
> ***Recognize:*** From the research you have conducted, what is the best example of when you have demonstrated this skill or attribute?
>
> I was collecting data in a school and had a whole class of children ready to complete an online study, but the IT system crashed and we could not access the study. Lots of work had gone into setting up the research link with the school, so I didn't want to waste the opportunity or the school's time. I had the study saved on a USB memory stick, so I asked the school if I could print up the materials. This meant that we were still able to collect data.
>
> ***Reflect:*** What are my strengths with regard to this skill or attribute? How can I further develop or improve them?
>
> I am able to think quickly and generate lots of possible approaches to a problem. This means that I can adapt to a situation, even when the most unexpected things happen. While I can think quickly about different solutions to problems, I tend to prefer to think things through on my own. This can be difficult when working with other people, so I need to work on talking through my thought processes with others. That would help the whole team to be flexible and adaptable together.
>
> ***Relate:*** Imagine you are being interviewed for your dream job or course. How would your skills in this area make you suitable for this position?
>
> I want to be a teacher, so being able to be flexible and adaptable is really important. While I will carefully plan all my teaching sessions, I know that it will be important to be flexible in the way that any teaching is delivered. If the session does not seem to go to plan, then I will need to adapt it within the session. I will also be flexible in terms of ensuring that students are able to work to their own skill level (i.e. giving more able students more advanced tasks within the session).

> **BOX 1.2 Hints and tips from psychology graduates and employers of psychology graduates**
>
> The student's perspective . . . Reflecting on independence and autonomy
>
> I learnt that I am confident enough to research novel topics on my own and create patterns across the different topics. This helped me in the long run when I was giving interviews and had to mould the research to match the criteria of the job description. With this, I also learnt to explore research across other fields such as Business and see cross-sectionality between my research topic and existing literature. This, too, enabled me to understand how I can apply my learnings to various career choices.
>
> Elizabeth, psychology graduate
>
> The employer's perspective . . . reflecting on being flexible and adaptable
>
> The reality of most jobs is that things won't go to plan. Clients are late, computers break, etc. Being adaptable is crucial so we can still deliver on our promise as a company, even when things aren't our fault. It is important to know that a student can adapt in unforeseen situations and that they can take on feedback. We'll often ask a question about this in interview.
>
> Hasan, neuroscience director

Wider reading

Pearson, *Skills for today: What we know about teaching and assessing social responsibility*. https://www.pearson.com/content/dam/one-dot-com/one-dot-com/global/Files/efficacy-and-research/skills-for-today/4008-SFT-Social-Responsibility.pdf

This document is a detailed consideration of how social responsibility can be developed in educational settings.

2 Different ways of developing research projects

 In this chapter you will learn . . .

- different ways the projects can be organized;
- factors influencing the development of your research project;
- several transferable skills that are essential to consider when developing your research project; and
- different ways of conducting your research project.

You are about to start your research project – how exciting! But where do you begin? When developing your research project, there are different factors that you need to consider that will ultimately influence your decisions about the type of project you want to conduct. We will start by talking about the different ways that research projects can be organized, and then think about the factors that may influence your decision-making. These factors may be internal (e.g. your personal preferences and abilities) while others are external, such as different academic and institutional influences. In this chapter, we discuss both internal and external factors, with the overall aim of helping you navigate the decision-making process underpinning the development of your research project. We also highlight several transferable skills that are important to consider when developing your research project.

2.1 How are student research projects usually organized?

Broadly speaking, there are three ways or models for conducting a student research project: individual, group, or research assistant. You can see each of these in Figure 2.1, along with the key transferable skills that you may develop when working within each model. It is important to bear in mind that there is no 'best' model of project organization. Each approach has its own strengths and each will allow you to develop different skills. The model used will usually be decided by the academics in your department and therefore the organization of the project overall may not be something you can choose. This makes it even more important to take some time to think about how to make the most of the opportunity offered to you.

Individual projects

An individual project is one of the models used for conducting student research projects. Within this model, a student works on their project independently and is supervised by a

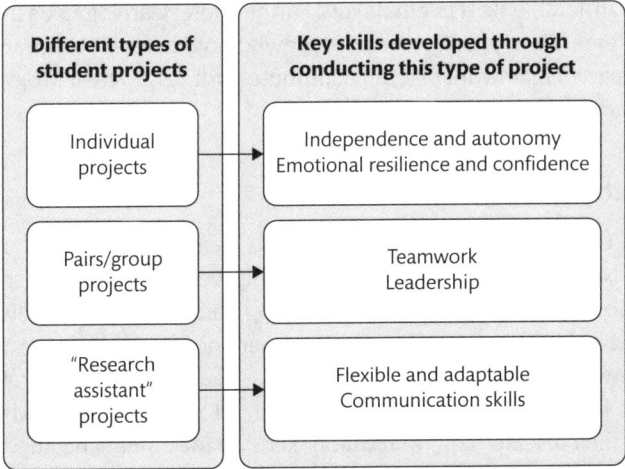

Figure 2.1 Different types of project organization and the key skills developed for each

member of staff. This has a number of advantages – for example, a student might be more likely to study a topic that they are particularly passionate about because they do not need to negotiate it with other students. They can develop a number of transferable skills within this model, such as independence, confidence, autonomy, and resilience. However, working on your own can sometimes feel a little lonely and isolating. Recently, there has been a move towards psychological research being a more collaborative process, partly motivated by the open science movement (we discuss this in detail in Chapter 5), and consequently student group projects are becoming more popular to reflect current practice in academic research.

Group projects

These usually involve two or more students working together on a project where certain aspects of the project are shared (e.g. core design, ethics application, and data collection) while others are independent (e.g. unique variables, hypotheses, data analysis, and the project write-up). Group projects have several advantages, the most obvious being working collaboratively and sharing tasks, such as preparation of study materials, writing the ethics application, recruiting participants, and data collection. Group members also share and negotiate ideas and, overall, group projects can contribute to the development of a number of key transferable skills, such as teamwork, leadership, and people skills. Another advantage of group projects is maximizing your sample size because more people collecting data means that more participants can be recruited. Having a larger sample size can help to make your sample more representative of the population and therefore your study more publishable.

However, a disadvantage of group projects is that individual students might have fewer options and be less flexible with the choice of research topic, questions, and methodology. They might also experience group conflict because working with other members may sometimes be challenging due to different personalities, priorities, etc. However, this could also be an advantage because group projects provide students with an opportunity to learn how to deal with challenging situations and to develop their resilience and people skills. These are very desirable transferable skills to employers. Furthermore, learning to be inclusive of peers who may be different from you in some ways, or who hold different views and perspectives, is an important part of teamwork that can contribute positively to their project experience as well as to your personal growth.

Research assistant projects

The final model is the research assistant model. This means that students' projects are integrated into an existing research project. Usually, this would be a project that the supervisor is already working on (or is currently setting up), either independently or as part of a larger research team. Clearly, this can be a great experience for students because they will be exposed to real-world research and become part of a group of professional researchers working in a research lab. For example, they may be invited to team meetings where they will be able to develop their research communication skills. On the other hand, they might not have so much independence and choice with such projects, although these could provide them with opportunities to learn to be adaptable and flexible.

2.2 Independence and supervision in a research project

Broadly speaking, there are two models for developing and conducting research projects: one more student-directed and the other more supervisor-directed. These exist on a continuum as you can see in Figure 2.2.

To illustrate this, I (Danijela) will use an example from my research. I regularly supervise student research projects and am currently interested in exploring the stigma towards invisible health conditions, both mental health (e.g. depression) and physical health conditions (e.g. chronic back pain). My students love this topic and always express a lot of enthusiasm for it. By 'invisible conditions', we mean that there are no obvious or visible symptoms or signs of a condition, which can lead to other people making assumptions, disbelieving and invalidating patients' symptoms and suffering. Currently, there is very little research comparing the stigma towards invisible conditions relating to mental health and physical health.

If I were supervising this project using the supervisor-directed style of supervision, which you can see at the top of Figure 2.2, I would have a leading role in the development of the project topic and the key research questions. For example, I would decide which health conditions my project students should focus on, as well as specific factors that should be studied in relation to this issue, such as sex, age, personality type, and empathy. In addition, I would be substantially involved in the design, methodology, and selection of materials for this project.

On the other hand, if I were supervising this project using a less supervisor-directed approach, I would propose some key research questions and then invite my students to contribute ideas in order to select the most appropriate question and negotiate the best way forward. For example, I would let them decide which specific health conditions they wanted to compare and which factors they wanted to focus on. Furthermore, I would propose a basic research design and invite them to provide their input into it – for example, by identifying appropriate measures, materials, and analysis. I would guide them through this process,

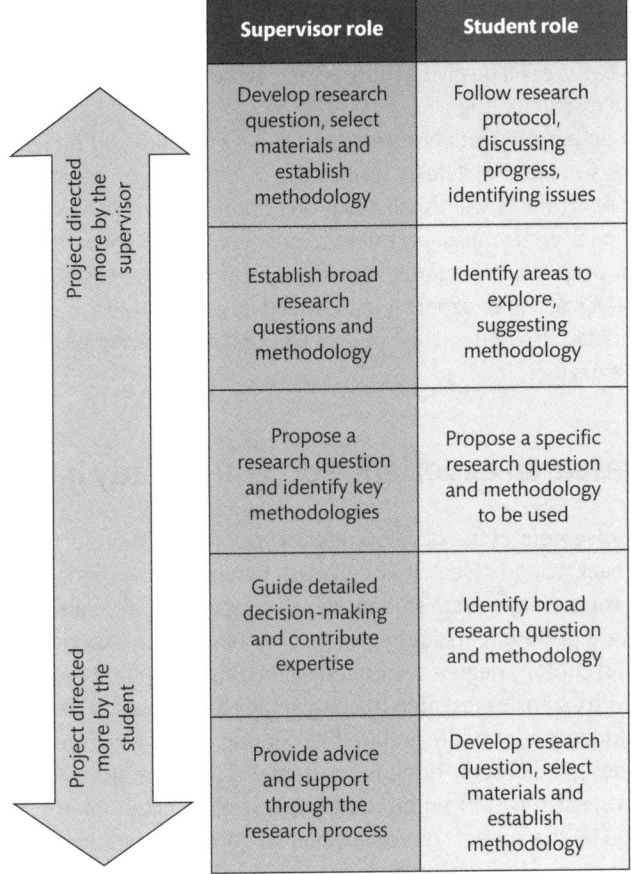

Figure 2.2 Levels of independence and supervision in a research project

direct them towards key literature, challenge their ideas, and help them moderate any overly complex or unrealistic plans. If you look at Figure 2.2, this type of project would be somewhere in the middle of the continuum and this is a style of supervision that I often adopt when supervising students' projects.

Finally, if I were supervising this project using the student-directed style, which you can see at the bottom of Figure 2.2, I would provide advice and guidance through the research process but let my students take a leading role. For example, I would tell them that their project should broadly focus on health stigma but that they would be expected to develop a research question, identify health conditions and factors they wanted to focus on, establish methodology, and find appropriate materials.

As we have said, the level of your and your supervisor's involvement can be observed on a continuum, and it may change and move along this continuum throughout your project. Your input and level of involvement will usually be discussed in your initial meetings with the supervisor. However, regardless of your level of involvement in the project, your supervisor should always ensure that the project you will be conducting is manageable and within the scope, resources, and time allocated to it by your department or institution. We will expand on this in Chapter 3 where we will be providing advice on how to work with your supervisor, and in Chapters 6–9 we will be giving more advice on how to develop research questions for different types of research design.

Whether you do a more student-directed or supervisor-directed project will depend on your supervisor's supervision style as well as the institutional or departmental set-up and requirements. Departments will usually take one approach across all students' projects, so make sure you check with your department to ensure that you know the approach that will be used for your project – for example, aspects such as their established way of supervising projects, their staff's research expertise and availability, and project resources. The department's approach may also depend on your background research knowledge and experience, which we discuss next.

2.3 What research experience do you already have?

Your level of involvement in the development of your research project is likely to be influenced by your background research knowledge, training, and experience. For example, if you are a final year undergraduate student developing your final year research project, you are likely to have a good understanding of research and some experience. Typically, a UK undergraduate psychology degree accredited by the British Psychological Society (BPS) provides students with extensive research training in the earlier years of their degree. As part of their training, students are usually required to conduct some group research projects that are usually pre-designed or semi-designed and small-scale. Therefore, final year undergraduate research projects might often be more supervisor-directed, or at least closely monitored and guided by the supervisor. However, if you are a postgraduate student, it is likely that you already have substantial knowledge and experience of conducting psychological research and have already made independent decisions as a researcher. This means that you will be able to carry out a more independent project.

Whatever your level of involvement in the development of your research project, whether you are adding a few variables to a semi-designed study or designing a new project from scratch, you will eventually have to make some research-based decisions. So, how might you go about making such decisions and which personal and academic factors can influence and inform them?

2.4 How might your personal situation influence your decisions?

Factors that can influence the development of your research project and your decisions may be personal – for example, your career plans or simply pastimes that you enjoy. Let us explore some of these in more detail.

Personal experiences and interests often play a major role when deciding what your project (or aspects of it that you control) should be about. Activities that you enjoy, interest you, you are good at or have confidence in will often inform your project-related decision-making.

For example, students are often interested in exploring current or popular topics or something that they or people close to them have experienced. Clearly, this approach to choosing a research topic is led by passion and enthusiasms, which have always been important for knowledge progression. Also, research can be laborious, lengthy, and challenging, and exploring a topic that you are passionate about can help you stay motivated and deal better with such challenges. However, it is also important to be realistic about your ideas. Before you decide on a topic, make sure to talk to your supervisor and do some preliminary research and reading to understand what your project will involve. Reading a few papers in your research area of interest will give you a more realistic idea as to whether you will be able to see the project through.

For example, you might be interested in cognitive deficits in dementia patients – an interest that may have been sparked by having a close family member diagnosed with dementia. However, after having read several papers and talked to your supervisor, you realize that such research involves securing access to dementia patients and that obtaining ethical approval for this is likely to take several weeks. You know that this is not workable, but you still want to examine this topic and are willing to adapt your research question by using alternative methods to explore it. After further discussion with your supervisor, you decide to focus on dementia carers' perceptions and experiences of dementia patients' cognitive defects. This is achievable within the scope and timeline of your project, and it is still very much of interest to you. This research would not require special ethical approval (e.g. NHS approval) and you could collect data online by posting your study on social media and advertising it to relevant support groups.

What this example shows is that it is really important to spend some time thinking and reading about your research topic in order to ensure that it is workable and attainable as well as interesting to you. Finally, we need to offer a word of caution about selecting a (sensitive) topic that has a very personal meaning to you (i.e. think about whether and how you might be emotionally affected by researching it for several months). If you have doubts about this, then it might be better to select a different topic.

Another personal factor that could inform your research project topic and the development of your project is your future career plan. We often have students asking us if their research project should be linked to the next step in their career. There is no straightforward answer to this question, but the simple answer, in most cases, is 'No'. For example, you may want to pursue a career in organizational psychology. However, you are not sure whether to do this for your research project because you also like neuroscience and would like to do research involving functional magnetic resonance imaging (fMRI) methodology. It is perfectly fine to explore questions that may not be relevant to your future career plans. In fact, this could demonstrate a number of desirable transferable skills and attributes like enthusiasm and a willingness to challenge yourself – for example, by engaging with advanced research techniques such as fMRI. However, there are some situations where it might be advisable to select a research topic and develop a project that will be linked to your next career step. For example, if you plan to apply for a PhD in a specific research area and want to start exploring this area of research before then, you might want to use your undergraduate or MSc project for that. However, please note that this is just an example and many PhD students will have done their undergraduate and even MSc projects in completely different research areas from those of their PhD.

2.5 How might your academic strengths and interests influence your decisions?

Your decisions may also be informed by academic factors, such as recognizing any areas of psychology where you have performed particularly well. If you are an undergraduate student, by the time you are about to select your final year research project, you will have been through at least two years of psychology modules covering an array of psychological topics. Undergraduate students often pick their final year research project based on these academic experiences. These could range from developing an interest in a broad area of psychology and wanting to examine any topic within that area (e.g. clinical psychology), to being interested in a particular topic or phenomenon (e.g. anxiety disorders), to wanting to examine a very specific aspect of that phenomenon (e.g. the role of perfectionism in anxiety disorders). This is a good approach to selecting your research project because you already have at least some knowledge of it.

Other academic factors influencing your research decisions might be more practical, such as maximizing your marks or selecting a supervisor whom you think you will get on well with. In order to maximize your research project mark, you may be inclined to choose a topic that you understand, feel confident about, and are sure you can do well in. These are important factors to consider, but you would still want to ensure that you have a genuine interest in the topic. Also, think about all the new skills and knowledge you could gain if you chose a slightly more challenging topic. Your decision might also be based on your being impressed by a particular lecturer – namely, their personal characteristics – and you think that you would work really well with them. This can be a sensible approach provided that you have an understanding and genuine interest in their area of research. However, being guided solely by lecturers' personal characteristics may not be the best approach when choosing your research topic. One last point to consider is that sometimes students are led by the unhelpful and wrong idea that they need to research a novel topic and/or get significant results from their analysis to obtain a good mark on their project. Actually, these concepts are not related. We will be discussing them more in Chapter 5 where we will consider the importance of replication studies and publishing non-significant results.

2.6 What transferable skills do you already have, and which do you want to develop?

Overall, it is important to balance personal and academic influences and different priorities when developing your research project. Considering the skills you have as well as those you want to develop are crucial for this. Take a look at Figure 2.3, where we use our *three Rs* (*3Rs*) model (introduced in Chapter 1) to help you think about this in a more structured way. Start by *recognizing* your skills, *reflecting* on them, and then *relating* them to your research project. For example, you may want to start by *recognizing* skills you have used in your previous research projects, such as those in Years 1 and 2. These could be specific research skills (e.g. learning new statistical software such as SPSS) or more generic skills and aptitudes (e.g. teamwork, resilience, and confidence).

The next step would be to *reflect* on these skills – specifically, to think about which skills you really excelled in and which you struggled with. While you no doubt want to bring some

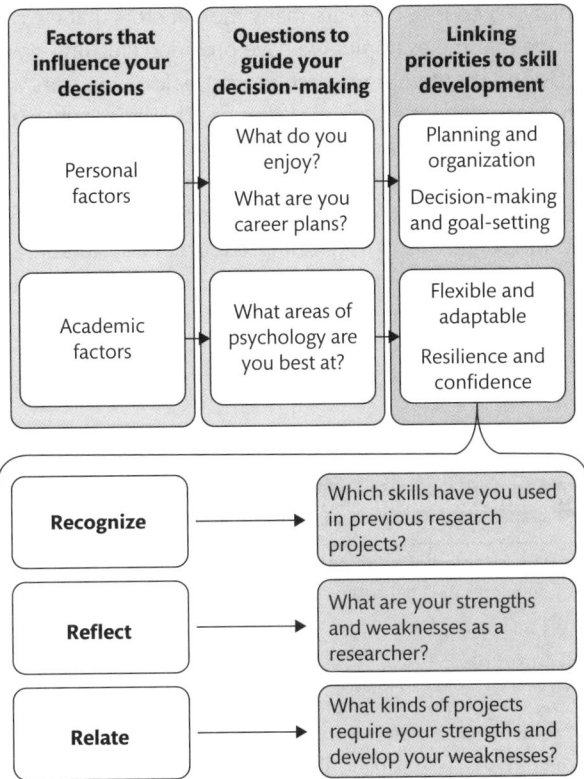

Figure 2.3 Examples of transferable skills and some questions that may help with decision-making about your research project

of your strengths to your research project, you may also see your project as an opportunity to improve some of your less developed skills or practise some new ones. While reflecting on your existing skills, go a step further and try to *relate* them to your research project, for instance, ask yourself what kinds of research projects require your strengths or, conversely, what kind of project might help you work on your weaknesses. For example, if you possess very good IT and technical skills, then engaging with a project that interests you but also requires the use of new or advanced technology (e.g. eye tracker) would be suitable for you. However, if you do not possess very good technical skills but are a highly motivated person and open to learning new skills, this project may be exactly what you need.

2.7 Summary: The key factors influencing your decision-making about the research project

To conclude, in this chapter we have discussed a number of factors that can influence your choice and the development of your research project. You can see (in Box 2.1) a case study of how these decisions also reflect part of your development of transferable skills. In Box 2.2, you can also see hints and tips from both the student's and the employer's perspective, reflecting on different skills developed through a research project and applied to enhance employability. Of course, there are many more factors that we could have covered. Nevertheless, we hope that the examples we have provided illustrate how important it is to make informed decisions about your research project before you start working on it. Once you begin work, there may be little scope for change. Therefore, you want to be confident that the chosen project matches your skills (both existing and those that you want to develop), interests, and aspirations. While engaging in this decision-making process, you are also developing and displaying a number of important transferable skills, such as planning, goal-setting, and decision-making. This in itself is an exercise in transferable skills development, which you might use in a future job application or interview as an example of your 'enviable' decision-making and planning abilities.

> **BOX 2.1 A case study showing reflection on the decision-making and goal- setting skills developed when conducting a research project**
>
> **Reflecting on your transferable skills and personal attributes**
> An example – decision-making and goal-setting
>
> **Recognize:** From the research you have conducted, what is the best example of when you have demonstrated this skill or attribute?
>
> I was torn between two areas for my research project. The first was cognitive psychology, specifically attentional biases. I was tempted to choose this because I was really good at it when I did it for my Year 2 lab report. I understood all background theory and methodology, and found it interesting and fun. I also got a first in the Cognitive Psychology module in Year 2. So, I thought that I would be comfortable with this project. However, I wanted to pursue a career in organizational psychology and saw myself working as a human resources (HR) manager one day. Having discussed it with my personal tutor, I realized that HR requires a specific set of skills and knowledge that I was yet to develop and learn. I realized that developing them would help me to achieve my goals and make me a more competitive candidate. Based on this, I made an informed choice to do a project in organizational psychology.
>
> **Reflect:** What are my strengths with regard to this skill or attribute? How can I further develop or improve them?
>
> I am capable of making well-informed and clearly thought-through decisions. I am aware that I often may lack experience to make correct decisions, but I always ensure that I speak to relevant people who can help me make the best possible choices.
>
> **Relate:** Imagine you are being interviewed for your dream job or course. How would your skills in this area make you suitable for this position?
>
> Doing this project taught me about new research designs and methodology, some of which were not my cup of tea. However, it paid off because I was learning new skills and it also reassured me that organizational psychology was indeed something that I wanted to develop in a future job. This experience gave me the confidence to make difficult decisions.

> **BOX 2.2 Hints and tips from psychology graduates and employers of psychology graduates**
>
> **The student's perspective ... reflecting on planning and organization**
>
> Start early, start now. Read a lot, find research from various sources, and discuss your ideas with your supervisor. I learned that pursuing your passion (i.e. researching a topic you are passionate about or at least interested in) is worth it. You will feel a lot happier at the end seeing your final draft and knowing that you worked on it from scratch until its final form! Also take the time to research how the topic applies to what career you'd like to go into. Then speak to your supervisor to make sure you are working towards building those skills during the time of your project.
>
> Rocco, psychology graduate
>
> **The employer's perspective ... reflecting on decision-making**
>
> I need to trust that the student can make decisions without constantly having to check in with me. This makes my workload more manageable without sacrificing the project/task. I always ask students to give an example of when they have made important decisions within the interview.
>
> Zarina, teaching fellow

Wider reading

Holliman, A., Rosenkranz, P., & Jones, T. (2020). How to make a 'promising' start to your dissertation: Development of a process mapping approach. *Psychology Teaching Review, 26*(1), 64–70.

This paper works through the process of selecting an appropriate topic for a research project.

# Working with a supervisor

 In this chapter you will learn . . .

- the importance of developing and maintaining a healthy and productive relationship with your supervisor and the key skills acquired through this;
- different ways to take a lead in both project tasks and your relationship with your supervisor; and
- how to approach issues in your relationship with your supervisor.

If you are an undergraduate student about to start working on your final year project, you might find the initial experience slightly daunting and confusing. So far in your degree, you have mostly attended lectures, participated in seminars, and asked your lecturers for advice about coursework and exams, but you probably have had very few opportunities to collaborate with them. For most undergraduate students, this will be the first opportunity to engage in a collaborative relationship with a member of staff. In this chapter, we provide advice about what you need to do to have a good working relationship with your supervisor and how you can get the most out of this experience. However, please bear in mind that different departments may have their own set of guidelines about what is expected of you as a project student. Therefore, always make sure that you check those guidelines because they will largely determine your role and involvement in the project.

3.1 Different ways that supervisors are allocated

There are several different ways that project supervisors can be allocated and we addressed these in Chapter 2. Project allocation will usually depend on institutional or departmental strategies. Some departments allocate according to research topic, providing a list of broad research topics to students who then select one and are then allocated a supervisor who is able to supervise that topic. A slightly different type of allocation uses rank order choices, whereby students select several potential supervisors from a list of those available, rank them in order of preference, and are allocated one of them. Some departments provide students with a list of supervisors and topics, which are then allocated to them on a 'first come, first served' basis. Individual negotiation is yet another way of allocating projects: this is designed so that a student approaches a supervisor they want to work with, and/or whose area of research they like, and they then negotiate a topic.

The result of many of these methods of supervisor allocation is that often students do not end up collaborating with the supervisor of their choice. However, this should not be seen as a disadvantage. In fact, working with a supervisor whom you have not chosen could be an

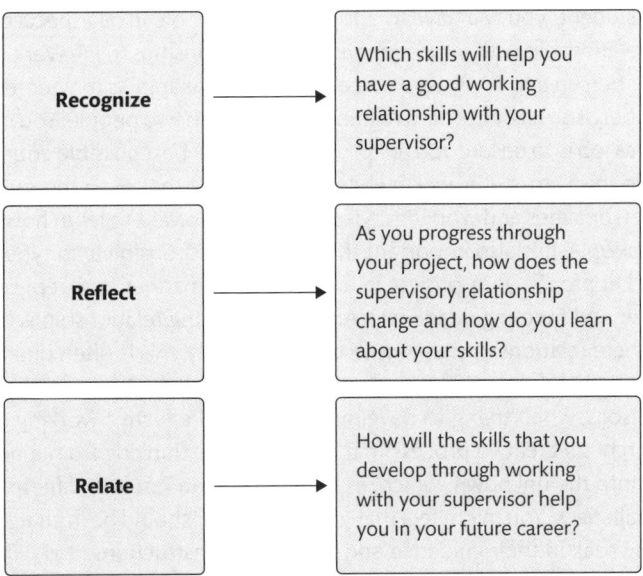

Figure 3.1 Reflecting on skill development through working with a supervisor on a research project

opportunity to develop a number of transferable skills. After all, when you enter the world of employment, you will rarely be able to choose the people you will be working with and employers value flexibility and adaptability in these circumstances. It can also be an opportunity for you to develop a number of other transferable skills, such as problem-solving, resilience, teamwork, and people skills. Try to reflect on this skill development as you progress through your project, and think about how you can relate it to your career plans. You can see some questions to help prompt this thinking in Figure 3.1. Consequently, if you are not able to work with your top choice supervisor, try to focus on the positives that you can take from this experience. If you are able to choose your supervisor, then, as discussed in Chapter 2, try to strike a balance between what you want to research (according to your career plans, interests, and skills) and who you want to work with. Remember, choosing a supervisor purely based on their personality or compatibility may not necessarily be the best approach and might even limit your skill development, career opportunities, and the overall project experience.

3.2 Understanding the student–supervisor relationship

In Chapter 2, we spoke about different levels of supervisor's involvement in the development of your project research question and design, from supervisor-led to student-led (see Figure 2.2). But what happens once you have designed your project and are ready to start conducting it? How closely will you be working with your supervisor? Who will be making the key decisions? Who should take the lead? How can you maintain a good working relationship? Does being part of a group project change any of this? These are just some key questions that you should consider before you start conducting your project.

As a project student, you will have to adopt a proactive role in all aspects of your project, including the relationship with your supervisor. No relationships in life work without adapting to the other person and applying some effort. The same applies to your relationship with your project supervisor. It is, after all, a relationship between two people. You might think that your supervisor's job is to ensure you are provided with the best possible educational experience and, while this is true, it is worthwhile remembering that even the most professional people have personalities and working styles, and it is important to learn how to work with a wide range of people. It is also important that you take responsibility for your own learning experience and approach your project in a professional manner (e.g. replying to emails in a timely manner and meeting deadlines). Any good working relationship is built on mutual respect and, where relationships are not working smoothly, this is often due to both people involved. It can be helpful to reflect on your own approach to the research project, as well as your supervisor's, when trying to develop a strong and effective working relationship. In addition, research is a creative process that often requires thinking from a new perspective and venturing into the unknown, which, in themselves, can result in differing opinions and relationship challenges. You might feel that your supervisor should be in charge and that your role is to simply soak in their guidance and follow their instructions. It is difficult to escape this feeling given that your supervisor will have a lot more knowledge and experience in your project area and will typically be marking your project. However, they will want to see you taking ownership of your project. A good supervisor will want to be involved in some intellectual discussion over the project topic even if it leads to you each coming to different conclusions.

All the above will help you approach your project management in a socially responsible manner whereby you are able to see yourself as an active and responsible participant in this process and to move away from a consumerist approach to your education. However, for some students, this can be anxiety provoking. When considering how to manage your relationship with your supervisor, you might start by considering how you can make the relationship comfortable and enjoyable – an odd choice of priorities, you might think. Well, not really, because a healthy and enjoyable relationship with your supervisor will help maximize your productivity and the success of the project, which, in turn, is likely to lead to a better project mark. The first step towards this is usually to address some ground rules and expectations.

3.3 Setting up ground rules and managing expectations

From the very beginning of your project, it is important to discuss and set up some ground rules and manage expectations. You can use the first meeting with your supervisor to do this. Consider bringing a set of questions with you to the first meeting so that you have an idea of what you want to ask and achieve. For example, you could:

- ask your supervisor what is expected of you and what you should expect of them;
- discuss your strengths and potential weaknesses or obstacles for meeting these expectations, and how you could address them;
- clarify the project's short- and long-term plans and key deadlines; and
- agree how often you should meet and the best way of communicating.

Some departments have set rules for the number and content of supervisory meetings; others do not. Make sure you familiarize yourself with any rules and clarify them with your supervisor. Some supervisors might be flexible while others might give you a strict schedule of meetings and tasks. You should also revisit and adapt this schedule later, negotiating with your supervisor if you need to communicate more or less often. Finally, make sure to agree the next meeting date and what exactly you should do in the meantime and bring to the meeting.

3.4 Being in the driving seat

Whether you are given a fully designed study, a broad research topic, or complete freedom to design your project, you will have the responsibility for it. Ultimately, it is your project and you should explore different ways to take a lead in both related tasks and your relationship with the supervisor. By coming prepared to your first meeting and following the steps we suggested earlier, you have already made a first step towards taking a lead. This helps you in developing not only your research skills but also your employability and social responsibility skills. Great work!

Overall, you should show that you are able to work independently. Your supervisor should guide you, but they should not be doing the work for you. It is actually you, rather than your supervisor, who should be taking the initiative when it comes to preparing the ethics application, data collection, etc. It is also important to monitor your own progress, keep your supervisor updated about it, and contact them should you need guidance and support. Do not get to the point where you are being 'chased' by your supervisor: they should be kept informed of your progress (including any drawbacks, delays, or successes) and be able to trust that you are in charge of the project. These are all examples of excellent and efficient leadership. Your supervisor might not be an expert in all aspects of your project and this can be an excellent opportunity to take a substantial lead. For example, I, like many other supervisors, often use students' projects to explore, adapt, or even develop new methodologies to test hypotheses. For instance, it is through my students' projects that I started using vignette-based experimental designs in my research. But, even if you feel there are not many aspects of your project that are novel to your supervisor, you should still work on having an overall ownership of the project as much as possible. As mentioned earlier in this chapter, regularly discussing ideas – or even challenging your supervisor's ideas – can help you achieve this and will make you feel more confident about your project.

While demonstrating your independence may feel daunting, and maybe even anxiety provoking, do not be afraid to ask questions or make suggestions. Your supervisor will not expect you to know everything about your project and exactly how to lead it. They will be well aware of the fact that you are learning, so sharing your concerns and asking for and following their guidance is another way of demonstrating independence and ownership of the project. Your supervisor will expect a positive and engaging attitude throughout your project and evidence that you are willing and able to learn, and prepared to take their advice on board as well as criticisms. This does not mean that you necessarily need to do exactly what your supervisor says. You may want to respond to any critique and back up your initial ideas, but you need to do this in an evidence-based and respectful way. Responding appropriately to criticism will be an excellent way of demonstrating willingness and independence. Finally, by adopting a proactive and organized attitude early on in your project, you will be better equipped to deal with expected and unexpected difficulties and will be maximizing your project mark. In many departments, a certain percentage of the project mark is allocated to the student's contribution, which usually reflects their dedication to the project, initiative, ability to meet deadlines, etc. As explained earlier, you should always try and clarify exactly what is expected of you at the beginning of the project. Even if your department does not have a contribution mark, it is most likely that your supervisor will be involved in the marking of your project. Therefore, your attitude and contributions can still influence the mark they give.

3.5 Consider your strengths and weaknesses

Starting a project of this magnitude and working closely together with an academic can sometimes feel overwhelming. To be able to build a healthy and productive relationship with them and to take ownership early in your project, you might start by *recognizing* and *reflecting* on your strengths and weaknesses, the skills you possess and those that you want to develop. Try to identify specific aspects of the project that you will be good at and those that might require more effort. This will help you develop a strategy for resolving issues early in the project, thereby managing your expectations and being more in control. Take a look at Figure 3.2, which depicts some key skills that will help you with that. Try to rate them according to how good you are or how comfortable you feel about them. You should try to use to your advantage the skills that you feel are your strengths. For example, consider all the

Figure 3.2 Key skills that will allow you to take ownership of your project while working effectively with your supervisor

possible ways your skills can enable you to demonstrate engagement, independence, and leadership in your project. Recognizing the skills that you excel at can also boost your confidence when you encounter tasks that you struggle with.

3.6 What to do if things do not go according to plan

Your supervisor will ensure that the project you will be conducting is manageable and within the scope, resources, and time allocated by your institution. However, they will not be able to ensure this without your input and feedback, including sharing and discussing potential obstacles. These obstacles, such as methodological or technical issues, can sometimes arise directly from the project itself. Nevertheless, it is often human factors, such as your or your supervisor's characteristics, situations in your personal life, or issues with communication that present prominent obstacles and can be the most difficult to discuss and resolve. While problems can occur during a research project, they are usually manageable. However, if you do encounter some obstacles that you are unable to resolve, you should approach the project's module coordinator (or other relevant person within your department) to discuss the situation. In this chapter, we will focus on the slightly more personal challenges that you may meet while working on a research project, and in Chapter 4 we will discuss some of the more practical challenges that can occur while conducting a piece of research.

Dealing with personal challenges

It is important to communicate clearly with your supervisor if there is anything that you cannot do or manage in your project. This will help you renegotiate goals and tasks, and receive the support you need. For example, if you are not keeping abreast of your project tasks, you might be tempted to avoid your supervisor or cancel meetings. It is always better to attend meetings and share your concerns with your supervisor so that you will be able to revisit your plans and adapt them to the circumstances. Always remember that your supervisor will be able to help you by providing advice, support, and resources.

Sometimes students can feel overwhelmed or experience personal challenges that might hinder their project's progress. Ask your supervisor for guidance in situations like this. Doing this will not make you appear weak or incapable – to the contrary, it will show that you are able to recognize issues, face them, and deal with them in a constructive and collaborative way. Dealing with difficulties well is itself an important skill that you will need in the future and throughout your working life. Taking the time to reflect on your response to a situation, and on your own strengths and weaknesses, can enable you to understand and further your own personal skills (this often comes up in interview questions!). In this sense, your research project is not very different from any other project you may carry out as part of a future job or study.

Working with different styles of supervision

Sometimes you may feel that you have taken all necessary steps to make your relationship with your supervisor work, but you are still finding it difficult to manage because of their unique supervisory style. Academics will have individual ways of working and years of experience. Everyone has different preferences and approaches, and styles of supervision can differ widely. No style is 'right' and each has its own strengths and weaknesses. To illustrate this, we have developed three brief and rather exaggerated supervisor profiles: Dr Over-enthusiastic, Prof. Control Freak, and Dr Hands Off, which you can see in Figure 3.3. Your first thought will likely be that these are extreme profiles. Yes, you are right! Most supervisors are nice, balanced people who do not fall strictly into any one of these categories, but you may experience some aspects of these characteristics when working with your supervisor. While you are unlikely to encounter one academic who fits into one of our caricatures, you may recognize some elements in the people you work with, and maybe even in yourself! The key issue is to take some time to reflect on how you can best work with people whose approaches to work may be different from yours. By introducing you to more extreme caricatures of imaginary supervisors, we hope to highlight some points to consider, help you manage expectations, and prompt you to develop your own strategies for managing your relationship with your supervisor.

Dr Over-enthusiastic: Is it not lovely to have a supervisor who oozes enthusiasm and passion for research? We often find such teachers the most memorable and influential in our lives. However, some supervisors can be just a little too enthusiastic, and this could be an obstacle to a productive and balanced student–supervisor relationship. Over-enthusiastic supervisors can sometimes be overwhelming, talk excessively in meetings, and yet be vague and unstructured in their explanations. In addition, they might have overambitious plans for your project and, as a result, you may feel lost and find it difficult to keep up with their ideas and plans. At the same time, they may not be aware of the impact of this on you

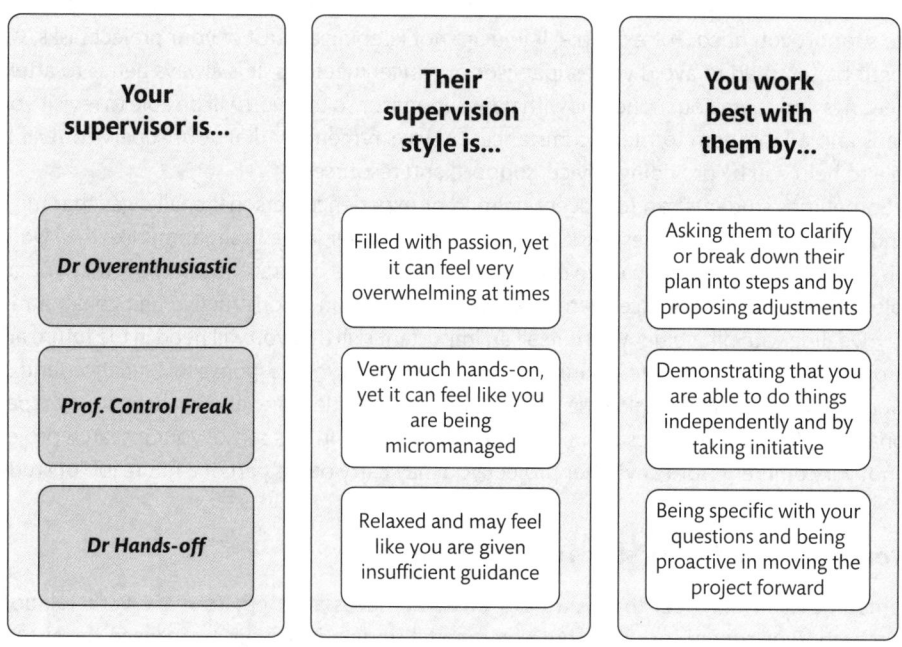

Figure 3.3 Different styles of supervision and how to work with each type of supervisor

and your project's progress. It is unlikely that they will be able to drastically change their supervisory style, so you will need to think carefully about how to deal with such a supervisor and come up with a strategy. One way to 'control' your supervisor's over-enthusiasm is to ask them to clarify and discuss some of their plans in more detail, and then negotiate the best way forward. Furthermore, you might want to follow up each meeting with an email asking them to clarify or confirm specific aspects of your discussion, and then propose adjustments to their ideas and plans if necessary. If you do this, make sure to explain clearly to your supervisor why this approach will work for you. This approach might allow you to make the moderations and adjustments that you need to assist you in your work. Importantly, this will not make you look incapable, but it will show that you are able to recognize and deal with issues and suggest resolutions. Following that, ahead of your next meeting with Dr Over-enthusiastic, you might think about sending an email with a clear plan of what you want to discuss.

Prof. Control Freak: Most supervisors are well aware that students have little experience of managing a project of this magnitude and will try to impose a balanced control over the project. However, Prof. Control Freak prefers being in control of all aspects and stages of the project. This might not be so bad and it can even be reassuring to know that they are in control. Try to think how you could use this to your advantage. For example, it might help you to learn more quickly and keep on top of project tasks. However, it can also be overwhelming (and annoying), because it might seem as though your supervisor is micromanaging your project, thereby limiting your opportunities to develop and demonstrate specific skills, such as independence, leadership, and initiative. One way to demonstrate that you have these skills is by actively reporting to your supervisor on the tasks you have accomplished, sharing plans for future steps, and asking for their input and feedback. In fact, adapting the advice and steps we provide in section 3.4 above will help you manage your relationship with Prof. Control Freak.

Dr Hands-off: A very different type of supervisor style is the hands-off. This means that your supervisor will let you be almost completely in charge of your project and may provide very little guidance. This type of approach can leave you feeling very concerned about your ability to pull the project off. Try and remember that a 'problem shared is a problem halved' and that you will need to be more proactive than usual with Dr Hands-off, taking not only the lead with the project itself but also with your communication with your supervisor. Supervisors are often very busy and you might get the sense that your project is not as important as other aspects of their work, but this will almost always not be the case. If you do feel this way, then try communicating your concerns in an open and diplomatic manner. If you struggle with this, then a good way to start the conversation is to share what you have done so far with your supervisor, invite them to comment on your plans, and then agree the next steps together. You can then repeat this at each stage of the project or whenever you feel you need a little more support.

Whatever their style of supervision, you will need to work closely with your supervisor, and it is therefore crucial that you maintain a good and productive working relationship with them. This is important not just for the success of your project but also for your well-being, development of transferable skills, and an overall positive experience of the task. It is also very important that you consider your own working style, strengths and weaknesses, and how these might interact with your supervisor's approach. For example, if you like to be proactive and independent in your work, you may have a more effective working relationship with Dr Hands-Off than with Prof. Control Freak. So do try to bear in mind that a good working relationship develops from the skills and attributes of both people. However, specific supervisor styles can sometimes make a relationship very challenging and, in exceptional cases, make the student feel like they cannot continue working with their supervisor. If this is you, you might consider consulting another member of staff for advice, such as the project module coordinator or your personal tutor. While this may feel like a difficult thing to do, remember that academic staff want to support you in your studies and for you to have a good educational experience. While conflicts within research projects are, thankfully, rare, they do occasionally occur and whomever you speak to will deal with yours sensitively and supportively. In this situation, make sure that you clarify what you want to achieve by talking to them. Apart from in very exceptional cases (where there might be issues regarding professional conduct), another member of staff should be providing advice and guidance – not taking your place in resolving your problems with your supervisor.

3.7 What about group projects?

When working in a group project, you should not expect your supervisor to manage your intergroup relationships. It is your project and you should take responsibility for managing it, including such relationships. However, if there are issues that you as a group may find difficult to resolve, your supervisor will assist you. We will discuss this in some more detail in Chapter 4.

3.8 Summary: Having a good working relationship with your supervisor

In this chapter, we have tried to illustrate the importance of developing and maintaining a healthy and productive relationship with your supervisor, while at the same time encouraging you to take the lead whenever possible. This relationship should be built on mutual respect and, in many ways, it mimics an employment setting. This means that this experience will enable you to develop several key transferable attributes, such as people skills, resilience, leadership, initiative, independence, and teamwork, which will also be required in your future employment or study. This will be an opportunity, too, to think about your project supervision and the overall management of your project in a more inclusive and socially responsible way. You can see an example of a self-reflective log, focusing on initiative and motivation, in Box 3.1. As you go through your project, you might want to keep a log of your interactions with your supervisor and the skills you have developed – these can be invaluable later with regard to job applications and interviews, and you can see some additional reflections in Box 3.2.

BOX 3.1 A case study showing reflection on initiative and motivation when working with a supervisor

Reflecting on your transferable skills and personal attributes
An example – initiative and motivation

Recognize: From the research you have conducted, what is the best example of when you have demonstrated this skill or attribute?

The first meeting with my supervisor was approaching and I was very excited about it. I was told that this meeting would primarily focus on my research project design. I was not sure whether we would discuss other project-related matters that I was also eager to find out about. So, instead of waiting for the meeting to find out, I decided to read all project guidelines and construct a list of the most pressing questions to ask in that meeting.

Reflect: What are my strengths with regard to this skill or attribute? How can I further develop or improve them?

I am a proactive person and able to channel my motivation and enthusiasm into taking initiative. Despite this, I still need to learn to be more confident with taking initiative, because sometimes I feel I'm being held back by the fear of not overstepping certain boundaries. Although I know this is not necessarily a weakness, I still feel that I could take initiative more often.

Relate: Imagine you are being interviewed for your dream job or course. How would your skills in this area make you suitable for this position?

I am interested in psychology of fashion and want to work in the fashion industry one day. I am a highly motivated person, and I enjoy making things happen and seeing a 'finished product'. These attributes and skills will be beneficial for my chosen career, and I plan to focus on developing them further and gaining more confidence in taking initiative.

BOX 3.2 Hints and tips from psychology graduates and employers of psychology graduates

The student's perspective . . . reflecting on taking initiative

With my supervisor's style, I had to take the initiative to arrange times to meet, which has helped me become confident in asking for help. Because they were responsive and supportive, it helped bring clarity to my research and the development of my project. Don't be afraid to ask questions and remember, this is not their first day on the job: they know what they're doing. Trust their methods and timelines.

Mei, psychology graduate

The employer's perspective . . . reflecting on people skills

I am looking for people to conduct research. This includes working with others to offer ideas, and partner with them in planning and implementing these ideas. Well-informed, collaborative, and succinct communication is therefore essential. Demonstrating good people skills is important and always appreciated.

Stefan, senior researcher

4 Managing yourself and your time

 In this chapter you will learn . . .

- the importance of thinking about your project over time and developing a timeline and Gantt chart for your project;
- the importance of developing your own strategy for effectively managing your project time, tasks, settings, and stakeholders; and
- about the strategies and skills needed to minimize and deal with challenges.

Whether you are doing an individual or group research project, making specific plans about how to manage your project effectively should be high on your priority list. Being a student requires constant planning and managing several things at the same time, from meeting deadlines and attending lectures to working part-time and volunteering. And let us not forget about the busy social life of a university student, which involves establishing new friendships and relationships. You might therefore wonder why managing your research project is any different from what has just been described, and why it warrants a whole chapter of this book.

The research project is the most complex and lengthy piece of academic work that you will undertake during your degree and, as such, is likely to put your planning and organizational skills to the test. It consists of multiple stages and tasks, many of which need to be conducted simultaneously. There are multiple deadlines to meet and several different stakeholders to manage and think about, such as your fellow students, your supervisors, and your participants. So, ultimately, your project is not only about you: it is also an opportunity to practise being open to and respectful of diverse perspectives and contexts. There is also a risk for you because both undergraduate and postgraduate projects commonly contribute a lot towards the overall degree mark, which creates additional pressure. All this is of course in addition to your numerous other academic and non-academic activities. Hence, it is important to devise a clear plan and precise timeline before you embark on your research project journey. To do this, you will need to have good planning as well as organizational and project management skills. Given that these skills are also required for a vast number of jobs that you may consider applying for after you graduate, your research project is an ideal and unique opportunity to develop these skills further. It is also the perfect way of showcasing these skills in job applications and interviews.

4.1 The importance of having an in-depth understanding of your project before you start planning

Before you start developing a plan for how to manage your research project, it is crucial that you gain an in-depth understanding of what exactly your project will involve. This will help you to develop a feasible plan and manage expectations. Without this knowledge, you are risking developing an unworkable plan and you could potentially face some unwelcome surprises along the way. There is actually a great deal you can do before you start planning, and we provide some examples here:

- Familiarize yourself with the project timeline. This will include the key deadlines and milestones.
- Carefully read the student project guidelines and understand what exactly is expected of you.
- Learn as much as possible about all the stages and tasks of the project, how long they take, and what they require.
- Learn about institutional/departmental procedures, such as those relating to research ethics and resources.
- Learn about potential project obstacles and challenges, and how to respond to those. This information may be included in your project guidelines or project informational sessions/lectures. If you want to learn more, your project supervisor will be best placed to help you with this.
- Discuss your project management plans with your supervisor.

Your very first task before starting your well-planned and well-managed project is to ensure that you are familiar with the various stages of conducting your research project. This will help you design a detailed and realistic plan. Being fully prepared will also minimize challenges (such as uncertainty, stress, and anxiety) and it will make you better equipped to respond to those when they do arise.

4.2 Thinking about your research project over time: timelines and Gantt charts

Planning out your entire research project is absolutely crucial. You will be provided with key project deadlines and milestones by your department. This might be in a form of a timeline, which usually includes the start and end dates of the project and the most important deadlines and milestones along the way, such as project proposal, ethics, draft, and final report deadlines. This timeline will also help you ensure that your project aims and design are not over- or under-ambitious.

Do bear in mind that the timeline provided by your department will only include information applicable to the entire student cohort: it will not be tailored to your specific project needs. All student projects are different, so we strongly advise you to create your own project timeline. This should include the major stages in completing your project (for the more granular planning, we will introduce you to Gantt charts in a moment). In addition to the deadlines and milestones provided by your department, this timeline should include information specific to your project, such as meetings with your supervisor and deadlines for your data collection. In Figure 4.1, you can see an example of a project timeline and – on the right – you can add your own notes, such as your departmental deadlines, your own deadlines, and perhaps the tasks that you will need to do to accomplish each stage. In order to meet your project deadlines and milestones, you will need to have a realistic picture of how long specific tasks will take to accomplish and what will be needed to accomplish them on time. To plan this, we recommend that you also

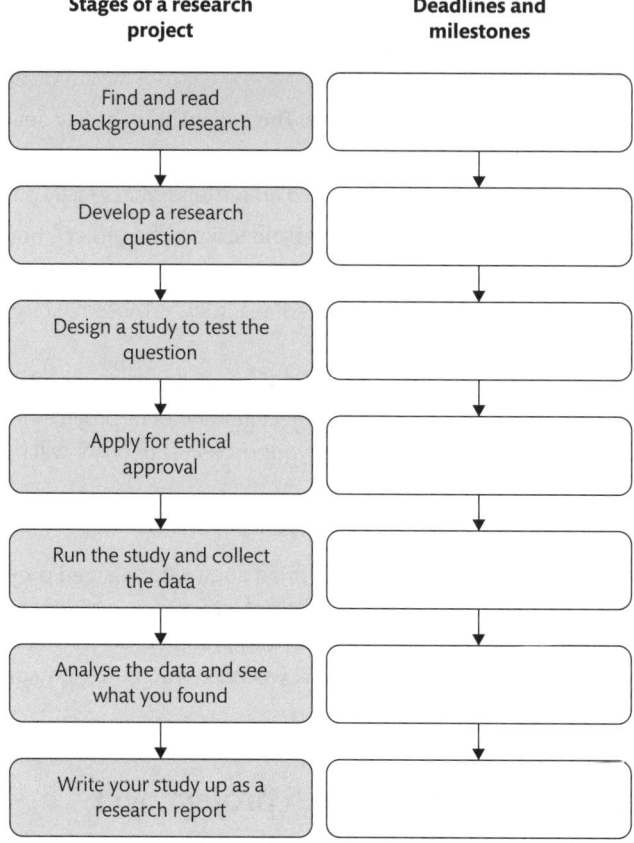

Figure 4.1 Make your own timeline for completing your research project, including both your departmental and your own deadlines for each stage

create a Gantt chart for your project. This is a detailed graphic plan for how and when you will complete each step of your research project, mapping every element of it from start to finish against the timeline that you have to complete the project within. The Gantt chart will help you determine the order in which you will complete tasks and any overlaps between them.

How long does research really take? Conducting research is a laborious process and it usually takes longer than expected. So, when planning your project, it is important to factor this in by over-planning a little and allocating extra time for certain project tasks. For example, preparing study materials such as questionnaires might be relatively straightforward and quick if you are using existing questionnaires, but it will take much longer if you need to develop them yourself. Furthermore, you may not have complete control over all aspects of your project, and an example of this is the data collection. Most psychological research relies on human participants – that is, on their availability and willingness to take part in your research. Both these aspects are largely beyond your control, so it is a good idea to factor them in and allocate some extra time for data collection.

	Month of the study					
	1	2	3	4	5	6
Find and read background research	✓	✓	✓			
Develop your research question	✓					
Draft your Introduction						
Design your study	✓	✓				
Review possible questionnaire measures	✓	✓				
Work on ethics application		✓				
Programme online data collection						
Draft your Methods				✓		
Collect the data						
Analyse the data						
Draft your Results						
Write-up your full draft report						
Revise and proofread your final write-up						

Figure 4.2 Gantt chart for an online questionnaire study with completed tasks ticked off

Also, different types of projects may need different timelines and schedules. For example, data collection for an eye-tracking study may take several months, while data collection using an online survey could be completed within days, although the data cleaning may take considerably longer. To reflect this, we have developed two different Gantt charts for two different research projects, with the completed tasks ticked off for each. Figure 4.2 shows the online questionnaire study and Figure 4.3 the eye tracking study. You can adapt them to your project or you might prefer to create your own Gantt chart. Whatever you do, we cannot recommend this strongly enough because a good Gantt chart will be your guiding star throughout the project.

4.3 Managing your research project time and tasks effectively

Now that you have a clear plan for managing your project and have developed a handy timeline and Gantt chart, you need to ensure that you meet all the deadlines and accomplish all the tasks successfully. This, of course, is much easier said than done: your research project is only one of many academic tasks and challenges you will face during the final year of your undergraduate or postgraduate degree. To help you stay on top of everything project-related, we recommend displaying your timeline and Gantt chart somewhere where you will be able to see them at all times – for example, on your notice board or your computer desktop.

	Month of the study								
	1	2	3	4	5	6	7	8	9
Find and read background research	✓	✓	✓	✓	✓	✓			
Develop your research question	✓	✓							
Draft your Introduction									
Design your study	✓	✓							
Create stimuli		✓							
Programme eye tracking		✓	✓						
Pilot stimuli and programme			✓						
Make changes to stimuli and programme			✓	✓					
Work on ethics application		✓	✓						
Draft your Methods									
Collect the data					✓	✓			
Data processing and cleaning						✓	✓		
Analyse the data									
Draft your Results									
Write up your full draft report									
Revise and proofread your final write-up									

Figure 4.3 Gantt chart for an eye-tracking study with completed tasks ticked off

We know that this might sound like a joy killer because nobody wants to be reminded of their deadlines every hour of every day, but it really is useful and comes with an added bonus: that feeling of joy when crossing off accomplished tasks!

Recognize and reflect on the skills needed for effective project management

Managing your time and tasks effectively will be crucial for the accomplishment and success of your project. How you do this will largely depend on your skills, attributes, personality, style of working, preferences and other responsibilities. This is actually the perfect time to *recognize* and *reflect* on a number of the skills and attributes necessary for developing a strategy for tackling individual project tasks and for your project as whole. In Figure 4.4, we have selected and described six skills that you will need to use and develop through managing your project. As they are crucial for effective project management, we recommend trying to self-assess how good you are at some of these skills now, at the start of your project. You can also consider a range of other skills, not included in this figure – in which case, you may want to revisit Chapter 1, Figure 1.4.

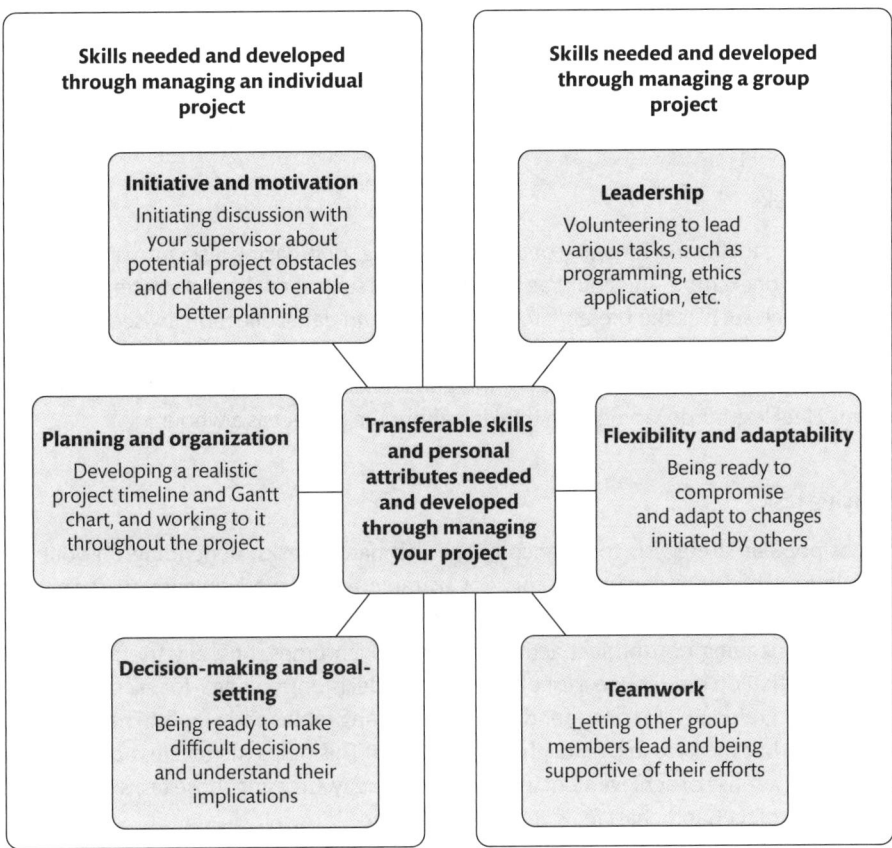

Figure 4.4 Key skills needed for an individual or group project

You may want to start by thinking about your usual ways and styles of working, and assessing any previous projects and situations where you had to accomplish a complex task over a period of time. Think about what you did well, how you managed to achieve that, which aspects you struggled with, and why. Then consider how you can use those strengths (the skills you are good at) in your current research project, and how you can deal with your weaknesses (the skills you are not so good at). For example, you might have realized that decision-making is not one of your strengths because you often take ages to make up your mind about things. This could indicate that project tasks that require decision-making might take longer than expected for you to accomplish – for example, deciding on study measures and materials. Because of this, you may decide to give yourself some extra time for this stage of your project. However, giving yourself too much extra time to make decisions may interfere with other scheduled tasks. Therefore, you need to consider how to develop your decision-making skills because this might be a potential hindrance to your project progress. This example illustrates how important it is to spend time self-reflecting on the skills needed for effective project management: it can save you a lot of time in the long run and help you to develop those skills.

Develop your own strategy to stay motivated and on top of things

Engaging in self-reflection and self-assessment should help you to develop your own strategy for tackling your project tasks. In this section, we include a few tips that may help shape your strategy.

Chunking tasks

One technique that works for many people is 'chunking', or breaking tasks into different levels or amounts. For example, this could be by time chunks such as days, weeks or terms; by stages of your project, such as the project proposal, ethics, and data collection; by sections of your project report, such as introduction, methods, results, and discussion; or some combinations of those. Breaking your project down like this and working towards accomplishing individual tasks may feel less burdensome than thinking about the project as a whole.

Balancing tasks

Another popular strategy is to balance easier and harder tasks, depending on your daily schedule, time of day, or personal factors. For example, when I work on my research projects, I usually avoid engaging in complex project tasks when I am very tired or when I need to focus on other demanding non-project activities. During such times, I usually try to accomplish project tasks that do not require a lot of thinking and decision-making – for example, reviewing my project reference list or appendices, or formatting tables and graphs. These tasks take a lot of time, but they are fairly straightforward to do. This helps me feel less overwhelmed and gives me a sense of achievement at the end of the day. Crossing those tasks off my 'to do' list and the project Gantt chart feels very rewarding too.

Rewarding yourself!

Yet another way of keeping yourself motivated – and a fun one – is by working towards a goal or a treat at the end of a working day. This could be something simple, like watching your favourite show or cooking a meal with your friends.

These are just some tips for how to manage your time and project tasks. There is no right answer to this and you will have to figure out your own strategy to help you manage your project in the best possible way. However, it is important that you think about this explicitly and early on in your project. It is also important to revisit your strategy and adjust it if necessary. Finally, do not forget that you are not alone in this, so do not hesitate to share project management ideas and strategies with your peers.

4.4 Considering your stakeholders and setting for ethical research

When planning your project, not only do you need to think about how to manage your time and tasks efficiently, you also need to think about your research settings and stakeholders. By stakeholders, we mean all the people who are either part of your research project, have an interest in it, or are in some way affected by its outcomes. Consequently, managing stakeholders and settings should be part of your project management plan and can be beneficial in developing your employability, social responsibility, and inclusivity skills.

The very first point to consider when thinking about stakeholders and settings is how to work as an ethical researcher. Applying ethical standards and reasoning in your research, and in particular in ambiguous situations, is a key social responsibility aspect that you should take very seriously (see the 'Wider reading' section in Chapter 1 for more information). You will be required to complete an ethics application as part of your project and submit it to your institution before you start collecting data. This application will cover all stages and aspects of your project, from the design to the write-up. As a psychology student, you have already received substantial training in research ethics, and you will be aware that all your actions should be guided by the British Psychological Society (BPS) Code of Ethics and Conduct (or the appropriate guidance for your institution).

However, it is also important to think beyond the standard ethics application and consider how you will be an ethical researcher throughout your research. In your ethics application, you will need to explain how you will treat your participants and key stakeholders. It is also important to be aware of your research settings and the people whom you may encounter during your project and who might not be specifically mentioned in the ethics application. For example, if you are recruiting patients in a hospital or a clinic, as well as the patients, you will need to consider the many other people whom you will likely encounter during your time there (practitioners, hospital administrators, patients' relatives, visitors, trainee practitioners, other researchers, and so on).

Continuing with this example, you should also consider appropriate conduct in a hospital setting. Hospitals are busy places where patients' health and well-being are the top priority, so professional conduct is important at all times. Showing humility and gratitude for having been given access to patients and to hospital staff who are willing to help with your research will go a long way. Being demanding and expecting patients and staff to help you with your research in any way would of course be unacceptable. Researchers like me have spent a lot of time in hospital waiting-rooms, where I spent much of my PhD time. It requires much patience and awareness of your surroundings. When working with patients, you should be especially mindful of ensuring confidentiality (given the sensitive nature of information being exchanged, such as patients' diagnoses and symptoms), by making sure, for instance, that your conversations with patients are not overheard by others.

If you are in doubt about any of this or have concerns, please consult the BPS guidelines and always discuss your concerns with your project supervisor.

4.5 Dealing with challenges

We discussed earlier how important it is to over-plan in case certain tasks take longer than expected. Research is rarely a linear process and it is possible that some aspects do not go according to plan. For reasons that may be outside your control, no matter how well you plan, you may encounter setbacks. For example, you may miss a particular deadline or there may be difficulties completing one stage of the project. Consequently, it is important to consider potential obstacles and have strategies in place for dealing with them.

Prevention is better than cure

Before you finalize your project management plans, you should discuss with your project supervisor any potential project obstacles and the likelihood of those occurring. To illustrate this, we will again focus on the recruitment of participants. Broadly speaking, the more inclusion and exclusion criteria you have, the more challenging it may be to recruit participants. For example, it is often difficult to recruit participants with specific health conditions, as many of my MSc project students would be able to testify. They often struggle with recruitment because their target population is people with chronic pain conditions. When this is combined with additional inclusion and exclusion criteria, such as certain age, sex, or occupation, the situation becomes more complicated. I always discuss these potential obstacles with my students in our initial meeting and ask them to come up with strategies to address them. One strategy that they often adopt is to recruit two groups of participants – a group with chronic pain and another without chronic pain (the control group) – and compare them on various outcome measures, such as academic and psychological outcomes. By adapting their design so that there is a comparison between groups, their recruitment target for participants with chronic pain is lowered and easier to reach.

Another strategy is simply relaxing the study inclusion and exclusion criteria by, for example, not having restrictions for age, occupation, or type of chronic pain.

The important point here is that it is crucial to think about potential obstacles during the design phase of the project. This is essential in order to avoid poor research practices such as HARKing, which we will discuss in Chapter 5. Also, implementing radical changes in your project design during the later stages of the project may considerably undermine the work you have already done. For example, introducing new variables or changing your study inclusion and exclusion criteria in the later stages might require drastic changes to the report's introduction where you discuss past research and justify the need for your study.

The need for resilience

Despite immaculate planning and preparation, even the best-planned projects can be presented with challenges and obstacles at any stage of the research process. You may encounter errors in programming, difficulties recruiting participants, large amounts of missing data, or personal difficulties that may prevent you from focusing on your project. These challenges will require you to respond appropriately and make difficult decisions. No research is perfect, but you need to show that you understand the consequences and implications of your decisions. Being able to deal with the unexpected, and thinking about alternatives will require you to be adaptable and resilient. While this may come more naturally to some than others, resilience is a key skill that we can all practise and enhance. Try not to compare yourself to others – instead, focus on reflecting on your own experiences and how you can work through this process in a way that will enhance your own skills and progression. To help you prepare for unforeseen challenges, you may want to evaluate your resilience skills early on in the project and think how you can develop them further. At this point, you may find Figure 4.5 helpful: it illustrates how we can engage in the process of *recognizing* and *reflecting* on this key skill, and then *relating* this to future experiences.

Furthermore, consider how you can develop your resilience through your project and relate this learning experience to the next step in your career. Being able to reflect on and assess your

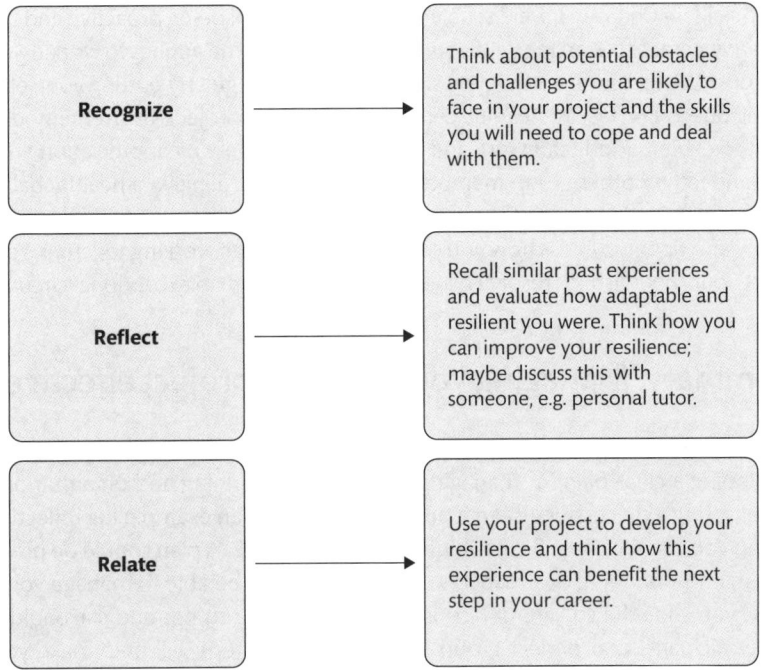

Figure 4.5 Building resilience through your research project using the *three Rs*

own progress is an important employability skill. We suggest that you write a reflective log of your project experiences because you may find this helpful once you start applying for jobs or further study. We designed a similar optional activity for undergraduate project students in our department. This involved their completing a self-reflective log on Moodle (our virtual learning environment) after each major project task. They were asked to write down how they found each task and what they learned from it. They found that this helped them reflect on their skills and think about how they may be able to use them in the future.

4.6 Working as an individual or within a group

As discussed in Chapters 2 and 3, depending on whether you are carrying out an individual project or a group project, you will need to adjust your project plans accordingly. There are some obvious advantages to doing an individual project – for example, not needing to worry about managing relationships and/or negotiating decisions and tasks with other group members. On the other hand, when working as part of a group, you can share many tasks and lighten your load. Tasks such as preparing your ethics application, study materials, and data collection can all be shared.

In a group project, you will need to make sure that you maintain good and productive relationships with your group members. This can be challenging because it is likely that you will be working with students who have different personalities, styles of working, and ambitions. However, it is also an opportunity to develop your communication, teamwork, and leadership skills. In Chapter 3, we discussed the importance of being proactive and taking initiative when it comes to working with your supervisor. The same applies to working with your project group. We recommend that you show initiative by regularly putting yourself forward for carrying out certain tasks or leading certain aspects of the project. But, remember, it is also important to exhibit good teamwork and people skills by showing appreciation and understanding, and letting other group members lead. In order to achieve a healthy balance and have a productive and yet friendly and supportive atmosphere in your group, you will need to regularly and openly discuss how you can achieve this when working together. You should not expect your supervisor to resolve issues for you, apart from in exceptional circumstances.

4.7 Summary: Managing your research project effectively

In this chapter, we have discussed the importance of thinking about your project over time and developing a clear plan for managing your project. Planning and organization are key skills in delivering a successful research project; you can see an example log reflecting this in Box 4.1 and you can see some further hints and tips in Box 4.2. A plan should be preceded by an in-depth understanding of all aspects of your project. To be able to manage your project effectively, you should also carefully consider your project settings and stakeholders, such as study participants and project group members. These steps will help make you better prepared for your project. However, they will not guarantee being spared from challenges as you progress through your project. Such situations will require you to adapt, be resilient, and use your problem-solving and decision-making skills. However, remember that all these potential challenges are manageable and you are not on your own in dealing with them. Do speak with your supervisor, other students, the module coordinator, your personal tutor, or anyone else with whom you feel comfortable. Being proactive in addressing any challenges you face will not only result in your conducting a better research project – it will also allow you to develop key employability skills that will be beneficial for you after you graduate.

BOX 4.1 A case study showing reflection on the planning and organization skills developed when managing a research project

Reflecting on your transferable skills and personal attributes
An example – planning and organization

Recognize: From the research you have conducted, what is the best example of when you have demonstrated this skill or attribute?

At the start of the final year of my undergraduate degree, I felt overwhelmed by the amount and complexity of the work ahead and the pressure to do well. In the past, I was not much of a planner – I simply went with the flow and somehow managed to do well. By self-reflecting like this, I realized that I needed to step up and improve my planning and organizational skills. As a result, I invested a lot of time in creating a detailed and feasible Gantt chart for my project, which ended up being the most visited and helpful document in my project folder.

Reflect: What are my strengths with regard to this skill or attribute? How can I further develop or improve with regard to these?

I have learned that I am able to design workable plans and actively engage with and follow such plans throughout my project.

Relate: Imagine you are being interviewed for your dream job or course. How would your skills in this area make you suitable for this position?

I need to ensure that I employ my planning and organizational skills, not just in complex and lengthy projects but also in small-scale projects and tasks.

BOX 4.2 Hints and tips from psychology graduates and employers of psychology graduates

The student's perspective . . . reflecting on developing resilience

Make sure you have a clear idea of what you'll research, your target population, your desired methodology, and keep close contact with your supervisor throughout the process. I learned how to effectively manage a high workload and how not to feel overwhelmed by it by taking small steady steps every day (e.g. writing a small amount every day). Being steady is the key, building that discipline is what will get you a high-quality project.

Angus, psychology graduate

The employer's perspective . . . reflecting on planning and organization

Working in HR is fast-paced with multiple projects on the go. At interview, we ask applicants to explain how they meet tight deadlines, manage competing demands, and deal with unexpected disruptions. It's handy to have an example of a challenge and how you overcame it, or how you were able to deliver a project alongside day-to-day responsibilities.

Talia, director of human resources

5 The current state of psychological research

In this chapter you will learn about...
- the impact the broader research context and environment have on the quality of psychological research;
- the replication crisis and questionable research practices contributing to it; and
- open science and the solutions it offers to improve the quality of psychological research.

Robust and trusted psychological research is essential not only for the advancement of knowledge but also for its positive real-world impact and social responsibility. Our research often informs public policy, clinical, educational, and organizational practices, and more. If our research is flawed or unreliable, it can lead to ineffective or even harmful policies and practices, ultimately resulting in a loss of public trust in our scientific findings. Reliable and replicable research is the foundation of scientific progress because consistency in findings under similar conditions allows us to develop a knowledge base and theories on which to build further research and knowledge that is useful to society. In this chapter, I (Danijela) will discuss some of the challenges and controversies that have had an impact on psychological research, and some of the ways in which psychological researchers have sought to improve the research that we conduct.

5.1 The replication crisis and open science

Scientific studies are often judged as successful by the replicability of their research evidence. Replicability is important for translating research findings into practice and for creating new lines of research, and, as such, it is a key aspect of science. However, in recent years, the scientific community has become increasingly concerned about replicability of published scientific evidence, with some researchers arguing that psychological research is undergoing a replication crisis. For example, the Open Science Collaboration (2015) attempted to replicate 100 experimental and correlational studies published in three psychology journals. While 97% of original studies had statistically significant results, only 36% of the replication studies led to significant findings. Yet, not everybody is convinced that replication studies are necessarily a good measure of research replicability because these studies can be prone to bias too. In spite of these disagreements around the term 'replication crisis', there is wide agreement among scientists about the need to improve the quality of psychological research.

Given that students are the next generation of researchers, it is important that you understand the various issues that have led to this 'crisis' in psychological research, and that you are aware of and able to use the strategies that have been developed to ensure that psychological research is more robust. Later in this chapter, we will give you some ideas about how you might apply the open science principles in your own research project, and we will come back to this again in later chapters.

Failure to replicate scientific findings has been attributed to poorly designed and underpowered studies (we will explain what this means later in this chapter under the heading 'Poor study design and low power') as well as problematic research practices, such as hypothesizing after the results are known (HARKing), lack of transparency about data, selective analysis, *p*-hacking, and selectively reporting positive results. In this chapter, we discuss each of these problematic research practices. We also discuss potential solutions, which fall under the broad umbrella of 'open science'. Open science is a movement that advocates transparency in all stages of knowledge generation and makes this knowledge publicly available. You can see a summary of this in Figure 5.1. This transition to open science has greatly benefited

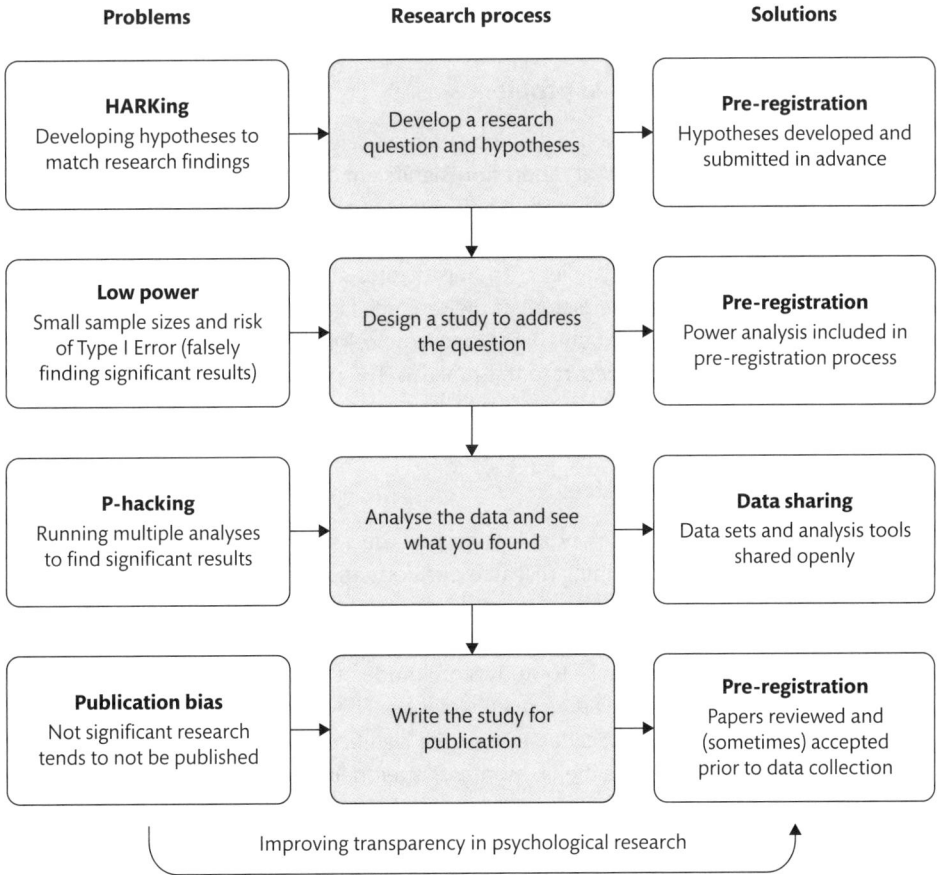

Figure 5.1 Some of the problems with the research process and some solutions offered by open science

psychological science, but it also requires more time, resources, and flexibility, so it has not been without challenges.

Why is this relevant to undergraduate and postgraduate students and early career researchers like yourself? Improving current science practices requires a better education of new generations of researchers, and familiarity with the replication crisis, the questionable research practices contributing to it, and the ways to overcome them are crucial if you are to be able to produce good-quality research. Being open to feedback, critiquing your research practices, and engaging with open science will help you develop several important transferable skills and prepare you for the world of work or further study. A good awareness of the principles behind open science will also allow you to produce research that is socially responsible and can make a positive contribution to wider society.

5.2 The problems leading to the replication crisis

Here, we outline some of the key problems leading to poor-quality psychological research and the apparent replication crisis. We also highlight that these problems do not exist in isolation and often interact with each other.

Publication bias or file drawer problem

Publication bias refers to the practice whereby journals selectively publish positive or novel results and rarely publish those that report non-significant or non-confirmatory results. This practice can influence researchers to report only their significant findings and dispose of their negative findings in a file drawer (Rosenthal, 1979). The file drawer problem means that it is difficult to establish how many studies with negative results have been conducted but not published, and therefore the true picture of the research landscape may be distorted. There are some indicators that the number is high. For example, John, Loewenstein, & Prelec (2012) found that over 70% of authors resort to this practice. The publication bias can give rise to a number of questionable research practices, which we now discuss.

Questionable research practices

Questionable research practices may, at least in part, be a result of the current competitive research 'climate', whereby obtaining research positions and promotions is heavily dependent on having published in high-impact journals, many of which prefer publishing significant and novel research findings. For example, if a researcher feels under pressure to obtain significant findings, they might choose to study a multitude of variables but present only those that produce significant results as their main variables. They might also resort to *p*-hacking, whereby they run several statistical analyses until significant results are found, and/or to HARKing, whereby they generate their hypotheses after their results are known. For example, a researcher might obtain non-significant results for their original hypothesis, but, after running several types and versions of unplanned or exploratory statistical analyses (*p*-hacking), they might obtain one significant result, which was not part of their original hypothesis. They might then decide to change their original hypothesis (HARKing) to fit their significant finding. They might also look for literature that would explain and justify their new hypothesis and finding. Therefore, their HARKing presents an exploratory analysis as if it were a confirmatory analysis. Why is this a problem? These practices go against the scientific method that forms the basis of knowledge generation: a basic premise of the scientific method is that researchers should start their inquiry with a specific hypothesis (usually informed by existing theory and knowledge) and have a pre-planned analysis for testing it, before they collect and analyse their data.

It is easy to think that these questionable research practices are only employed by a small number of dishonest researchers. This could not be further from the truth, because a large number of honest researchers use them too. This statement probably makes little sense to you, so let us try to unwrap it. There are a number of reasons why this happens to perfectly honest and well-meaning scientists, and these are nicely outlined and discussed by Nuzzo (2015). One issue is that the current research environment is very competitive, and it has become an ideal to produce large quantities of exciting and novel findings that have the potential to speed up the progress of conducting and publishing research. This has led to the quantity over quality problem, and it is usually significant rather than non-significant findings that are considered exciting. Many researchers do not deliberately produce potentially misleading results. Instead, in order to deliver what is expected of them, they try to find something significant and exciting in their data. In addition, science is all about innovation, so these questionable practices might be justified (consciously or unconsciously) as being innovative rather than problematic. Nuzzo (2015) argues that, because the human mind is susceptible to self-deception, it is easy to get into this trap without realizing that what we are doing might be wrong. It is therefore important to regularly reflect on and evaluate our research practices. This will ensure that psychological research is robust and beneficial to specific groups and society more broadly.

Poor study design and low power

The reliability of scientific research is also undermined by poorly designed and underpowered studies. Research shows that low statistical power is a consistent problem in a number of disciplines, including psychology (Button et al., 2019). The statistical power of a study is defined as the probability that it will reject a false null hypothesis (also referred to as a 'Type II error'). Essentially, this means that you may have missed finding a result that really does exist. A false null hypothesis is concluding that there is no effect when, in reality, there is an effect, but the study was not powerful enough to detect it. If a study has sufficient power, it is more likely to detect an effect, provided an effect exists in the real world. Statistical power is influenced by the size of the effect that exists in the real world. For example, if you are comparing scores on a memory test between patients who have a brain injury and control participants who do not have a brain injury, then you would probably expect quite a large difference between the groups, or a large effect size. In contrast, if you were to compare memory scores between two subtle stimuli manipulations, then you may expect a relatively small difference, or a small effect size. The key point here is that different effect sizes are suitable for different research questions, so a large effect size is not necessarily 'better' than a small effect size – it just depends on the research question that you are asking.

The size of the sample you need is in part determined by the size of the effect you expect to find. Larger effects are easier to detect and require smaller sample sizes, while detecting smaller effects will require larger samples. Low statistical power, meaning that you may not have enough participants to detect the effect that you are looking for, does not only lead to a Type II error. If a study with a low statistical power produces a large effect size, it reduces the likelihood that that result is true. If an inappropriate effect size is used, it may be hard to draw reliable conclusions from such studies. Therefore, low statistical power can also lead to an inflated effect size and potentially a Type I error (obtaining a false-positive result). Overall, underpowered studies undermine the production of reliable knowledge and lead to wasted resources. Underpowered studies can be a result of the current research climate whereby quantity over quality resides and a lack of resources and limited understanding of the importance of statistical power abide.

Lack of transparency in planning, conducting, and reporting research

Another example of poor research practice that has contributed to the current crisis in research is the lack of transparency in planning, conducting, and reporting research. Credible and reliable scientific claims should be always supported by evidence. This includes the collected data as well as the methodology used to acquire and deal with the data. Lack of transparency about the way research is conducted makes re-analysis, synthesis, independent verification and evaluation difficult. To improve the credibility and replicability of their research findings, researchers should make their research practices as transparent as possible, and this should include every stage of the research process. However, improving the transparency, and consequently replicability of research findings, necessitates involvement from all research stakeholders: researchers, institutions, and journals (Munafò et al., 2017). Often, there are institutional and dissemination barriers to transparency of research, such as different financial interests and manuscript length restrictions. This can result in partial reporting of research – for example, study protocols, raw data, and analytical procedures are usually not available to readers.

5.3 The solutions open science offers

In this section, we introduce and discuss several potential solutions to the questionable research practices and ways to improve the quality of psychological research. The list is not exhaustive so, if you would like to do further reading, please see the list of useful references at the end of this chapter.

Pre-registration of research designs and Registered Reports

Pre-registration refers to a practice whereby researchers pre-register their study hypotheses, basic study design, and planned analyses before commencing their data collection. Any additional analyses they decide to carry out, after they have their data, are classed as exploratory analysis. These are distinguished from their planned or confirmatory analysis. This is a simple yet efficient way to protect against many questionable research practices, such as HARKing and *p*-hacking. To demonstrate that their study was not subject to questionable research practices, researchers can include their pre-registration form when they submit their finished study to a journal. This has been an established practice for a number of years for certain types of research such as clinical trials and systematic reviews, and it is now being embraced within other types of research and variety of disciplines. Researchers can pre-register their study plans on research platforms such as AsPredicted,[1] Open Science Framework[2] and PROSPERO.[3] The latter was specifically designed for the pre-registration of systematic reviews and meta-analyses.

However, because pre-registration forms are not subject to peer review, researchers are not guaranteed that their finished studies will be published. The good news is that some journals now accept Registered Reports. Registered Reports are similar to pre-registration, but they are peer reviewed. They also include a much more detailed study plan whereby both the research question and the proposed methods to address it are carefully examined. If a Registered Report is accepted and the study plan is followed, the manuscript resulting from it is guaranteed to be published, irrespective of its results. This means that, in addition to addressing HARKing and *p*-hacking, Registered Reports also address publication bias.

When you complete your research project, you may not yet be thinking as far ahead as publishing your work, but a number of psychology departments are now including a form of pre-registration as a standard process within student research projects. This means that you may be asked to write a project proposal or pre-registration document when you are designing your study. It will help you to clearly plan out your project, your methods, and the research question you will address.

Improving study design and power

An essential step towards rigorous research designs is education. Providing proper and continuous research training in the principles of scientific research to both experienced and new generations of researchers is necessary for creating competent researchers and good-quality research. One key target area for training is improving the statistical power of research studies. Poorly designed and underpowered studies are often a result of the current competitive research environment and inadequate understanding of statistical power. Statistical power is influenced by the size of the effect that exists in the real world and the size of the sample a study uses to detect it. However, many researchers do not report effect sizes and/or state a justification for their sample size. These practices should be encouraged and relevant training should be provided to researchers. Poorly designed and underpowered studies can also be due to a lack of resources. Collaborative research efforts, such as 'team science' could be used to tackle this problem. Team science refers to collaborations whereby scientists from different fields and with diverse skills work together to address a research question. In some ways, student group research projects are a form of team science with people bringing together their different interests, research skills, and life experiences. This may involve aspects such as multi-site data collection and cross-disciplinary expertise, and it can result in highly powered designs and also contribute to the generalizability of findings (Button et al., 2019).

---

[1] http://AsPredicted.org   [2] http://osf.io   [3] https://www.crd.york.ac.uk/prospero

If you are completing a project pre-registration form (or proposal), then you are likely to be asked to include information about your anticipated sample size and to justify this on the basis of power calculations. With this in mind, you can be confident that your design is powerful enough to detect any meaningful effects that may exist.

Improving research transparency, sharing of data, and analysis tools

The term 'open science' indicates that scientific knowledge generation should be open, transparent, and available to others. In line with this, an increasing number of researchers are making their research plans (e.g. research protocols), procedures (e.g. analytical workflows) and raw data available. However, many of these practices cannot take place without support from relevant institutions and journals, which are now enabling this change to happen by introducing specific open science policies and guidelines (Munafò et al., 2017). An example of this is the Transparency and Openness Promotion (TOP) guidelines.[4] Another example is the Open Science Framework (OFS), which is a free, open platform for sharing research processes and supporting research collaboration.

TOP and OFS are designed to improve research quality and transparency in general, while other guidelines have been designed to address the transparency and quality of research reporting of particular research methodologies. A great number of specific guidelines now exist for various types of research, such as observational studies, randomized controlled trials, systematic reviews, meta-analyses and so on. An example of this is the Preferred Reporting Items for Systematic Reviews and Meta-Analyses (PRISMA) guidelines[5] for the reporting of systematic reviews and meta-analyses.

Pre-registration is an important part of improving transparency around psychological research, but you may also engage with the research tools and data that other researchers share as part of your research project. For example, if your project involves a replication study, you may use the research protocols and materials shared by other researchers. Or you may use secondary data, made available by other researchers, as a part of your project. Beyond this, you may also be asked to share your own research protocols and the data that you collect as a part of your research project, particularly if the project that you complete is submitted for publication in a peer-reviewed journal.

Rapid sharing of psychological research

One way to improve quality of psychological research is to open it more to scrutiny, and another way to achieve this is via a rapid dissemination of research ideas and findings. Publishing research in journals can be a very slow process. To overcome this problem, researchers can use various research platforms to publish their research 'preprints'. Preprints are finished research manuscripts shared publicly without undergoing peer review. Research platforms such as OSF Preprints[6] allow researchers to share their work publicly and receive quick feedback. There are also discipline-specific platforms: for example, PsyArXiv[7] is a free preprint service for the psychological sciences and it is hosted by the Centre for Open Science. It is

---

[4] https://cos.io/top/   [5] http://www.prisma-statement.org/   [6] https://osf.io/preprints/
[7] https://psyarxiv.com/

important to clarify that preprints are usually not considered publications. Some journals will accept articles that have been previously shared publicly as preprints while others will not.

When you are reviewing the previous research for your project, it might be helpful to also check these platforms to ensure that you are aware of the most recent developments within your area of research. Bear in mind that while research shared in this way may be very current, it may not have been through the usual peer review process (for more on this, see Chapter 11). Therefore, it is important to acknowledge this if you use these papers in your write-up.

5.4 Open science practices and developing transferable skills

In this chapter, we have discussed the current state of psychological research. We have argued that the current research climate contributes to various questionable research practices. We have also described several solutions to these issues and introduced the concept of open science. Open science practices require a change in how research is planned, conducted, disseminated, and funded. It is incredibly important for students starting out in research to be familiar with these problems, to learn how they can produce good-quality research, and to think about the skills developed through engaging with open science practices. You can see some examples of this in Figure 5.2.

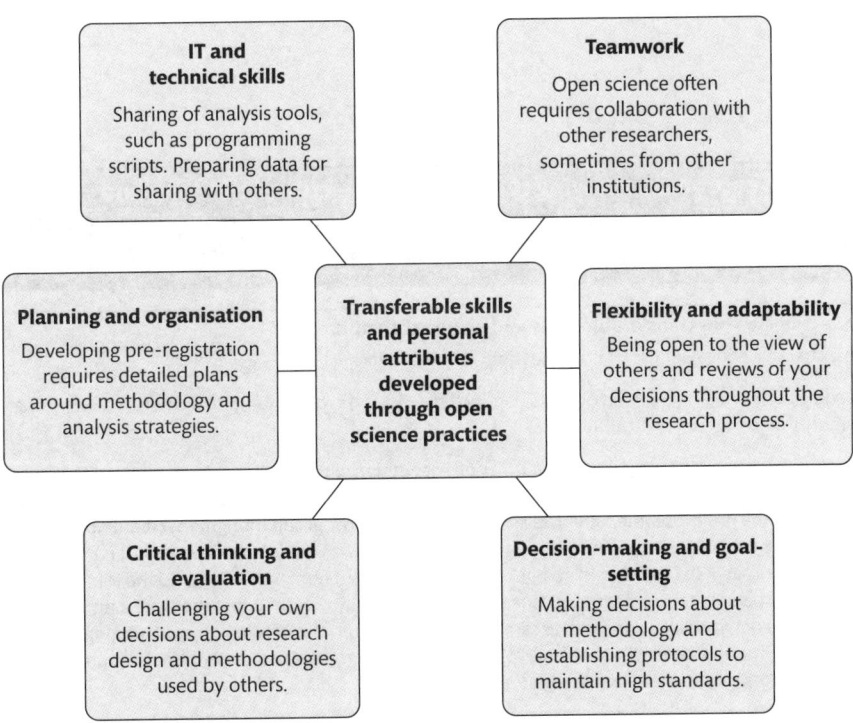

Figure 5.2 Key transferable skills and personal attributes that may be developed through open science practices

Engaging with open science will also help you develop a number of transferable skills. Producing good-quality research requires good planning and organizational skills. By challenging your own and others' research practices, you will be developing your critical thinking and evaluative skills. If you are part of a team, you can encourage your team members to think critically about your project and also assist them in adapting open science practices. This can be an opportunity for you to work on your teamwork and leadership skills. Being open to criticism from your supervisor, reviewers, and colleagues about your research practices will help you become a more resilient, adaptable, and confident researcher or future employee.

5.5 Summary: Reflecting on open science and research

Throughout the research process, it is important to take the time to *recognize* the skills that you are developing and demonstrating, *reflect* on your strengths and weaknesses, and *relate* your skill development to your future educational and career aspirations. These are the *three Rs (3Rs)* that we talked about in Chapter 1. Engaging in open science practices gives you some unique opportunities to develop some quite high-level skills that are invaluable in postgraduate education and which are highly sought after by many employers of graduates. In Box 5.1, you can see an example of how a student might reflect on the transferable skills and personal attributes that they have developed while working on a research project and engaging with open science practices. You can also see some helpful hints and tips in Box 5.2.

BOX 5.1 A case study showing reflection on the critical thinking and evaluation skills developed when conducting research according to the principles of open science

Reflecting on your transferable skills and personal attributes
An example – critical thinking and evaluation

Recognize: From the research you have conducted, what is the best example of when you have demonstrated this skill or attribute?

I was working on my undergraduate final year project design with my project team. We had to come up with a recruitment strategy, and this included deciding how many participants we needed to recruit. This part of the project seemed relatively straightforward, so my group thought that it did not require extensive reading of literature and learning and the decision was made quickly. I was not entirely happy with this approach, so I decided to go back to my old lecture notes and read around the topic to check whether we needed to approach this issue more systematically. I learned that there are a number of strategies to determine an appropriate sample size and I shared this with my group. By being able to think critically about research, I was able to help my group re-evaluate our recruitment approach and make an informed decision about sample size.

Reflect: What are my strengths with regard to this skill or attribute? How can I further develop or improve with regard to them?

I am an inquisitive person and always like to question and evaluate what I hear and read. This attribute has helped me to develop my critical thinking skills. I believe I am able to think critically about others' and my own research practices. I have always enjoyed my research methods lectures and reading scientific research papers, which helped me to develop my critical thinking skills. To improve these skills still further, I should try to learn about and be more engaged with current trends and issues in research beyond my degree, such as open science initiatives.

Relate: Imagine you are being interviewed for your dream job or course. How would your skills in this area make you suitable for this position?

I want to study for a PhD in clinical psychology. Being able to produce good-quality unbiased research is important for this position. It requires excellent critical thinking and evaluation skills. I am hoping to publish my research, so it is important to ensure that it can help my readers to make informed decisions. I am aware that my research can potentially have an impact on health practices and policies, hence being critical about my own research is crucial.

BOX 5.2 Hints and tips from psychology graduates and employers of psychology graduates

The student's perspective . . . reflecting on planning and organization

Through completing my project, I learned the importance of good planning and consistency in preparing and executing the methodology. This contributed to producing valid and reliable research, making a meaningful contribution to the field of study.

Natalya, psychology graduate

The employer's perspective . . . reflecting on critical thinking

Critical thinking and evaluation are essential for a policy research role. We are often researching topics with which we are not familiar, so being able to assess the evidence base and the robustness of research methods is really important. We often ask applicants to write a sample briefing, or ask in interview how they assess research.

Lucas, statistical advisor

Wider reading

Button, K.S., Chambers, C.D., Munafò, M.R. et al. (2019). Grassroots training for reproducible science: A consortium-based approach to the empirical dissertation. *Psychology Learning & Teaching*, 19(1).

In this paper, the authors present a model of consortium-based (i.e. team science) student projects to train undergraduates in reproducible science and the production of high-quality research. They also outline the pedagogical benefits of this approach and how it can be aligned with the current educational practices, such as those relating to student assessment.

Munafò, M.R., Nosek, B.A., Bishop, D.V. et al. (2017). A manifesto for reproducible science. *Nature Human Behaviour*, 1(1), 0021.

In this paper, the authors argue for the adoption of certain measures (e.g. pre-registration, team science) to deal with questionable research practices, improve key elements of the scientific process, and increase the transparency and reproducibility of research. They discuss why these measures are important and how they can be implemented.

6 Doing an experimental research project

  In this chapter you will learn . . .

- how to design a robust and complex experimental research study;
- how to plan out an appropriate analysis strategy and interpret your findings; and
- how to write up your study and think critically about experimental designs.

By this stage in your training to do psychological research, you are probably very familiar with experimental designs and the basics behind designing and analysing experimental studies. However, as you progress to become a more independent researcher, you are likely to design rather more complicated designs, and these require rather more complicated analyses. In this chapter, I (Victoria) want to work through one of these more complicated designs – a 2*3*3 three-way mixed design ANCOVA. Don't worry: we will go through exactly what this means, along with many hints and tips to help you to design, analyse, interpret, and write about more complex experimental psychological studies. If you want to revise some of the core concepts underlying experimental design and ANOVA (analysis of variance), then there is some recommended reading at the end of this chapter (Section Two of Bourne et al., 2021, has nine chapters going through experimental design, analysis, and write-up in lots of detail). Depending on your design, you may also find that parts of this chapter are less relevant than others. For example, the ANCOVA section may not be so necessary if you are not including a covariate in your design. Similarly, if you are only manipulating two variables, then the section on three-way designs may not be such essential reading.

6.1 Skills required to be a good experimental researcher

Designing, running, analysing, and interpreting an experiment involves lots of detailed planning to ensure that your experiment clearly addresses your research question in a robust and rigorous way. This means that you will develop a wide range of transferable skills, which you can see in Figure 6.1. In addition to the planning, decision-making, and initiative that you will need to design your experiment, you may also develop some new IT skills through learning software to develop stimuli and programme your experiment. Experiments also often require working within a research team and much time recruiting and testing participants, making people skills and communication essential to ensure that your experiment runs smoothly.

DOING AN EXPERIMENTAL RESEARCH PROJECT 55

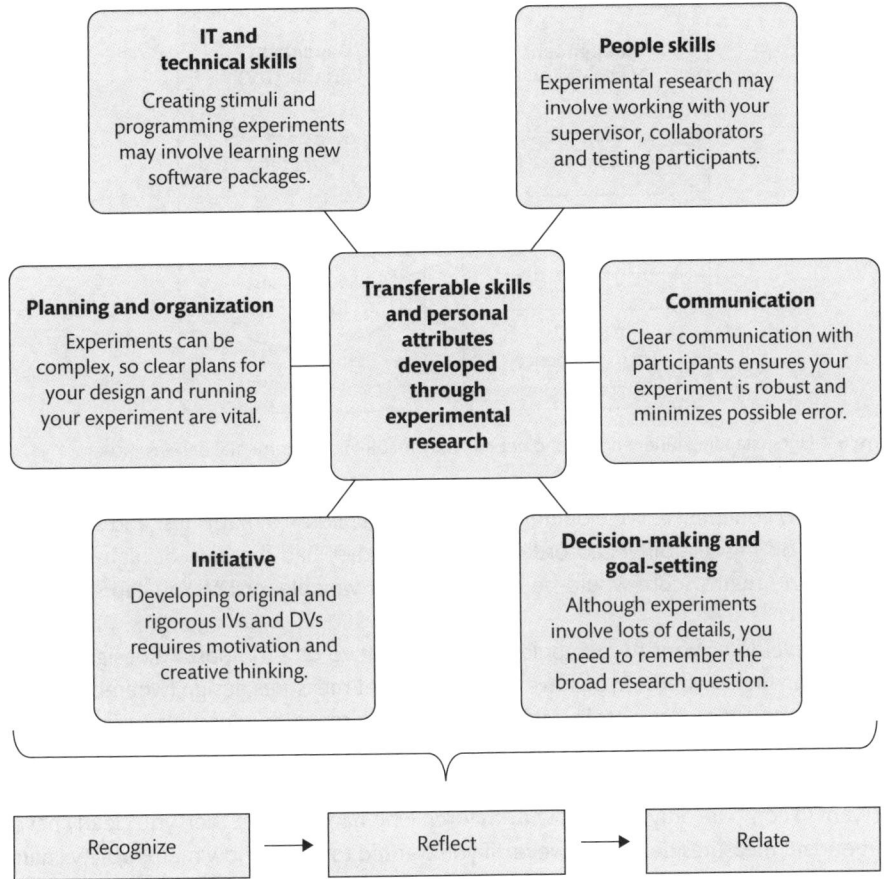

Figure 6.1 Transferable skills and personal attributes developed through experimental research

6.2 A quick revision of the basics

When we design experiments, there are a number of technicalities, and it is important to get these right to ensure that your study is well-designed, appropriately analysed, and accurately interpreted. While you should be familiar with the basics of experimental design, we will have a quick refresher while I explain the fictional experimental design that we will be working through in this chapter.

Experimental manipulation and types of design

The main aim of an experiment is to manipulate one or more variables to see the impact that this has on a measured variable. For example, if we were interested in how teachers' confidence influences children's academic performance, we might develop a manipulation whereby we compare teachers with either high or low confidence in teaching maths. This manipulation would be our independent variable, or IV, and it would have two conditions:

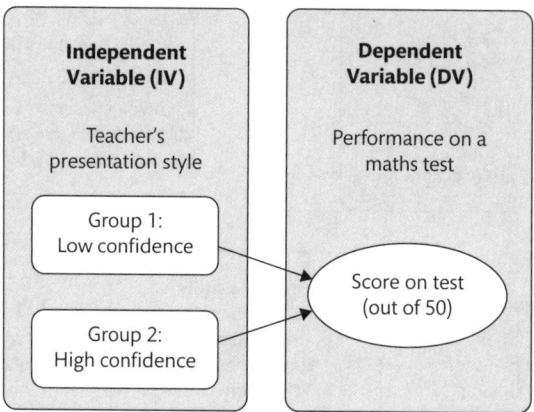

Figure 6.2 Understanding independent and dependent variables in experimental designs

high and low confidence. We would then give all the children a maths test and see whether their score on this test differs according to whether they had the low- or high-confidence teaching. This maths score would be our dependent variable, or DV. You can see these in Figure 6.2.

When developing your IV manipulation, there are two other important design decisions to make. The first is whether you have an independent measures design (whereby you have separate groups of participants in each condition) or a repeated measures design (whereby you have one group of participants who take part in all the conditions). Sometimes it is obvious whether you should have an independent or repeated measures design. For example, if you want to compare only children with children who have siblings, then you clearly have an independent measures design. However, if you wanted to look at how maths ability changes over time, you would have a repeated measures design. Sometimes, though, it is not quite so obvious, and this is where it is important to think carefully about the decision you make and the possible implications that this will have for your findings. For our teacher's confidence IV, this could be either an independent or a repeated measures design. I'd probably not use a repeated measures design because of possible carryover effects from repeatedly doing a maths test – either practice effects (getting better with practice) or fatigue effects (getting worse due to boredom). Either of these effects would create random variance in the dataset, making it difficult to work out what variability in the scores had been caused by our manipulation. Therefore, for the teachers' confidence IV, an independent measures design would be more suitable. This means that we will have two separate groups of children: one group in the low teachers' confidence condition and the other group in the high teachers' confidence condition.

The second design decision is whether your design is a pure experiment, meaning that you can randomly allocate participants to the conditions, or whether it is a quasi-experimental design, meaning that whatever defines which conditions participants are in cannot be randomly allocated. For example, with our teachers' confidence IV, we could randomly allocate the children to being in either the low or the high teachers' confidence group. Therefore, it is a pure experiment with random allocation. Imagine that, instead, we wanted to compare 5-year-olds with 10-year-olds: that would have to be a quasi-experimental design because we can't manipulate a child's actual age and randomly allocate them to be either 5 or 10 years old! Wherever possible, a pure experimental design is preferable but, if the IV that you are interested in requires a quasi-experimental design, then that is fine.

Understanding variance in experimental designs

Before talking more about experimental design, I want to take some time to go over what it is that we are looking for, statistically, when we do an experimental study. It is easy to fall into the trap of thinking that the main aim of an experimental study is to look for differences between conditions but, statistically, it is not quite as simple as that. When we analyse data collected in experiments, we are actually looking at the variability that exists in a dataset and trying to understand what has caused that variability. There will always be variability in data because some people will get higher scores and some lower. We analyse the data to find out what is causing this variability, of which there are two types. Experimental (or 'between groups') variability is the simple difference between two conditions, whereas random (or 'within groups') variability is the remaining variance that cannot be explained by our manipulation. Instead, random variance is likely to result from some kind of measurement error or confounding variables. If you imagine all the variance in the dataset as a cake, all we are doing in the analysis is dividing the cake up into slices, whereby each slice represents a different type of variance. The more complex the design, the more slices we will have in the cake. We will come back to experimental and random variance later in this chapter!

The important point here is that it is not just the size of the difference between the conditions (the experimental variance) that determines whether the result is significant or not. It is to do with whether the variability in the data is best explained by the experimental manipulation or whether it is random, and this is what an ANOVA will look at. If you look at the two examples in Figure 6.3, the difference between the two conditions (the experimental variance) is exactly the same. However, the amount of random variance is very different, which you can see in the variance 'cakes'. In the example on the left, there is relatively little random variance and this analysis would most likely be significant, whereas, in the example on the right, the large amount of random variance means that the analysis would probably not be significant. Through every stage of doing an experimental project, always remember that it is not just about the difference between the conditions – any random variance in the data you collect will have an impact on the conclusions that you draw.

6.3 Designing an experimental study

So far, we have a very simple experiment, with just one IV being manipulated. You may see this described as a 'one-way design' because there is just one IV. However, in this chapter, we want to focus on more complex experimental designs, including those where multiple IVs are manipulated, which are called 'factorial designs'. If two IVs are manipulated, this is a two-way design; with three IVs, it is a three-way design, and so on. Again, if you would like to revise the basics of experimental design, there is some recommended reading at the end of this chapter (from Bourne et al., 2021).

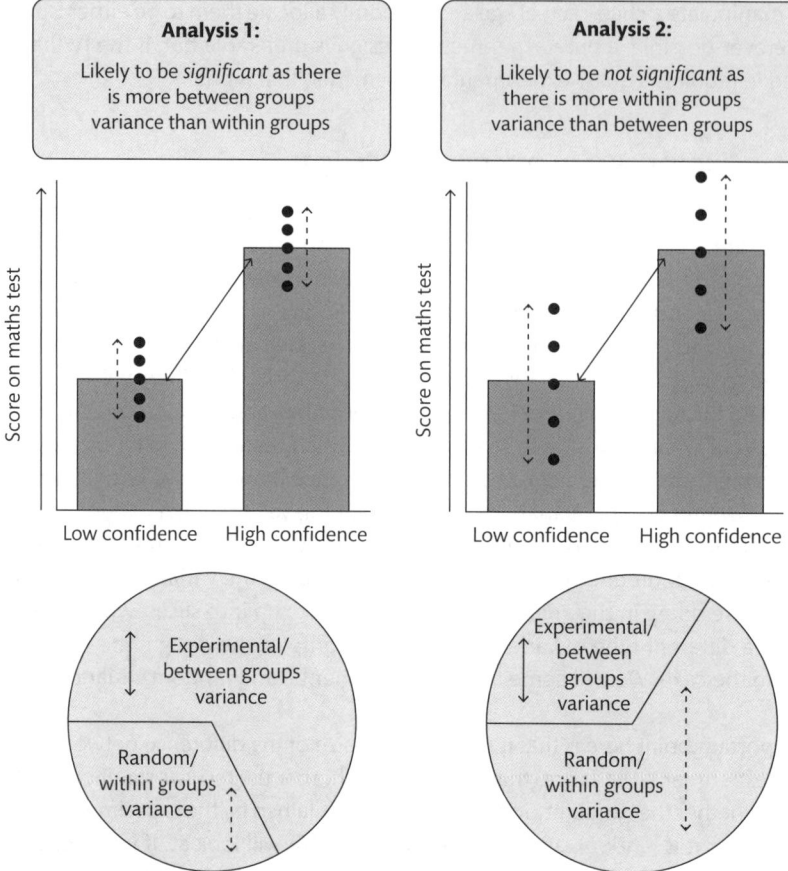

Figure 6.3 Experimental and random variance in a simple experimental design

Developing a two-way factorial experiment

Let's add an extra IV to our design and make it a two-way design. Our second IV will be test difficulty, with three conditions: easy, medium, or difficult. This will be a repeated measures IV, so each child will complete three maths tests, one at each difficulty level. This would be described as a 2*3 mixed design. The '2' is because of the two conditions in the teachers' confidence IV, and the '3' is because of the three conditions in the test difficulty IV. It is a mixed design because it includes both an independent measures and a repeated measures design. You can see this broken down in Figure 6.4.

With a two-way factorial design, our analysis still focuses on understanding the experimental and random variance cakes. However, there are now rather more slices in the cake, reflecting the various experimental effects that we will want to analyse and understand. With a two-way design, we will end up with three statistical findings, reflecting three different sources of experimental variance, which you can see in Figure 6.5. There are two important points to remember with experimental effects in factorial designs. The first is that each main effect looks at the amount of variance uniquely explained by an individual IV, ignoring any variance explained by other IVs. The second is that the two-way interaction looks at the variance

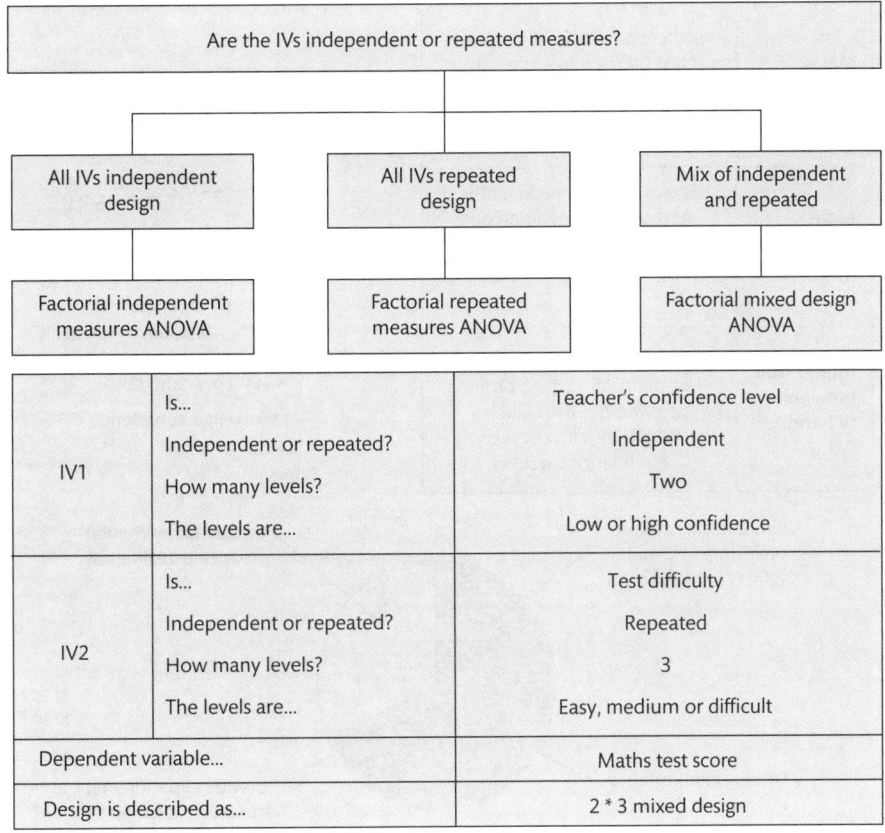

Figure 6.4 Describing factorial experimental designs

uniquely explained by the two IVs in combination. In our example, this might mean that the differences according to test difficulty might vary depending on the teachers' confidence. The fictional interaction in Figure 6.5 shows how maths test scores are very similar across the difficulty levels when the teacher has a low level of confidence whereas, for high-confidence teachers, the children do far better with the easy test than the medium and difficult tests.

Developing a three-way factorial experiment

Until this point, everything is probably revising what you already know but, for this chapter, we are going to take a step further and look at a three-way factorial experiment! We will now add a third IV, which relates to the children's self-esteem. For this variable, the children are asked to fill in a self-esteem questionnaire, which gives a score by adding up all the item responses. This continuous variable is then converted into a categorical variable with three groups: low, mid, or high self-esteem. This means that IV3 is the child's self-esteem and it is an independent measures variable with three conditions, making our new three-way design a 2*3*3 mixed design. You may not have come across three-way designs before and at first they can look a little daunting, but there are ways to help understand these more complex designs. You can see this in Figure 6.6. I often find it helpful to map out the final design in this

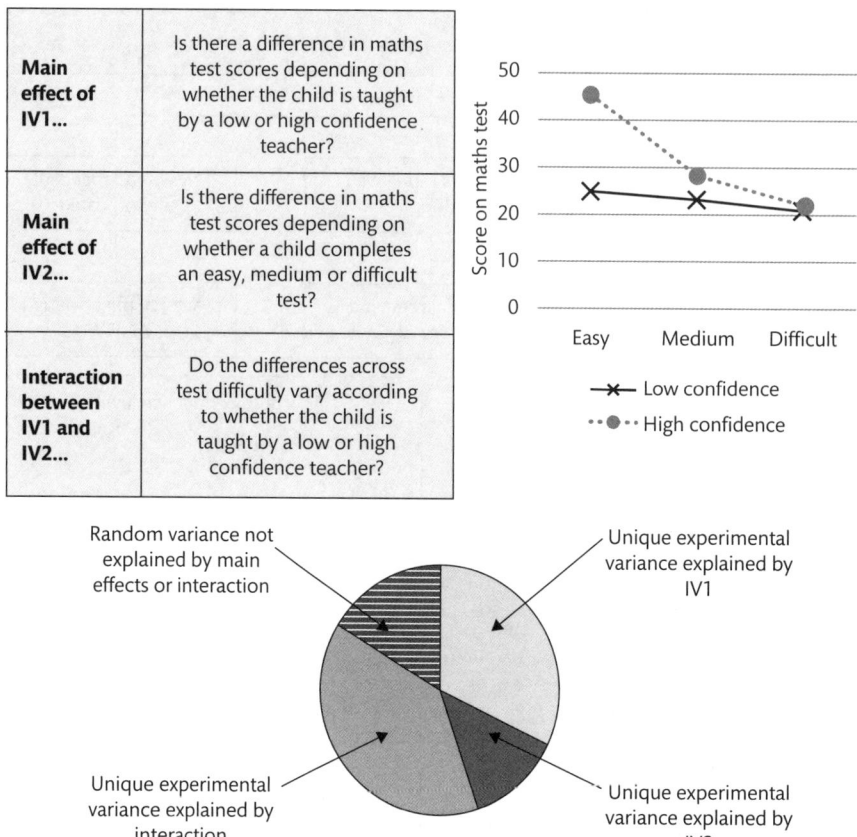

Figure 6.5 Experimental effects in a two-way factorial design

way before getting into the next steps of designing the experiment, and I would recommend that you try to do this too.

Possibly the most difficult thing about doing a three-way experiment is that the number of effects that we now need to analyse and interpret increases, and there are now seven different findings! In Figure 6.7, you can see how we have three main effects: three two-way interactions and one three-way interaction. This means that, ultimately, we will need seven hypotheses and our ANOVA will have seven different effects that we will need to write up and interpret! Looking at the variance cake, there are now eight slices: the seven effects and one slice of random variance. In this example, it appears that the variance in the data mainly comes from the main effect of IV2, the interaction between IV2 and IV3, and the three-way interaction.

Designing a robust experimental study

We now have the three IVs and the DV for our factorial experiment, but there are still a number of methodological issues to consider and decisions to make in the hope of designing a robust and rigorous experiment. Essentially, a number of different factors can lead to random variance in our data, and we want to try to minimize this so that we increase our chance of

DOING AN EXPERIMENTAL RESEARCH PROJECT 61

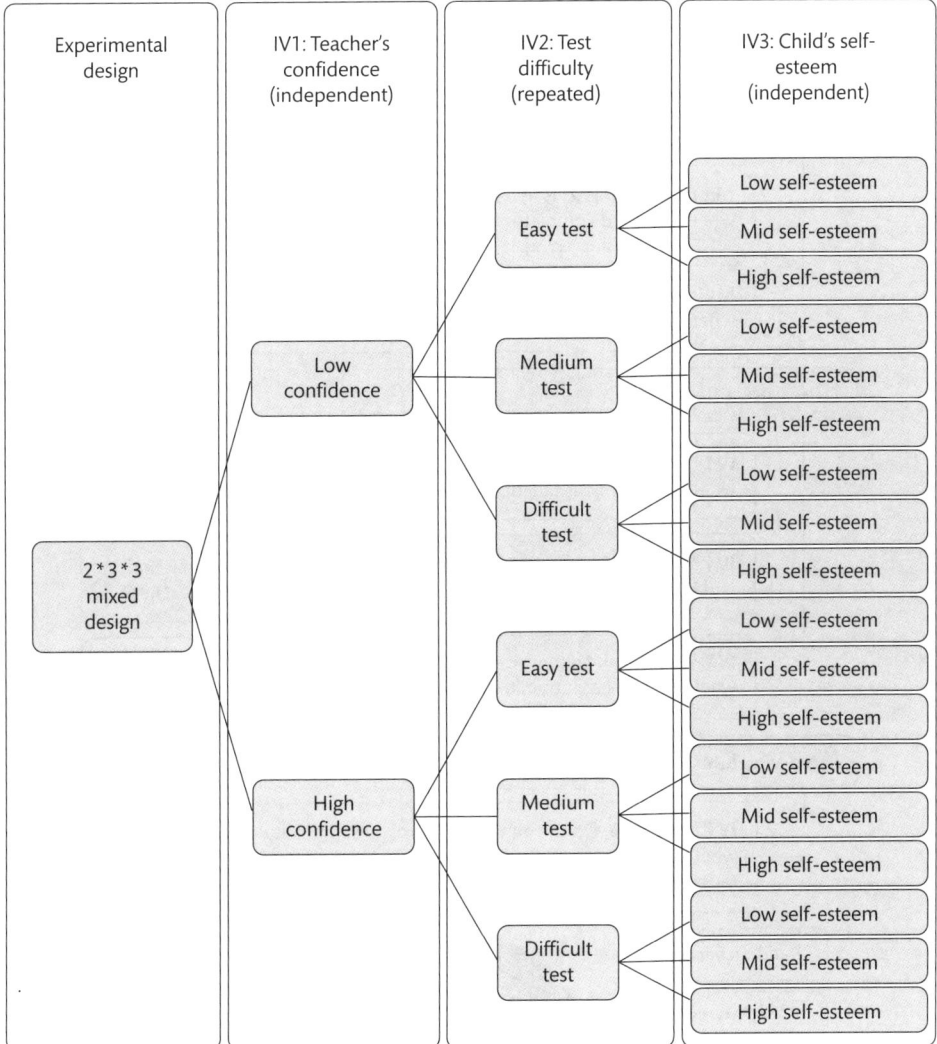

Figure 6.6 The full experimental design for a 2*3*3 mixed design

seeing the different sources of experimental variance. We will now look at four different ways that we can do this: considering confounding variables, use of randomizing and counterbalancing, recruitment decisions, and sample size.

Confounding variables

Hopefully, you will already have come across confounding variables, but, as a quick reminder, a confound is a measurable variable that is likely to explain some of the variability in our dataset. However, it is not a variable that we are interested in exploring. Typically, a confounding variable will already be well-established in the existing research, so we know that it is likely to

Main effects of independent variables

- **Main effect of IV1:** Is there a difference in maths test scores depending on whether the child is taught by a low or high confidence teacher?

- **Main effect of IV2:** Is there difference in maths test scores depending on whether a child completes an easy, medium or difficult test?

- **Main effect of IV3:** Is there difference in maths test scores depending on whether a child has low, mid or high self-esteem?

Two-way interactions

- **IV1 * IV2:** Do the differences across test difficulty vary according to whether the child is taught by a low or high confidence teacher?

- **IV1 * IV3:** Do differences in maths test scores in children with low, mid and high self-esteem differ according to the confidence of the teacher?

- **IV2 * IV3:** Do the differences across test difficulty vary according to whether child has low, mid or high self-esteem?

Three-way interaction

- **IV1 * IV2 * IV3:** Do the differences across test difficulty vary according to whether child has low, mid or high self-esteem and whether the child is taught by a low or high confidence teacher?

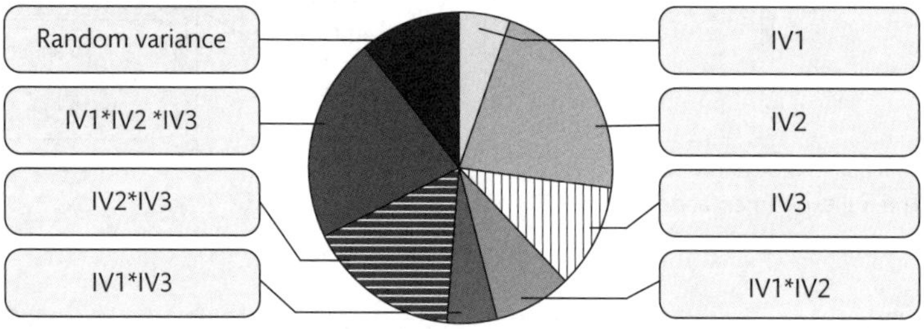

Figure 6.7 Experimental effects in a three-way factorial design

explain some variance in the data we collect: the covariance. We therefore want to measure the confound so that we can analyse our data to remove the covariance from it and see the remaining effects in our experimental data.

For our design, we know that a child's level of concentration is likely to influence their ability to learn information and their performance in academic assessments. Therefore, we will give all the children a frequently used questionnaire to measure their typical levels of

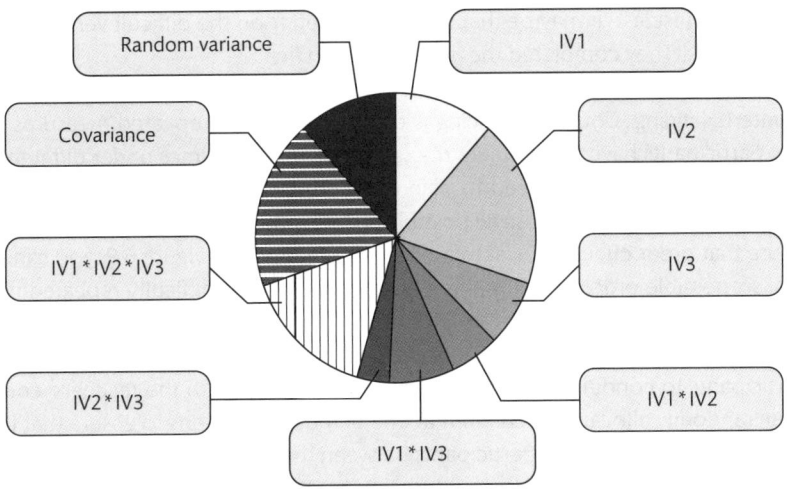

Figure 6.8 The variance cake for a three-way ANCOVA

concentration. We can then include this within our analysis, which would make it a 2*3*3 mixed design analysis of covariance, or an ANCOVA.

Now, there are two important points to bear in mind when planning an ANCOVA. First, our variance cake now has an extra slice, which explains the amount of covariance in the design. For our study, this now means that there are nine slices in our variance cake, which you can see in Figure 6.8. The covariance can, effectively, be taken from any of the existing sources of variability in our design: from a main effect, an interaction, or the random variance. Indeed, it could soak up some of the variance from across a number of these. Second, adding a covariable to our analysis can mean that any of our effects (the main effects or the interactions) can increase or decrease in significance, or perhaps just stay the same.

When you design an experiment and include a measured confound, it is important to bear in mind what the analysis (typically an ANCOVA of some kind) will actually do. Although you will usually see all the output from the analysis in one go, essentially what happens is that any of the variability that can be explained by the covariable is first analysed and taken into account. Then the remaining variability is analysed to determine how much of the variability each of the main effects and interactions can explain. This means that our main findings for this analysis will be *after* taking into account any of the variance explained by the measured confound, or (in our case) *after* taking into account any of the variance explained by the children's concentration levels. We will need to keep this in mind when we develop our hypotheses, when we write up our statistical analyses, and when we interpret our findings.

Randomizing and counterbalancing

When designing an experiment, we want to try to avoid any possible sources of bias in our design. For example, if all the children with higher mathematical ability were allocated to the high-confidence teaching condition, we would not be sure whether any significant effect we might find occurred due to the participant allocations or the IV manipulation. Or, if there are practice effects when completing the easy version of the test first, then the medium difficulty and the hardest test last, it may be that children do better on the difficult version of the test than they would if they completed the difficult version first.

We can avoid both of these potential methodological limitations through randomizing and counterbalancing. Counterbalancing is usually relevant to repeated measures designs, whereby participants have to complete the same task multiple times under different conditions. To counterbalance, you need to plan out all the ways you could possibly order the conditions and ensure that you use all possible orders within your experiment. This way, you can ensure that order effects cannot influence your findings. In Figure 6.9, you can see that there are six possible orders that the three tests within the test difficulty repeated measures IV could be completed in.

Randomizing is typically relevant to independent IVs where it is possible to randomly allocate participants to conditions (i.e. not quasi-experimental). With the teachers' confidence IV, we can randomly allocate the children to one of those conditions to ensure that there are no systematic differences in the participants between the two groups. We can also randomly allocate participants to one of the counterbalanced test orders, meaning we end up randomly allocating the participants to one of twelve groups (two teacher confidence levels by six counterbalanced orders), and you can see these in Figure 6.9.

With the child's self-esteem IV, it is not possible to randomly allocate children to conditions because we are putting them into groups depending on their own self-esteem, which we cannot manipulate (i.e. it is quasi-experimental). With some variables, counterbalancing and randomizing are not possible, but, if you can put these methodological safeguards in place, you reduce the chance of coming to conclusions about your data that may be the result of methodological decisions you made, rather than your IV manipulations.

Recruitment strategy

With an experiment, one of the most important aspects of recruitment is to ensure that participants who are placed into different conditions do not systematically differ in a way that might influence the data you collect by increasing the random variability, and therefore your analyses and conclusions. One of the key ways to achieve this is through the random allocation to conditions that we have just discussed. However, there may also be some participant characteristics that we are aware of in advance, which we can also use to inform our recruitment strategy. This may be that we want to ensure that all our participants have a particular characteristic – an inclusion criterion – or that they do not have a particular characteristic – an exclusion criterion.

With both inclusion and exclusion criteria, it is often helpful to include these in your recruitment advertising. For example, if you are running a functional magnetic resonance imaging (fMRI) experiment about language, it may be essential that all your participants have English as a first language. This could then be an inclusion criterion that you include in all your recruitment and advertising. Given that the study is fMRI, you would also have an exclusion criterion of not testing people who are pregnant or have any metal implants. For our teaching confidence study, our inclusion criterion would be children who are in Year 2 in participating schools, and we may decide to exclude any children who have additional educational support in place due to additional educational needs. It is very important to decide on your inclusion and exclusion criteria in advance of recruiting participants in order to minimize the possibility of recruiting

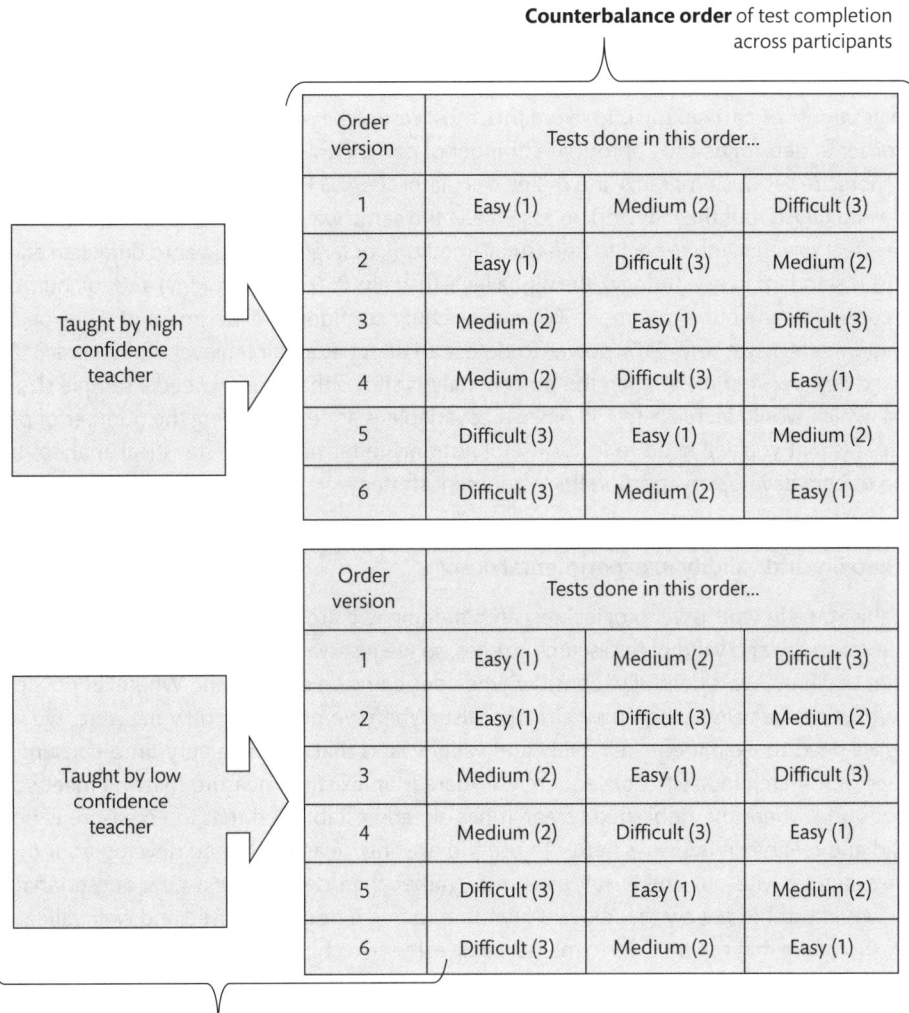

Figure 6.9 Randomizing and counterbalancing within an experimental design

participants whom you are unable to test. Ultimately, this is an inconvenient waste of time for both the experimenter and the participant, and it is potentially an ethical issue because you are unnecessarily asking someone to participate and give up their time. Ensure that you plan your recruitment clearly and carefully so that you avoid being in this situation.

Sample size

Before collecting data, you will also need to decide how many participants to recruit. While you may have a good idea of what is an appropriate sample size from reading research papers on similar research questions, it is also possible to statistically determine an appropriate sample size. In Chapter 5, we discussed that one explanation for the replication crisis in psychological research is that some studies have been underpowered (i.e. they have a relatively small sample of participants). To avoid this, most researchers now conduct a power analysis in order to determine the appropriate number of participants for a study design.

There are various programs and online calculators (e.g. G Power) that you can use to run a power analysis, but they all work in essentially the same way. You need to know in advance the effect size that you expect to find (small, medium, or large), the power to detect an effect (80% is standard in psychology), the alpha level (usually .050 in psychology) and the number of conditions in your experiment. For our teaching confidence experiment, if we expect a medium effect size, with 80% power to detect an effect at an alpha level of .050 in a 3*2*3 mixed design experiment, then the power analysis shows that we will need a sample size of 144, which would increase to 155 when a covariable is added. Knowing the number of participants that you will need to test is useful not only in terms of your statistical analyses but also to help develop an appropriate recruitment strategy.

Reliability and validity in experimental designs

By this stage in your psychological research training, we are assuming that you are familiar with reliability and validity in research studies, so we just wanted to pick up on one general point that it is always helpful to consider when designing an experiment. Wherever possible, use existing measures when they already exist. When we develop a new measure, we will always need to examine its reliability and validity, and that can be a very time-consuming piece of research in itself! Consequently, if there is an existing measure that will meet your needs and where the published research has already established that the measure is both valid and reliable, it is always better to use the existing measure than to develop your own. For example, with our child's self-esteem IV, rather than developing a new questionnaire, we would want to review the relevant literature to find a frequently used and well-validated questionnaire that can be used to measure self-esteem in children aged 6 to 7 years old. Even when using an existing measure, it is still good to run a reliability analysis on the data you collect, just to be confident that your data are reliable. We would only consider developing a new questionnaire for our study if a suitable, reliable, and valid measure did not already exist.

Ethics for an experimental study

With any piece of psychological research, you will know by now that there are certain ethical considerations that must be met. You will be familiar with the idea of informed consent and the right to withdraw, avoiding active and passive deception, protecting participants from potential harm, and the importance of anonymity and confidentiality, so we will just raise a couple of points that are particularly relevant to experimental research.

Experimental IVs usually involve some form of 'manipulation' and it is important to consider the possible ethical implications of this manipulation and any deception, either active (i.e. telling the participant something that is untrue) or passive (i.e. not disclosing something). For some designs, there are no ethical concerns. For example, in our teaching confidence experiment, the IV where we measure children's self-esteem to create low, mid, and high groups is unlikely to have any negative ethical impact on the participants. However, imagine a different experiment, whereby we wanted to examine different clinical interventions to improve self-esteem: here, our manipulation is far more active and actually aims to change a person's self-esteem. This would have a range of ethical implications to consider. For example, how much would you tell the participant about the manipulation in the informed consent? You would need to ensure that they were aware of what they would be asked to do, but without potentially influencing their response to the intervention. In doing this, are you using passive or even active deception to ensure that your IV manipulation is implemented with validity and reliability? In aiming to manipulate people's self-esteem, might this have an impact on their perception of the right to withdraw from the study or risk possible psychological harm?

Even if the chance of a negative impact on a participant is quite small, it is still necessary to consider this when you are designing your study and applying for ethics. As you move towards becoming a more independent researcher, and possibly towards conducting more complex research studies with more nuanced ethical considerations, it is important to bear in mind that research might not be ethically 'perfect' due to the research question that you are asking. There may be some level of deception or risk in your design that raises some ethical concerns, but that does not mean that you cannot conduct that study. The key point is to openly consider the implications of your experimental design decisions, and to have safeguards in place to minimize any possible risk to participants. For example, if your manipulation aimed to change a person's self-esteem, then you might want to have exclusion criteria for anyone with a diagnosed mental health condition, and your debriefing should include referrals to sources of support in case a participant feels concerned after participating. Wherever possible, it is always best to design the most ethical experiment that you can, but, if there are potential areas of concern, you should be honest about this in your ethics application and include plans for how to minimize possible risk and protect the participants in your experiment.

Developing hypotheses for an experimental study

When developing hypotheses for a complex experimental design, you can end up with quite a lot of predictions because you will need one for every effect in your analysis. Remember that a hypothesis should explain how you predict that a manipulated IV (or IVs) will have an impact on a DV. Back in Figure 6.7, we set out all the main effects and interactions within our design, and we need a hypothesis for each of these. For our three-way ANCOVA, this means that we will need seven predictions, which you can see in Figure 6.10. Importantly, if you have any covariables included in your design, such as our covariable of the child's concentration, then you will need to first include that you predict that the covariable will explain a significant amount of variance in the data, and that all the other effects will be after taking into account this covariance.

With this clearly set up, you need to go through all your hypotheses and you should aim to do this as a paragraph (not as a bullet-point list). You can have a combination of one-tailed (directional), two-tailed (not directional), and null (no effect) hypotheses across the effects, but the most important thing is that these should be justified by the research that you have reviewed in your Introduction. It is also important to remember that your hypotheses should be developed before you collect any data. While you may find it tempting to develop your

Hypotheses for main effects

Prediction for IV1: Maths test scores will be higher for children taught by a high confidence teacher than for children taught by a low confidence teacher.

Prediction for IV2: Maths test scores will be highest for the easy test, lower for the medium test and lowest for the difficult test.

Main effect of IV3: Maths test scores will be lowest for children with low self-esteem, and higher but comparable for those with mid or high self-esteem.

Hypotheses for two-way interactions

Prediction for IV1 * IV2: When taught by a high confidence teacher, performance will not differ according to test difficulty, whereas when taught by a low confidence teacher, scores will be highest for the easy test, lower for the medium test and lowest for the difficult test.

Prediction for IV1 * IV3: There will be no interaction between children's level of self-esteem and the confidence of the teacher in terms of maths test scores.

Prediction for IV2 * IV3: For children with high self-esteem, maths test scores will not differ according to test difficulty, whereas for children with low or mid self-esteem, scores will differ according to test difficulty.

Hypothesis for a three-way interaction

Prediction for IV1 * IV2 * IV3: Maths test scores for children with mid or high self-esteem will not differ according to teacher confidence or test difficulty. However, for children with low self-esteem, when taught by a high confidence teacher, performance will not differ according to test difficulty, whereas when taught by a low confidence teacher, scores will be highest for the easy test, lower for the medium test and lowest for the difficult test.

Figure 6.10 Developing hypotheses for main effects, two- and three-way interactions

hypotheses after you have analysed your data and seen your results, this is the exceptionally bad research practice of HARKing, which you can read more about in Chapter 5. It is perfectly acceptable for your findings to not support your hypotheses as long as you take the time to consider in your Discussion why that may have happened.

When you develop a hypothesis for a main effect, the prediction is very simple if there are only two conditions – you simply need to say how you think the two conditions will differ (such as for IV1 in Figure 6.10). If you have more than two conditions, you will need to think through how you will want to break down this main effect, and follow this through with the contrasts you will select. You also need to make sure that all the conditions are included within your prediction, although it is fine to combine them, such as with IV3 in Figure 6.10.

With a hypothesis for a two-way interaction, it is important to ensure that both IVs and all the conditions are included within the prediction. You can combine the mention of some of the conditions, such as with the IV1*IV2 interaction in Figure 6.10, but the entire interaction needs to be included in the hypothesis. The same goes for a three-way interaction. However, this can be a little more complex due to the number of IVs and conditions involved. It can help to start by separating out one of the IVs and then, effectively, you can make two-way interaction predictions for each condition of the IV that you have separated out. In Figure 6.10, you can see that the three-way prediction separates out the children according to the self-esteem IV, and then makes different two-way predictions for the teachers' confidence and the test difficulty.

6.4 Running an experimental study

When you are running an experimental study, one of the key things to constantly keep in mind is the need for consistency. If there are differences in the way that the study is run, there may be additional random variance in the data you collect, and the more random variance there is, the more difficult it can be to identify any significant differences that may arise from your experimental manipulation. So always keep in mind the need to be consistent in what you do.

Running a study with others

Conducting experimental research can involve working with lots of different people, especially if you are working on a group project and collaborating with other students. With any kind of research project, the ability to collaborate and communicate is essential, particularly during the design process. It is important to be well informed about the prior research so that you can make an informed contribution to the design of your study, but also be mindful of the views of others. In Chapter 3, we talked a lot about how to work with your supervisor, so please do follow that advice but with the additional guidance that attention to detail is particularly important when putting together and running experiments. Your supervisor is likely to have run experiments using the methodology a number of times, so they will be a fantastic resource to ensure that your design is rigorous, but don't be afraid to make your own informed contributions to the discussions you have with your supervisor and others in the research team.

If you are working in a group, you will need to work closely with that group to ensure that you are all following the same protocol for the recruitment, testing, and debriefing of participants. For each of these, even small differences in the things that you do risk an increase in the random variance in the data you collect. Try to work together to develop a protocol to ensure that you are all working in the same way. It can even be helpful to write a script to help you explain the experimental procedure to participants. Not only will this help to ensure that everyone runs the experiment in the same way, it will also help you to remember everything that needs to be said. Although consistency is important, it is also important to recognize when things are not working as well in practice as hoped. For example, while experimental instructions may seem clear to you, if participants are consistently asking for clarification around an issue, then it might be worth discussing the protocol with your supervisor and colleagues to see if any tweaks might improve the situation. Keep communicating with your supervisor and colleagues throughout the study. If you are proactive in communicating, you may feel that you end up 'nagging' others, but don't let this put you off showing initiative and leadership to ensure that your research project is a success.

Finally, running an experiment may mean testing lots of participants and every single one needs to be treated in the same way. With the first few participants, you may feel a little nervous; then, with the next few, you will get into the swing of things, although at some point you may find yourself getting bored of all the repetition! While this is understandable, be aware of this and try to ensure that every participant is treated exactly the same. Not only is this important in terms of your experimental procedure, it is also important ethically to ensure that all participants are fully informed as to the purposes and expectations of the study, and also debriefed fully and appropriately. Having a checklist can help to ensure that you always cover the necessary points, and taking a break occasionally from testing can help to reduce boredom! It can also be helpful to run a few participants as a pilot study before running the main study to practise the procedure and to smooth out any potential issues.

Different ways of collecting data

Essentially, there are two ways of collecting data: either in person in the lab or online. In the past, in-person data collection tended to be the norm for experimental studies but, with the increase in online research platforms (such as Qualtrics or Gorilla) that allow for highly controlled experimental designs, online collection is now more common for experimental research. When considering whether you should collect your data online or in person, there is no single or correct answer: it really depends on your design and which method is most appropriate when you weigh up the advantages and disadvantages of each approach.

For example, one advantage of online data collection is that the method is highly controlled and there is a high level of consistency across participants because they all get exactly the same instructions, procedure, etc. In contrast, there can be more variability with in-person data collection, both within one individual experimenter and across different researchers if a team are collecting data together. With online data collection, there is less chance of experimenter bias (either intentional or unintentional) occurring. It can also be helpful to collect data online if your research involves sensitive topics, because participants may be more open in completing a study in the safety of their home and without being directly observed by a researcher. On the other hand, some experimental research requires the use of technical equipment that may only be available in a lab – for example, eye tracking or virtual reality research. Obviously, for these research studies, in-person data collection is likely to be necessary.

One final issue to consider is the impact of online or in-person data collection on the actual data that you collect. With online data, you may be more likely to have incomplete datasets because participants may cease to take part before the end of the study, they may miss parts of the procedure, or they may ask for help or input from other people. All of these are hard to control but may increase the random variance in the data you collect. This may mean that online data needs more cleaning and quality control before you have a dataset that you can analyse. You may also have less control over who your participants are, because it is difficult to verify the demographic information that they give you. Again, you need to consider your own project and what your priorities are. Neither in-person nor online methods are 'better': it is just a case of balancing up which is most appropriate for your study and thinking through how to reduce any possible limitations of the approach you choose.

Recruiting participants

For many psychological research studies, recruitment relies on word of mouth, personal links, social media, or recruitment pools, such as those run by departments or online (such as Prolific). If your study is being run online, then most of the subsequent communications with participants will be very standardized and likely within the online set-up that you use (e.g. study information, consent). This makes things very easy to run in many ways because you, effectively, only need to 'present' the information once, and then reuse that for all participants, thereby ensuring consistency. However, do make sure that all participants have an easy way to get in touch with you in case they do have any questions. If you are running your study in person, try to create scripts to use for all interactions with participants. This will mean that you are consistent with all participants, something that is particularly important if there are multiple people running the experiment.

If doing research outside a university setting, such as at a school or hospital, there are almost two stages of recruitment. First, you need to make links with the relevant person to arrange for the project to be conducted at that institution. This is a vital part of developing the research project and setting up the collaboration. Second, you need to work with the institution to recruit the individual participants, and with this it is important to follow any required protocol or process of the institution, as well as of your own university. Your supervisor is likely to have gone through this process a few times, so do make the most of their guidance and experience.

Finally, when you are running an experimental study, think carefully about how you communicate with every single participant from the initial invitation to participate through to debriefing them and thanking them for their participation. As well as ensuring that you are consistent in your communication, also bear in mind that your participants may not be psychology students, and therefore the research setting and some of the terminology used may be unfamiliar to them. Try to make your communications with participants and the information that you give them as accessible as possible, so that they feel comfortable taking part in your study.

Collecting, coding, and storing data

When you are collecting and storing your data, it is important that you do this in a way that ensures the participant's anonymity. If you need to link a participant's data to other data sources (e.g. if you are repeating testing on a different day or you are linking scores to their educational records), then you need to establish ways to ensure that their confidentiality is maintained. For example, you might get them to create a unique identifying code (e.g. the date of their birthday, their house number, and the year they were born to give a code like 8301982) that can be used across all phases of testing to link the participant's data reliably without the risk of identifying them. This is also important to ensure that you are conducting your research in a highly ethical manner.

If there are multiple people working on coding and/or entering the data, then you need to ensure that you have a clear protocol in place for how you deal with issues like data cleaning, dealing with missing values, creating variables, and so on. If there are differences in the way the data are treated, this can reduce the reliability of the data collected and introduce random variance into the data. After all the work to carefully control the experimental design and minimize the random variance in the dataset, it would be a shame not to have consistency at this stage! Once you have collected all your data and it is entered into a spreadsheet of some kind, make sure that you have back-ups and that they are digitally secure. For example, consider adding passwords either to the files or the folders that they are in. There are usually recommendations for how to store data, where to store it, and how long it should be stored for after a research study has ended. However, this can vary depending on the institutional guidelines and whether the research is funded by an external agency, so check these matters with your supervisor.

6.5 Analysing experimental data

There are various statistics packages that you can use to run your ANOVA, but they should all give you the same results, so use whichever package you have learned with and feel most confident using. I have used SPSS, so the figures will be SPSS output and they may look different from your output if you are using R, JASP, or any other package, although the numbers should be the same. I am not going to go through the steps of how to run your analysis – hopefully, you are already familiar enough with ANOVA to do this with the help of your preferred statistics textbook. Instead, I will concentrate on guiding you through how to pull out and interpret the relevant bits from the analysis to help you understand your findings and to apply these to your hypotheses.

Developing an analysis strategy

The most appropriate time to develop your analysis strategy is when you are actually developing your experimental research methodology. You should absolutely not be thinking about how to analyse your data after you have collected it (you can find out more about why this is such a bad thing in Chapter 5)! If you have spent the time designing a clear and robust experiment, then it should be relatively obvious which type of ANOVA you need to run (you can look back at Figure 6.4 as a reminder), and, if you have a covariable, you will need to run an ANCOVA. However, developing an analysis strategy is not just about working out what kind of ANOVA or ANCOVA you need to run – you also need to think about how you will break down each main effect and interaction in your analysis.

Breaking down main effects is relatively straightforward. If you have only two conditions, then you do not need any additional contrasts: just look at the means to interpret the main effect. If your main effect has three or more conditions, then you will need to use planned contrasts if you have a one-tailed hypothesis or post hoc contrasts if you have a two-tailed hypothesis. Breaking down interactions can be a little more complex, but it might help to try to focus on looking at the differences across one IV and then looking at each condition of the other IV separately. Remember that these analyses are intended to test your hypotheses, so look back at Figure 6.10 and, for each hypothesis, map out the analysis that you need to conduct to test it. For example, if you look at the IV2 * IV3 hypothesis in Figure 6.10, you will see that I break this down by making predictions for each self-esteem group separately and then hypothesizing about the differences for each test difficulty within each self-esteem group. If this interaction is significant, my analysis strategy would need to map onto this prediction, so I would split my datafile according to the self-esteem groups, and then run a one-way ANOVA on test difficulty for each of the three self-esteem groups separately.

Again, it is important that you develop your full analysis strategy before you even start collecting data. So plan out how you would break down every single main effect and interaction in your analysis. However, also remember that you would only actually statistically break down significant main effects or interactions, which means you may end up not using some of your planned analyses if you find yourself with findings that are not significant.

Preparing data for analysis

Before you start running your analyses, it is important to spend some time ensuring that your dataset is appropriately set up and structured (this will differ depending on the statistics software you are using) and to spend some time cleaning the data. Two key aspects of this are to look for and deal with missing data points and outliers (scores that fall outside the range of scores that would usually be expected).

When cleaning your data, there are two steps: first, you need to look for any possible problems and, second, you need to fix any you find. It is important to have your strategy for identifying issues and any criteria needed before you start working on your data. In line with the open science principles discussed in Chapter 5, rectifying any problems with your data should be done in a systematic and planned way, without consideration of how your results may change. For example, if you are looking at outliers, you should not be checking on how your results may change with or without particular outliers in the dataset. All these decisions should be based on your analysis strategy. To look for missing data points, it is usually simplest to run a frequency analysis and check for any variables where the number of data points is fewer than you are expecting. There are various ways to deal with missing data. You might decide to remove the participant entirely or you may replace the missing data with a calculated estimate (e.g. the mean from the participant's other data or from the overall sample). To identify outliers, you might want to look at a histogram or box plot of the data, or you can use the descriptive statistics. Talk with your supervisor about how to deal with missing data and outliers because different research areas tend to have different standards, but make sure that you are clear about this in your data analysis strategy and report this in your write-up.

Making sense of your findings

When you write up your analyses, you should always structure your analysis in the following way (which may be in a different order to how it appears in your output). First, consider whether the assumptions of the analysis have been met. The reader should know of any possible issues with your data before they read the main analysis findings. Second, if you have a covariable, then you report these findings next. Finally, you report the various effects from your analysis, usually starting with all the main effects, then all the two-way interactions and, finally, the three-way interaction. Within this, you should report all the effects, both significant and not significant, as well as all of the relevant descriptive statistics.

Analysis of the assumptions

For an ANOVA, you need to first look at whether the assumptions of normal distribution of data and homogeneity of variance (for an independent IV) or sphericity (for a repeated IV) have been met. For all of these, you want the analyses to be not significant in order to be confident that the assumptions have been met and that your analyses are robust. You can see all the relevant output in Figure 6.11, and you would report these using the usual APA formatting.

Looking at the distribution analysis (Figure 6.11, top), out of the 16 analyses, only 3 show significant skew, which is probably fine in terms of overall meeting the assumption. However, if you want to be a little cautious and ensure that your findings have not been influenced by the skewness, you can transform your DV using either a log or square root transformation, which usually reduces skewness. You can then run the analysis again using the transformed DV scores and see if the pattern of significant and not significant results changes or remains the same. You do not necessarily need to report this secondary analysis in full.

Tests of Normality

Child's self-esteem	Teaching confidence level		Kolmogorov-Smirnov[a]			Shapiro-Wilk		
			Statistic	df	Sig.	Statistic	df	Sig.
Low SE	Low confid	Easy test score	.138	33	.116	.955	33	.187
		Middle test score	.100	33	.200*	.961	33	.282
		Hard test score	.129	33	.180	.903	33	.006
	High confid	Easy test score	.133	33	.148	.940	33	.069
		Middle test score	.129	33	.175	.933	33	.043
		Hard test score	.107	33	.200*	.964	33	.340
Mid SE	Low confid	Easy test score	.129	33	.181	.944	33	.089
		Middle test score	.121	33	.200*	.961	33	.274
		Hard test score	.109	33	.200*	.953	33	.159
	High confid	Easy test score	.167	34	.017	.922	34	.018
		Middle test score	.127	34	.178	.948	34	.107
		Hard test score	.229	34	.000	.860	34	.000
High SE	Low confid	Easy test score	.131	34	.148	.951	34	.135
		Middle test score	.124	34	.200*	.953	34	.147
		Hard test score	.122	34	.200*	.942	34	.069
	High confid	Easy test score	.086	33	.200*	.973	33	.558
		Middle test score	.166	33	.022	.919	33	.017
		Hard test score	.137	33	.123	.955	33	.192

*. This is a lower bound of the true significance.
a. Lilliefors Significance Correction

Three analyses (out of sixteen) show significant skew

Mauchly's Test of Sphericity[a]

Measure: MEASURE_1

Within Subjects Effect	Mauchly' SW	Approx. Chi-Square	df	Sig.	Epsilon[b]		
					Greenhouse-Geisser	Huynh-Feldt	Lower-bound
Test_difficulty	.992	1.459	2	.482	.992	1.000	.500

Levene's Test of Equality of Error Variances[a]

	F	df1	df2	Sig.
Easy test score	1.775	5	194	.120
Middle test score	1.503	5	194	.191
Hard test score	1.242	5	194	.291

Assumptions of sphericity and homogeneity of variance met (not significant) for all variables

Figure 6.11 Evaluating the assumptions in an ANOVA

In published research, you will often see a footnote within the reporting of the assumptions, and the footnote will very briefly explain the alternative analysis and how the findings changed or remained the same. The main analysis reported is then based on the original untransformed DV, but with the knowledge that the findings are not the result of any skewness in the data.

Looking at the bottom of Figure 6.11, you can see the analysis for the assumptions of sphericity for the repeated IV and homogeneity of variance for the independent IV. For these to be met, they should be not significant, so we can see that all these assumptions have been met. If the assumption of sphericity was not met, you could have used the Greenhouse-Geisser correction when interpreting any of the effects involving the repeated IV. If the homogeneity of variance assumption had not been met, unfortunately there isn't a simple correction, so you may be limited to acknowledging this and the possible implications for your interpretation in the Discussion. For example, if the variance were particularly large in one condition, what does that mean for your understanding of the results and your research question?

Analysis of the covariable

If you have a covariable in your analysis, you need to report this before getting into your main effects and interactions. This is because an ANCOVA, essentially, first looks at how much variance in the data is explained by the covariable, and then the main effects and interactions are analysed based on the remaining unexplained variance. For this analysis, the covariable is significant: $F(1, 193) = 4.6$, $p = .033$. You can see this in the output in Figure 6.12 in the next section of this chapter. This means that the children's concentration explains a significant amount of the variance in the maths test score, and therefore the main effects and interactions that we are about to look at have all been analysed after removing this variance from the DV, meaning that the effects cannot be explained by the covariable and we can be more confident that our findings reflect the impact of our IV manipulation.

Analysis of the main effects

We can now get into the actual analysis that will allow us to answer our research question and address our hypotheses. First, you need to look at your main effects and we have three in our 2*3*3 mixed design ANOVA. In SPSS, the main effects and interactions are all mixed up and distributed across the output, but hopefully Figure 6.12 shows where the various numbers come from. When a main effect only has two conditions, such as with our IV of teachers' confidence, all we need is the ANOVA result and the means in each of the conditions to fully interpret this finding. For the main effect of teachers' confidence, the result is not significant ($F(1, 193) = 3.7$, $p = .057$, partial $\eta^2 = .019$), showing no difference in maths test score between teachers with low confidence ($M = 26.7$, $SE = 0.7$) and teachers with high confidence ($M = 28.6$, $SE = 0.7$).

If a main effect has three or more conditions and is significant, then remember that you will need to also report the planned or post hoc contrast that is appropriate for breaking it down. Also, remember that if the assumption of sphericity was not met for any of the effects, you should be taking your ANOVA statistics from the Greenhouse-Geisser correction

Tests of Within-Subjects Effects

Measure: MEASURE_1

Source		Type III Sum of Squares	df	Mean Square	F	Sig.	Partial Eta Squared
Test_difficulty	Sphericity Assumed	2591.457	2	1295.729	15.349	.000	.074
	Greenhouse-Geisser	2591.457	1.985	1305.540	15.349	.000	.074
	Huynh-Feldt	2591.457	2.000	1295.729	15.349	.000	.074
	Lower-bound	2591.457	1.000	2591.457	15.349	.000	.074
Test_difficulty * Concentration	Sphericity Assumed	133.528	2	66.764	.791	.454	.004
	Greenhouse-Geisser	133.528	1.985	67.270	.791	.453	.004
	Huynh-Feldt	133.528	2.000	66.764	.791	.454	.004
	Lower-bound	133.528	1.000	133.528	.791	.375	.004
Test_difficulty * Teacher_confidence	Sphericity Assumed	279.145	2	139.572	1.653	.193	.008
	Greenhouse-Geisser	279.145	1.985	140.629	1.653	.193	.008
	Huynh-Feldt	279.145	2.000	139.572	1.653	.193	.008
	Lower-bound	279.145	1.000	279.145	1.653	.200	.008
Test_difficulty * Childs_self_esteem	Sphericity Assumed	1399.875	4	349.969	4.146	.003	.041
	Greenhouse-Geisser	1399.875	3.970	352.619	4.146	.003	.041
	Huynh-Feldt	1399.875	4.000	349.969	4.146	.003	.041
	Lower-bound	1399.875	2.000	699.938	4.146	.017	.041
Test_difficulty * Teacher_confidence * Childs_self_esteem	Sphericity Assumed	960.913	4	240.228	2.846	.024	.029
	Greenhouse-Geisser	960.913	3.970	242.047	2.846	.024	.029
	Huynh-Feldt	960.913	4.000	240.228	2.846	.024	.029
	Lower-bound	960.913	2.000	480.456	2.846	.06t	.029
Error(Test_difficulty)	Sphericity Assumed	32586.111	386	84.420			
	Greenhouse-Geisser	32586.111	383.099	85.059			
	Huynh-Feldt	32586.111	386.000	84.420			
	Lower-bound	32586.t 11	193.000	168.840			

(IV2: Test difficulty; IV2 * CV; IV2 * IV1; IV2 * IV3; IV2 * IV1 * IV3)

Tests of Between-Subjects Effects

Measure: MEASURE_1
Transformed Variable: Average

Source	Type III Sum of Squares	df	Mean Square	F	Sig.	Partial Eta Squared
Intercept	46093.434	1	46093.434	900.050	.000	.823
Concentration	236.135	1	236.135	4.611	.033	.023
Teacher_confidence	188.235	1	188.235	3.676	.057	.019
Childs_self_esteem	95.478	2	47.739	.932	.395	.010
Teacher_confidence * Childs_self_esteem	29.710	2	14.855	.290	.749	.003
Error	9883.934	193	51.212			

(CV; IV1; IV3; IV1 * IV3)

Figure 6.12 Main effects and interactions in SPSS output

row. For our example, our test difficulty IV is significant ($F (2, 386) = 15.4$, $p < .001$, partial $\eta^2 = .074$) and a planned repeated contrast was used to break this down, showing no significant difference ($p = .055$) in scores between the easy (M = 31.1, SE = 0.7) and medium difficulty tests (M = 29.5, SE = 0.7), but scores on the medium difficulty test are significantly higher ($p < .001$) than on the difficult test (M = 22.3, SE = 0.7). For the IV of self-esteem, there are three conditions, but the main effect is not significant ($F (2, 193) = 0.9$, $p < .395$, partial $\eta^2 = .010$) and therefore there is no need to report the contrast because there is no significant main effect to break down.

Analysis of the two-way interactions

If a two-way interaction is significant, then you will need to follow this up with some contrasts to break this down. In our analysis, two of the two-way interactions are not significant: test difficulty * teachers' confidence ($F (2, 386) = 1.7$, $p = .193$, partial $\eta^2 = .008$) and teachers' confidence * self-esteem ($F_{(2, 193)}$ = 0.3, p = .749, partial η^2 = .003). While these not significant findings do need to be reported, no further analysis is needed.

With the remaining interaction between test difficulty and self-esteem, there is a significant interaction ($F_{(4, 386)}$ = 2.9, p = .024, partial η^2 = .028), and therefore we need to break this down. There are various ways we can achieve this (e.g. planned contrasts or Bonferroni corrected t tests or ANOVAs), but the key point is that the approach taken allows us to directly test the hypothesis for this interaction. Our hypothesis (you can see this in Figure 6.10) is best tested by separating out our participants into three groups according to self-esteem, and to then run a one-way ANCOVA on test difficulty for each group (still controlling for concentration). We then need to Bonferroni correct our alpha to account for running three analyses and therefore artificially inflating our familywise error and risking a Type I error. Therefore, the one-way ANCOVAs used to break down this interaction will only be significant if the p value is equal to or less than .017 (α = .050/3).

You can see a condensed version of the relevant output for the one-way ANCOVAs in Figure 6.13 (the table is huge, so I've just cut out the unnecessary bits). Mauchly's test of sphericity is not significant for any of the ANCOVAs (all p values ≥ .486), so we can use the 'Sphericity assumed' output, which shows that all of the ANCOVAs are significant, with all three having p values below the Bonferroni corrected alpha level of .017. You can see the main effects from the one-way ANCOVAs and the planned contrasts that you need to break down any significant main effects in Figure 6.13. The graph for the two-way interaction is also

Tests of Within-Subjects Effects

Measure: MEASURE_1

Child's self-esteem	Source		Type III Sum of Squares	df	Mean Square	F	Sig.	Partial Eta Squared
Low SE	Test_difficulty	Sphericity Assumed	1128.868	2	564.434	7.837	.001	.109
		Greenhouse-Geisser	1128.868	1.972	572.403	7.837	.001	.109
		Huynh-Feldt	1128.868	2.000	564.434	7.837	.001	.109
		Lower-bound	1128.868	1.000	1128.868	7.837	.007	.109
Mid SE	Test_difficulty	Sphericity Assumed	1607.031	2	803.515	8.240	.000	.113
		Greenhouse-Geisser	1607.031	1.979	812.098	8.240	.000	.113
		Huynh-Feldt	1607.031	2.000	803.515	8.240	.000	.113
		Lower-bound	1607.031	1.000	1607.031	8.240	.006	.113
High SE	Test_difficulty	Sphericity Assumed	826.775	2	413.387	4.574	.012	.066
		Greenhouse-Geisser	826.775	1.956	422.612	4.574	.013	.066
		Huynh-Feldt	826.775	2.000	413.387	4.574	.012	.066
		Lower-bound	826.775	1.000	826.775	4.574	.036	.066

Tests of Within-Subjects Contrasts

Measure: MEASURE

Child's self-esteem	Test_difficulty		Type III Sum of Squares	df	Mean Square	F	Sig.	Partial Eta Squared
Low SE	Level 1 vs Level 2		101.746	1	101.746	.633	.429	.010
	Level 2 vs Level 3		2048.042	1	2048.042	15.448	.000	.194
Mid SE	Level 1 vs Level 2		610.719	1	610.719	3.256	.076	.048
	Level 2 vs Level 3		1013.201	1	1013.201	5.550	.022	.079
High SE	Level 1 vs Level 2		1088.769	1	1088.769	5.268	.025	.075
	Level 2 vs Level 3		16.670	1	16.670	.096	.758	.001

Figure 6.13 Output to break down a significant two-way interaction (note the output has been cropped, so will look different from the full SPSS output)

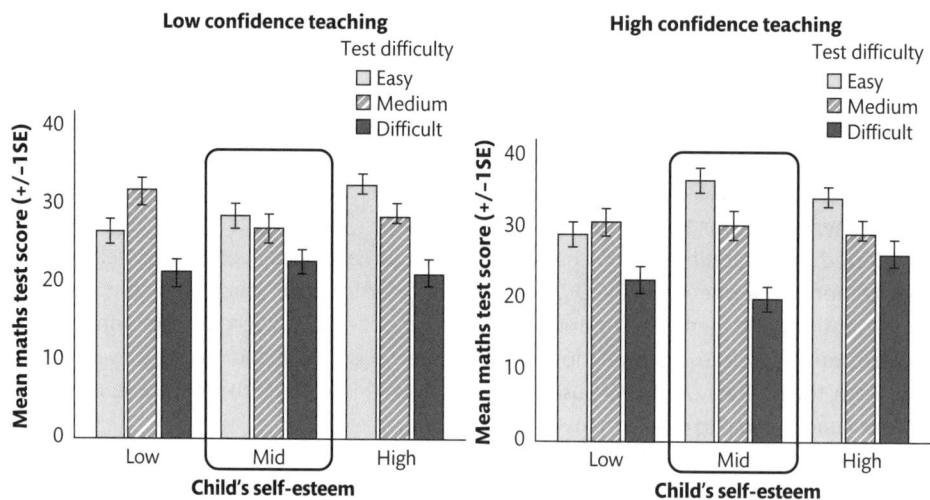

Figure 6.14 Graph showing the significant three-way interaction

shown to help understand the effects, and here you can clearly see how the performance across the levels of test difficulty depends on the child's self-esteem.

Analysis of the three-way interaction

Now we get to possibly the most interesting, but also the most complex part, of the analysis – the three-way interaction! Looking at the output in Figure 6.12, we can see that this interaction is significant ($F(4, 386) = 2.9$, $p = .024$, partial $\eta^2 = .029$). This suggests that the differences in the data are dependent on all three of the IVs, all contingent on each other. To break this down and understand what is actually going on, we need to look back at our three-way interaction hypothesis in Figure 6.10. The simplest way to break down a three-way interaction is to split the data according to one of the IVs, and to then run two-way ANOVAs on the remaining IVs. The hypothesis clearly frames the test difficulty * teacher confidence interaction being different according to the child's self-esteem, so we will split the data according to self-esteem and then look at the two-way ANOVAs for each of the three groups.

When we do this analysis, we find that there is no significant two-way interaction between test difficulty and teacher confidence for children with low self-esteem ($F(2, 126) = 0.8$, $p = .468$, partial $\eta^2 = .012$) or high self-esteem ($F(2, 128) = 1.0$, $p = .389$, partial $\eta^2 = .015$). However, for the children in the middle self-esteem group, the interaction is significant ($F(2, 128) = 5.1$, $p = .008$, partial $\eta^2 = .074$). If you look at the graph in Figure 6.14, you can clearly see where the three-way interaction is coming from, although in a full write-up you would want to follow this up with the relevant statistics for breaking down the two-way interactions. However, it seems that for children with mid-level self-esteem, when taught by a low-confidence teacher, there is no difference in their performance according to test difficulty. When taught by a teacher with a high level of confidence, this pattern changes and there is greater differentiation in performance across the three levels of test difficulty.

6.6 Writing up an experimental study

By this stage in your research training, you may have written up a few lab reports, so your project write-up should be relatively familiar to you. It will probably just be a little longer and with a more complex design. Reading lots of research papers within the area can be really helpful in demonstrating the style that you should be aiming for. Typically, your write-up should follow the APA style and standards, but check with your supervisor (the expert!) because the standards can be applied slightly differently across areas of psychology. Also make sure that you follow any requirements that your department or university sets. When writing your project, try not to compartmentalize each section too much. While there are clearly distinct parts within a research report, the research question that you are aiming to address should guide each section and form the bigger picture of what you are aiming to achieve in your write-up.

Title

Your title should be short, around 10–20 words. Make sure it gives an accurate indication of your research question and avoid being too vague. It can help to include your main variables in your title.

Abstract

Your abstract should be about 150 words or so, and it is often easiest to write your abstract last, after you have completed all the other sections. This is because your abstract should be a summary of your report, and aim to have each of the four sections equally covered in the abstract. So, write one or two sentences to summarize each of the Introduction, Methods, Results, and Discussion.

Introduction

It can be helpful to think about your Introduction as a bit like a funnel: it starts very broadly by setting out the bigger picture of the research question you are exploring and it ends with your very specific predictions about your design that will allow you to answer your research question. As such, the first and last paragraphs should be relatively straightforward to write. What goes in between them should be a critical analysis of the existing relevant and current research, framed in such a way that you can explain and justify your experimental design and your hypotheses. It is important to remember that your Introduction is not an essay. Instead, it serves a very specific function in setting up your experimental design. Every single paragraph should explicitly relate to your design, reviewing the existing research, and explaining to the reader how this has helped to inform your own research question, predictions, and design.

One thing that can help you to structure your experimental Introduction is to set out all the variables that you will be manipulating and measuring (i.e. your independent variables, your dependent variable(s) and any covariables in your design). Also check your design for any elements that you need to explain or justify in your Introduction. For example, if you choose to sample a particular age group, use a particular questionnaire, or select a particular type of stimuli, it can be helpful to explain this and the research that helped you to make these decisions in the Introduction. When someone reads your Methods section, nothing should be unexpected or require too much explanation if you have covered everything you need to in the Introduction.

Methods

By now, you are probably quite used to the typical structure of a Methods section: Participants, Materials, Procedure, Design and Analysis. While this structure may work really well for your experimental design, with more complex research studies, sometimes a researcher will decide to use a different structure. From reading the relevant previous research, you should have a good feel for the structure typically used within your research area, and of course your supervisor will be an invaluable source of information! Within the Participants section, if you have independent measures IVs, make sure you include how the participants were allocated to each condition and the number of participants in each group, and summarize any participant characteristics that are particularly important for each group separately. In the Design and Analysis section, remember that you need to set out your entire analysis strategy, not just the type of ANOVA that you used. All the contrasts that you may need to break down significant main effects and interactions should be explained, even if you end up not using them where findings are not significant.

If you have a Materials section and a Procedure section, then you should explain all your materials (e.g. stimuli, software, questionnaires) in the first and then explain how the experiment runs from start to finish in the second. However, it may be helpful to separate out the Materials section into further subsections if your design is particularly complex and involves different aspects. For example, in our teaching confidence experiment, I might split the Materials into four subsections: teaching confidence manipulation, the maths test (including the difficulty manipulation), the self-esteem questionnaire and creating of low/mid/high groups, and the concentration questionnaire (the covariable). This would help to ensure that the Methods are clearly structured and make it easier for the reader to follow.

Results

Earlier in this chapter, we went through how to analyse and interpret your experimental dataset, and, if you work through the hints and tips there, you should be well prepared for how to report on your ANOVA (or ANCOVA). It is really important to report everything in the right order, so start with the assumptions, then the effect of the covariable (if you have one), then the main effects, then the two-way interactions, and so on. You should report the full statistics for your covariable, main effects, and interactions, even if they are not significant. However, you should only go on to break down any significant effects that you find.

In a complex experimental design, you are likely to have lots of descriptive statistics to report, because you will report these for all your effects and interactions, even if not significant. I find it easiest to have these as a big table, such as the one at the top of Figure 6.15. This way, all the values are there for the reader if they are interested enough to spend time looking through the table. However, a big table of numbers can make it difficult to interpret and understand the main findings of the study. Therefore, it can be helpful to pick out the main finding(s) and create a graph to represent this visually for the reader, such as the two-way interaction shown in Figure 6.15. Remember to include a table or figure legend (which you can also see in Figure 6.15), and don't forget to refer to the table or figure in the written text, so that the reader knows to look at it (e.g. 'see Figure 3 for the

DOING AN EXPERIMENTAL RESEARCH PROJECT 81

Table 1 *Descriptive statistics for the three-way interaction*

Teaching Confidence	Test Difficulty	M	SE	M	SE	M	SE
		Low Self-esteem		Mid Self-esteem		High Self-esteem	
Low Confidence	Easy	26.5	1.7	28.5	1.8	32.1	1.7
	Mid	31.7	1.5	27.0	1.7	28.4	2.0
	Difficult	21.3	1.7	22.7	1.9	21.0	1.8
High Confidence	Easy	29.2	2.0	36.7	1.6	33.8	1.5
	Mid	30.7	1.8	30.2	1.9	28.9	2.1
	Difficult	22.7	1.9	20.1	2.0	26.1	1.

Figure 1 *Graph showing the two-way interaction between test difficulty and self esteem*

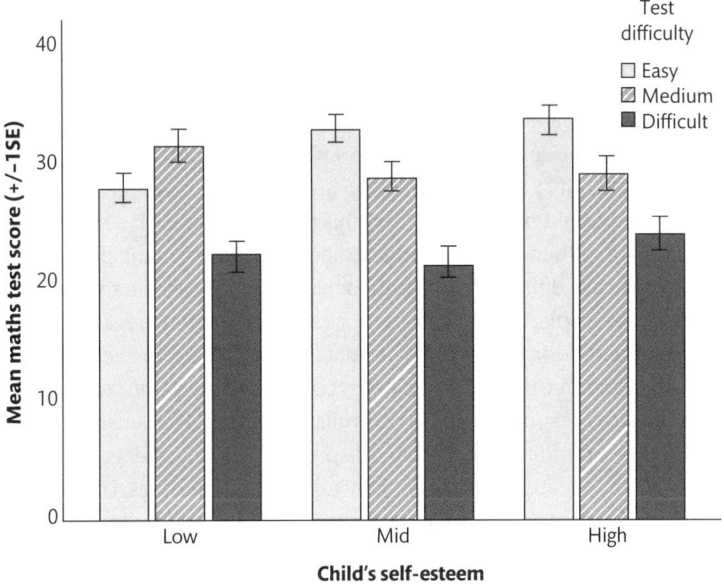

Figure 6.15 Two different ways of presenting descriptive statistics following APA style

descriptive statistics relating to the significant two-way interaction between test difficulty and self-esteem'). In psychological research, we would typically follow APA guidelines for the presentation of tables and graphs, and those in Figure 6.15 meet the APA expectations. While it is good to aim for APA style presentation, do check with your supervisor about any departmental expectations that you should follow.

Discussion

The main aim of your Discussion is to critically consider the implications of your findings, and you can divide this up into three key parts. First, you need to summarize your findings, without repeating the actual statistics, and then consider these within the context of the relevant previous research that you reviewed in your Introduction. Are your findings in line with the previous research and your predictions, or are there unexpected or contradictory findings? If you did not support your hypotheses, how might you explain that?

Second, you need to critically evaluate your study, and here it is particularly important to think carefully about the points that you choose to consider. You don't want to pick too many points. It is better to discuss a small number of issues in detail than to list a load of potential issues. You should also select points that are more like to actually influence your findings somehow. For example, in our teaching confidence experiment, we might have two points that relate to our sample. One might be the impact of level of attendance at school (i.e. low attendance may be associated with lower academic performance and self-esteem) or the impact of a diagnosis of dyscalculia (a specific learning difficulty that relates to the perception and processing of numbers). Now, both of these could theoretically have an impact on our findings. However, the attendance criticism would be a far stronger criticism to consider than the dyscalculia criticism. This is because every child will have an attendance score and there is likely to be a fair amount of variability in the attendance data, so we could include this as a covariable in any future study we conduct. A diagnosis of dyscalculia is relatively rare, especially in children as young as those in our study, so the vast majority of the children in our study will have no diagnosis and consequently dyscalculia is unlikely to have much of an impact on our findings (although we might want to consider making this an exclusion criterion for recruitment in future studies).

If you have an independent measures IV, you should also consider whether a potential evaluation point would affect all your participants, or just the participants in one condition. If all your participants would be affected, then this might not be such a strong critique point because, while it might influence the amount of random variance in the data collected, it may not explain any significant difference you find, because all the participants would have been equally affected. For example, if the self-esteem questionnaire that we used lacked reliability, that may explain more random variance in our dataset, but it couldn't actually explain any of the differences we found because all participants completed the same self-esteem questionnaire and all participants' responses would be similarly affected. However, if the point you are making only affects one condition, or perhaps disproportionately affects one condition, then this is a bigger problem because it might actually explain your findings. For example, imagine that – after running the experiment – we discovered that the teacher in the low-confidence condition was far less experienced than the teacher in the high-confidence condition. This actually could provide an alternative explanation for the differences we found, because they may be due to experience rather than confidence, which may be correlated but may also reflect quite distinct variables. So, when thinking critically about your design, try to avoid detailed consideration of issues that affect all participants, and instead focus on those that could explain the differences that you find, or perhaps did not find.

Finally, you need to consider the next steps in answering this research question. It can be tempting to jump ahead to a big and applied next step, perhaps developing treatments for dyscalculia or transforming the way that teaching is delivered and assessments designed in schools. While these are certainly interesting and valuable aims, it is better to focus on what you would want to achieve in the next research study or two that you run. Try to use the points you raised earlier in the discussion to justify the next steps you suggest. For example, you might want to research a contradictory finding between your study and the previous research, or you might want to resolve a limitation in your recruitment that you identified and considered. What is the next study you would actually want to run, and why?

6.7 Building transferable skills through experimental methodology

In this chapter, we have worked through how to do an experimental project, from developing the initial idea through to writing up your project. Two recurring issues are the importance of consistency and of controlling the experimental design to maximize your chances of finding differences that really reflect the IVs that you are exploring. Good people skills can be vital in achieving this, whether it is receiving feedback from your supervisor, developing your ideas with your research group, or recruiting participants and running the study. In Box 6.1, you can see an example of how a student might reflect on the people skills they needed and developed while conducting an experimental study. You can also see some helpful hints and tips in Box 6.2. Overall, conducting an experimental project and adhering to the scientific practices and tips provided in this chapter will help you develop advanced research and transferable skills, enabling you to contribute to the knowledge base and make a significant impact on your applied field and society more broadly.

BOX 6.1 A case study showing reflection on the people skills developed when conducting experimental research

---

Reflecting on your transferable skills and personal attributes
An example – people skills

Recognize: From the research you have conducted, what is the best example of when you have demonstrated this skill or attribute?

Our research group had to run lots of participants for this study, which meant recruiting lots of people, explaining the experiment requirements to them and then debriefing them. This meant that our group needed to work together so that we all communicated with participants in the same way, and gave exactly the same instructions and the same level of debriefing.

Reflect: What are my strengths with regard to this skill or attribute? How can I further develop or improve with regard to it?

Developing the research protocol for recruitment and running the study needed me to work closely with the rest of my research group. I took the lead in ensuring that everyone was able to contribute their ideas and that everyone was comfortable with the protocol that we had in place. For the debriefing, some participants asked some questions that were a little challenging to answer although, reflecting back, I did know the answers, I was just too nervous to give a quick response. As the experiment progressed, I gained more confidence and I think I probably need to work more on my own confidence in my knowledge and skills in working with other people.

Relate: Imagine you are being interviewed for your dream job or course. How would your skills in this area make you suitable for this position?

I would like to be an educational psychologist, and you need to be very sensitive in the way that you communicate with others, whether it is the children, their parents, or their teachers. In this project, I was able to show how I can work with other people in my team, as well as giving participants clear instructions and sensitive debriefing. I feel that these skills will help me when working with others as an educational psychologist.

> **BOX 6.2 Hints and tips from psychology graduates and employers of psychology graduates**
>
> The student's perspective... reflecting on people skills
>
> I learned how important it is to ensure clear communication between group members and your supervisor on expectations around data collection and detailed methodology execution, to ensure consistency throughout the group and study.
>
> Elias, psychology graduate
>
> The employer's perspective... reflecting on communication skills
>
> In particular communication skills, asking questions, giving and receiving feedback, and emotional/social intelligence. More typically work involves small teams which may well include client members too, and understanding the need to be flexible, adaptive and sensitive are all key skills, because no one has all the answers or can do everything, we all need help sometimes and the goal of any team is to be greater than the sum of its parts.
>
> Jelena, clinical psychologist

Wider reading

Bourne, V., James, A.I., & Wilson-Smith, K. (2021). *Understanding Quantitative and Qualitative Research in Psychology: A Practical Guide to Methods, Statistics and Analysis*. Oxford University Press.

Section Two of this book has a number of chapters covering different aspects of designing, analysing, and writing about experimental research. If you want to revise any of these aspects, or read more, then this would be a good place to look.

7 Doing a correlational research project

 In this chapter you will learn...
- how to design and run a robust advanced correlational research study;
- how to analyse and interpret your findings; and
- how to report your study and think critically about correlational research.

Correlational research is very popular and psychology students start training in it early in their degree. Hence, in this chapter, we will assume some existing knowledge. Basic correlational research entails simple binary correlations whereby two continuous variables are correlated. This is very simple to design and conduct. However, for your final year project, you are likely to be expected do a little more than just a simple correlation. So, in this chapter, we focus on a more advanced correlational design and analysis – regression, with a specific focus on hierarchal regression. Please do not worry if you are not too familiar with, or do not feel confident about, this design! We will start with a simple correlational design/analysis and develop it gradually to hierarchical regression but, if you would like to revise the basics of correlational design and analysis, there is some recommended reading at the end of this chapter (in particular, Section 3 from Bourne, James, & Wilson-Smith, 2021).

7.1 Skills required to be a good correlational researcher

There are many skills that are important when designing, conducting, and writing up correlational research and in Figure 7.1 we outline just some of them. One skill that for me (Danijela) stands out is teamwork. Correlational research usually needs a lot of participants. It also typically involves surveys that consist of several questionnaires. Furthermore, if your study is conducted online, this can present an additional obstacle because participants may leave the survey incomplete. Working well as a team can help overcome these obstacles. Another key skill in correlational research is critical thinking. Students sometimes confuse correlational research with experimental research. For example, they talk and write about it using cause-effect terminology (e.g. the effect or impact of one variable on another). It is important to think critically about what correlational research can and cannot do, and we discuss this later. Other key skills we chose for this chapter are IT, leadership, taking initiative, and independence; Figure 7.1 provides some examples of these. Recognizing the importance of these skills will help you reflect on how you use them in your research and relate them to your present and future career. We will provide an example of this at the end of the chapter, but first let's talk about correlational research!

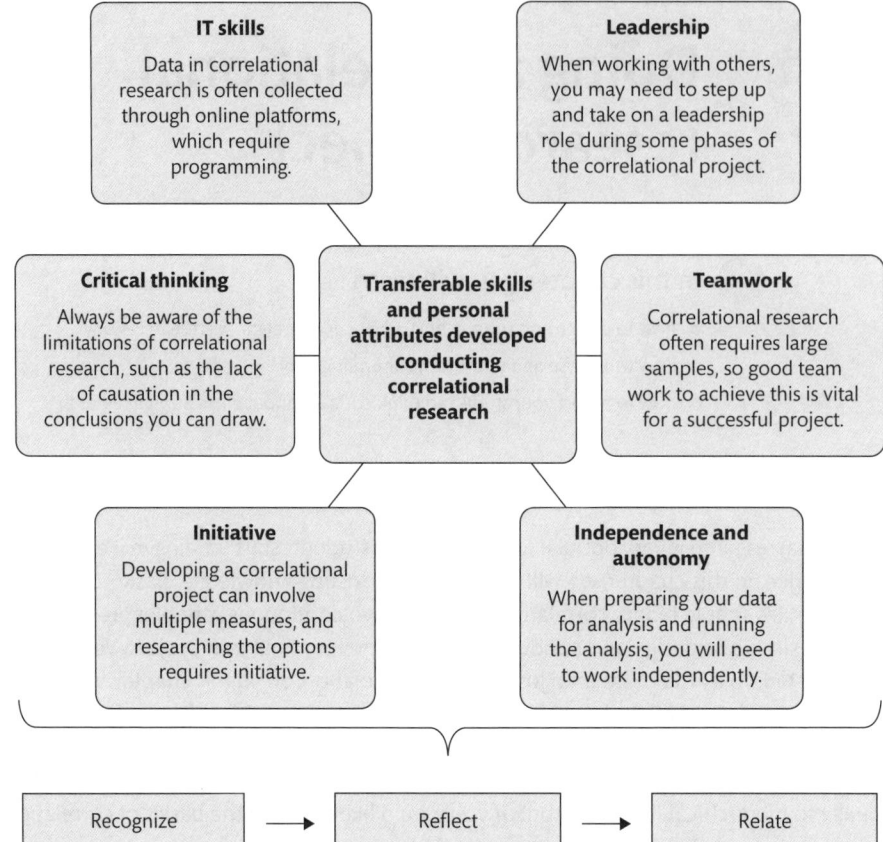

Figure 7.1 Key skills and attributes developed through running a correlational study

7.2 A quick revision of the basics

Before we start developing a more advanced correlational design, we want to remind you of a couple of fundamental aspects of correlational research.

Main aim of correlational design

The main aim of correlational research is to examine a relationship (correlation, association – these terms are used interchangeably) between variables. The simplest correlational design involves correlating two variables. This is called 'simple correlation'. It is also sometimes called 'zero-order correlation', 'binary correlation', 'bivariate correlation' or 'Pearson correlation' (with 'Spearman correlation' being its non-parametric equivalent); all these names are used interchangeably. In addition to the simple correlational design, there are also advanced correlational designs that will require you to use more complex statistical analysis such as regression. Regression is the main focus of this chapter! But let's first illustrate a simple correlational

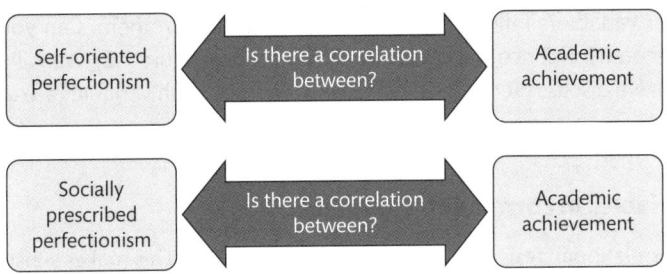

Figure 7.2 A simple correlational research design

design. To do this, we will use a fictional design. This design will also be used later to develop our advanced correlational design.

As illustrated in Figure 7.2, we are interested to see if perfectionism is correlated with academic achievement, so do people who are more perfectionist tend to achieve higher (or lower) grades? To examine this relationship, we can correlate perfectionism with academic achievement to check if an increase (or decrease) in one variable is associated with an increase (or decrease) in the other. Academic achievement will be measured using the end of academic year average mark, ranging on a scale 0–100. Perfectionism will be measured with the Multidimensional Perfectionism Scale (MPS; Hewitt et al., 1991) which consists of three subscales that measure three different facets of perfectionism: self-oriented perfectionism (unrealistic expectations of oneself to be perfect), socially prescribed perfectionism (the belief that significant others expect oneself to be perfect) and other-oriented perfectionism (imposing unrealistic standards on others and expecting them to be perfect). For this chapter, we will use two of these facets: self-oriented perfectionism and socially prescribed perfectionism because, in contrast to other-oriented perfectionism, they both assess own perfectionism. We will test these relationships using 300 fictional participants' data.

Important to note here is that we need to run two separate correlations to see whether each type of perfectionism is correlated with academic achievement (see Figure 7.2). So, in a simple binary correlation, we can correlate only two variables at a time.

Correlation versus causation

A key aspect of correlational design is that it can only examine whether two variables are correlated: it cannot examine whether one variable has an impact on or produces a change in another. So, if your research question requires this kind of examination, then you should be looking at an experimental design instead. Correlations examine whether an increase/decrease in one variable is associated with an increase/decrease in another. For this reason, in a simple correlational design, variables are just called 'variables'. We do not call them 'independent' or 'dependent' variables: this terminology is exclusive to experimental designs where an independent variable is manipulated to observe a change in the dependent variable. You can see this in Figure 7.2 where we used a double-headed arrow to indicate that the two variables are correlated and no causal relations are assumed. This also means that there could be other variable/s influencing the correlation between them. Can you think of any variables that could influence the correlations depicted in Figure 7.2? We will come back to this later when we discuss hierarchical regression whereby such variables are used as control variables.

Types of variables in correlational designs

In a simple correlational design, we use continuous variables. This makes sense because, in a correlational design, we want to assess the *strength* of a relationship between two variables along their continuum. We would not be able to assess this if their scores were categorical (e.g. yes/no). So, in our study, academic achievement is measured using participants' end of year average marks (on a scale 0 to 100), whereby higher scores mean better academic achievement. Perfectionism is measured on a scale 1 (strongly disagree) to 7 (strongly agree). Each perfectionism subscale has 15 items and therefore a total score for each subscale can range between 15 for a participant with the lowest score (15*1=15) through to 105 for a participant with the highest score (15*7=105). In advanced correlational designs where regression is used, our variables can be both continuous and categorical. We will talk about this more later in the chapter.

Positive, negative, and no correlation

To establish whether your two variables are significantly correlated, you should inspect the r statistic and its associated p value, most likely using the Pearson's correlation. If you find a significant relationship between them ($p < .050$), you would need to go a step further and inspect whether this relationship was positive or negative. r values range between -1.0 (a negative relationship) and $+1.0$ (a positive relationship). If it is a positive relationship, this means that the scores on one variable increase as scores on the other variable increase. On the other hand, a negative correlation between two variables means that, while scores on one variable increase, scores on the other variable decrease. For our two correlations, which you can see in Figure 7.3, we found a significant positive correlation between self-oriented perfectionism and academic achievement: $r = .189$, $p = .001$. We also found a significant positive correlation between socially prescribed perfectionism and academic achievement, $r = .178$, $p = .002$. So, this means that people who are more perfectionist tend to achieve higher grades. We will not elaborate further because some existing knowledge is assumed but, if you are still struggling with these concepts, please see other resources (e.g. Bourne, James, & Wilson-Smith, 2021).

7.3 Designing an advanced correlational study – regression

We can also use correlational designs to address more complex research questions – instead of just *correlating* two variables, we can try to *predict* one variable from another. This can be tested with regression. Regression is used in advanced correlational designs that typically include multiple variables that are divided into predictor and outcome variables.

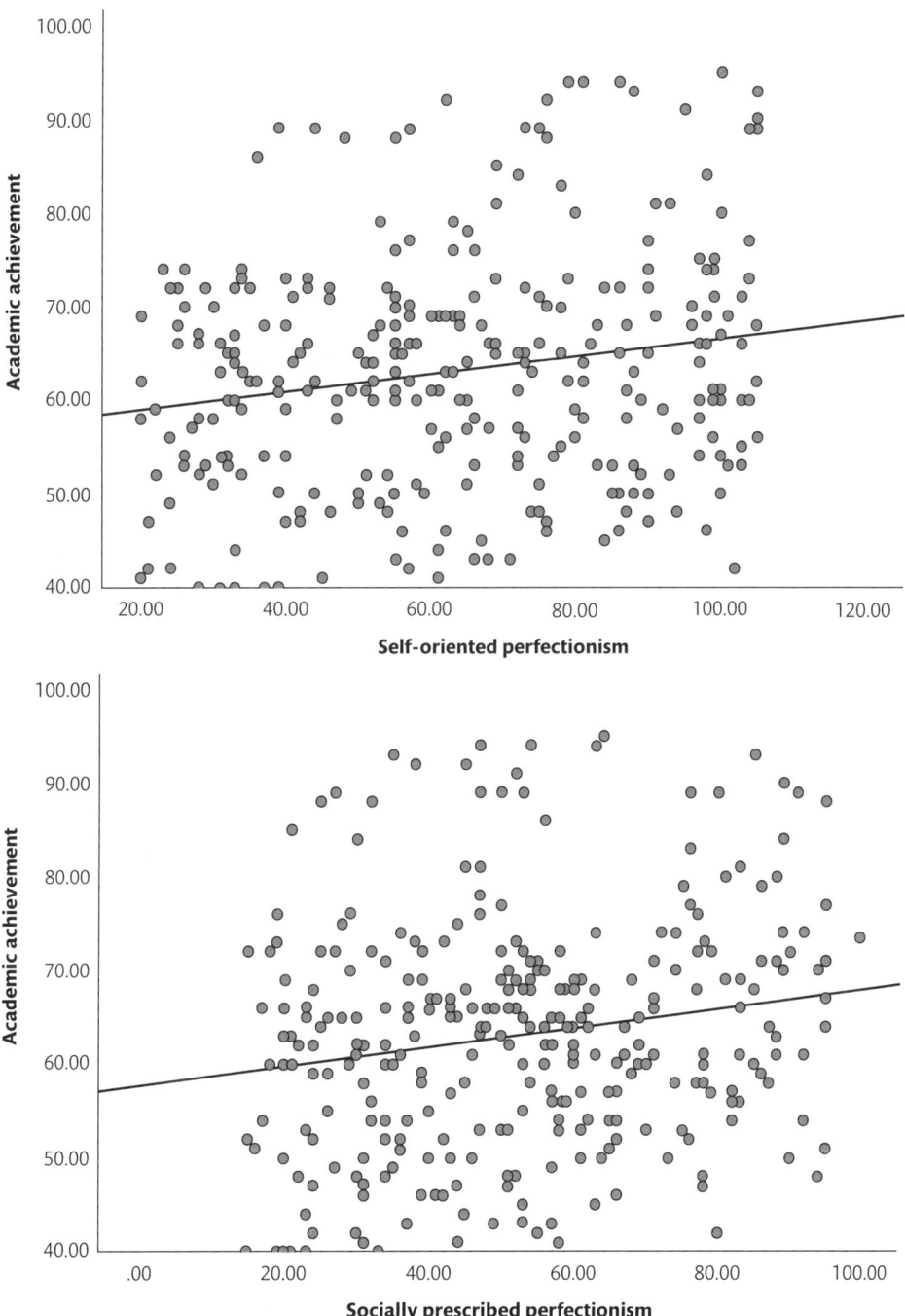

Figure 7.3 Scatterplots showing two positive correlations

Types of variables in regression

In a typical regression analysis, there is always only one outcome variable, but we can have one or more predictor variables. Your predictors can be either continuous or categorical. However, when using a categorical predictor, you need to ensure that it has no more than two categories, which must always be coded 0 and 1. You will sometimes see these described as 'binary variables'. Most types of regression have a continuous outcome variable (see Figure 7.7), with the exception of logistic regression where the outcome is a categorical variable.

From correlation to regression

We will now go back to our fictional design and use it as a basis for our regression. We will use academic achievement again, this time as an outcome variable. We will use both perfectionism scores again, this time as our predictor variables. Furthermore, we are going to add two new variables as predictors: helicopter parenting and first-generation student. Helicopter parenting refers to an overprotective parenting style, whereby parents 'hover' over their children like a helicopter. It will be measured with the Helicopter Parenting Scale (HPS; LeMoyne & Buchanan, 2011). This measure consists of 10 Likert-style items, 1 (strongly disagree) to 5 (strongly agree), with a total score ranging between 10 and 50. Higher scores represent higher levels of helicopter parenting perceived by respondents. Our second new predictor is whether a participant is a first-generation student or not. This is a categorical binary variable with either a yes first-generation student (coded as 1) or a no first-generation student (coded as 0) response options.

So, we want to examine how these four predictors relate to our outcome variable. The four predictors form a regression model, which is shown in Figure 7.4, where you will see that a regression analysis has two aims: first, to inspect whether the model as a whole (all predictors together) significantly predicts our outcome variable; second, to inspect how individual predictors predict the outcome variable. But what do we really mean by 'prediction' and what is the purpose of regression anyway?

What is the purpose of regression?

In our simple correlational design depicted in Figure 7.2, we found a positive significant relationship between both types of perfectionism and academic achievement. We can look more closely at this relationship and ask: 'If a student has a particular self-oriented perfectionism score, what will their grade be?' What we are trying to understand here is how the changes observed in academic achievement (outcome variable) are associated with the changes in self-oriented perfectionism (predictor variable). So, the difference between correlation and regression is that the first simply examines the *strength* of a relationship between two variables. Regression, on the other hand, examines how changes in one variable (predictor) are associated with the changes in another variable (outcome). You will see later that the term we use a lot in regression in *variance*. Variance is a measure of variability and, in simple terms, it measures how much the changes in the outcome variable are associated with the changes in the predictor variable/s.

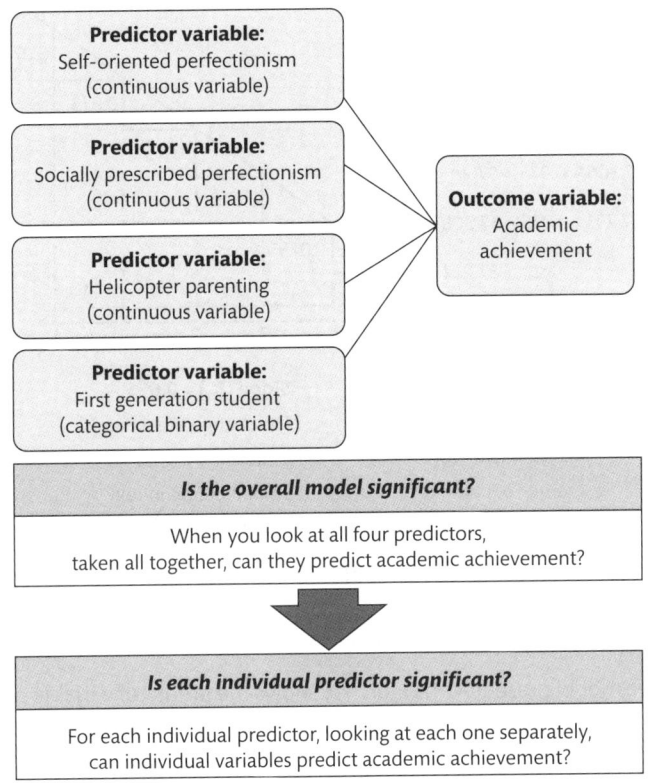

Figure 7.4 A simultaneous multiple regression, with the two aims of the analysis

This is closely linked to the concept of 'prediction'. A key feature of regression is 'predicting'. This means that we can use existing regression models (like the one depicted in Figure 7.4) to predict outcomes for the future (e.g. for variables and situations where we do not have the data yet). What do we mean by this? If we want to know how well a random student (could be you) will achieve academically if they had a particular perfectionism score, we could use our existing model to predict that person's academic achievement. To understand this, we need to look at the regression equation and consider the very basics of regression. Again, we assume some existing knowledge here so, if the next section goes a little too quickly for you, maybe look back at a more introductory text, such as the one recommended in the 'Wider reading' section of this chapter.

Basics of regression

In Figure 7.5, you can see the regression equation that shows how our outcome changes with any given change in our predictor. We can use this equation to make a regression line, which should be straight, meaning that it should show a linear relationship (hence 'linear' regression). The direction in which the regression line slopes will depend on whether the relationship is positive or negative.

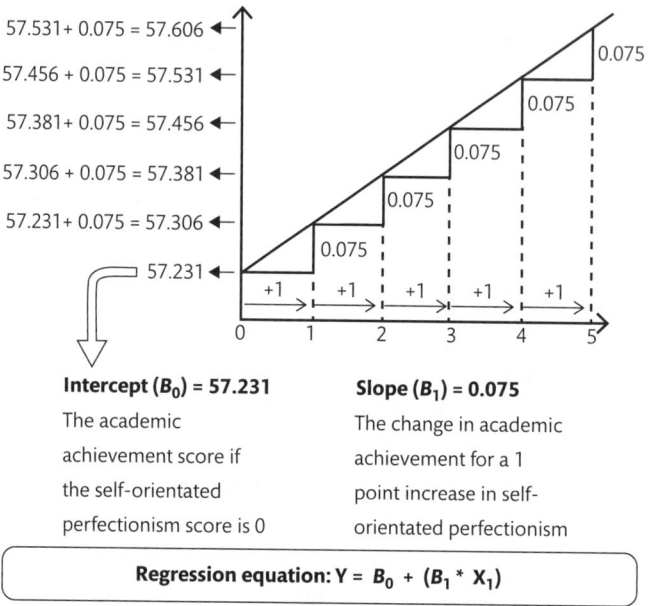

Figure 7.5 Understanding slope and intercept values in a regression analysis

The predictive model presented in Figure 7.5 shows the predictor variable on the x axis and the outcome variable on the y axis. To build this model we used the following:

a) the unstandardized beta (B_1) value (also called the 'slope'). To remind you, this tells you how much variance in academic achievement (our outcome variable) is explained by self-orientated perfectionism (one of our predictors). Specifically, how much academic achievement increases/decreases for one unit increase in self-oriented perfectionism. After running our regression analysis, we found that our B_1 is .075 so, as self-orientated perfectionism scores go up one unit, academic achievement goes up by .075.

b) the intercept value (B_0), which is also referred to as 'baseline' or 'constant' (you can find this in the coefficients table in your results output, see Figure 7.8). This simply tells you what the outcome score would be when the predictor variable score is 0. In our case, this value is 57.231. This means that, if the score for self-orientated perfectionism were 0, the academic achievement score would be 57.231. So, using the regression equation shown in Figure 7.5, we can calculate that if, for example, our imaginary student had a perfectionism score of 4, their mark would likely be 57.531.

$$Y = B_0 + (B_1 * X_1)$$
$$Y = 57.231 + (.075 * 4) = 57.531$$

Two key steps in regression

In any regression analysis, we are interested in two outcomes (see also the bottom of Figure 7.4): first, whether our model (all predictors together) predicts the outcome variable. This is assessed with the R squared (R^2) statistic. Specifically, it gives you the percentage of the

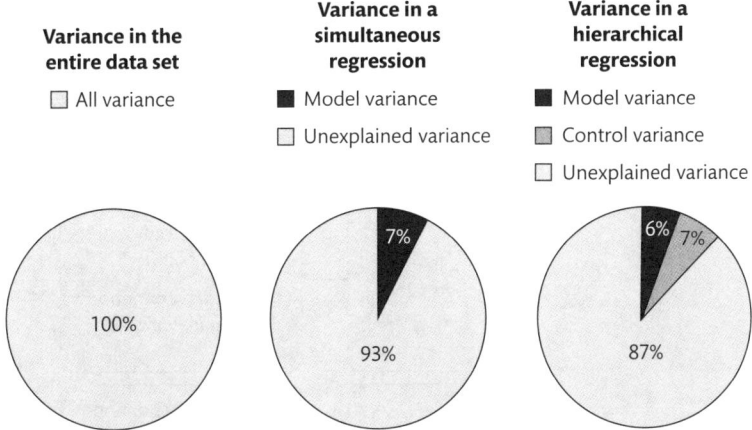

Figure 7.6 Understanding different sources of variance in a regression analysis

variance (0%–100%) in the outcome variable explained by all the predictors together. It is hard to talk about variance without the help of the variance cake, so here we go: have a look at Figure 7.6. For now, just focus on the first two variance cakes – we will come to the third one a little later.

The second point we want to examine is the individual contribution that each predictor has on the outcome variable. This is the second part of your regression analysis and is assessed with beta values (*B*). We have already covered the meaning of this but, just to remind you, a beta value measures the change in the outcome variable for one unit increase in the predictor. So, the question is: *If our self-oriented perfectionism score goes up one unit* (this would be one point on the self-oriented perfectionism scale), *how much change can we see in the outcome variable?* Similar to the *r* statistic, betas can be either positively or negatively associated with the outcome variable. If the relationship is positive, as the predictor score increases, the outcome score increases too, while the reverse is true when the relationship between them is negative. You can also have categorical predictors, for example our first-generation student (yes/no) predictor is a binary variable (see Figure 7.4). The two groups are always marked as 0 and 1 in a regression analysis. So, when you inspect beta for this predictor, if the beta is a positive value (indicates a move from 0 to 1, in a positive direction), this is associated with an increase in the outcome variable. If the beta is a negative value (indicates a move from 1 to 0, in a negative direction), this is associated with a decrease in the outcome variable.

Types of regression

There are several types of regression and we outline them in Figure 7.7. Note that the regression model shown in Figure 7.4 is a simultaneous regression. This is probably the simplest type of multiple regression analysis because all predictors are treated equally and entered at the same time. This means that we do not assume that any of them are more important than the others. We often choose to do this when we do not have previous research evidence to show that they should be treated differently. A key feature and advantage of regression

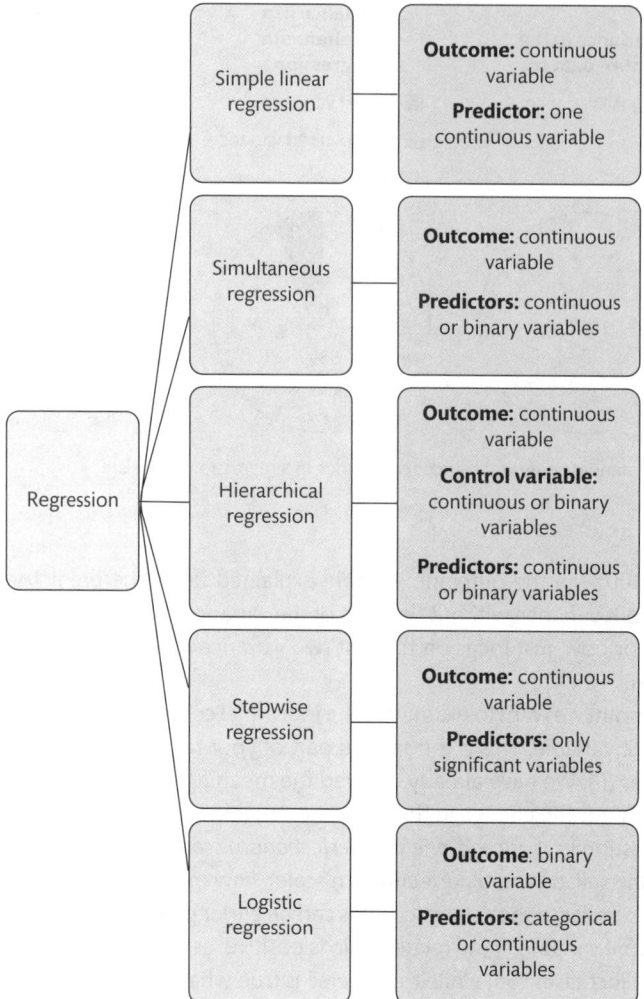

Figure 7.7 Understanding different types of regression models

analysis is that it can be used to understand patterns that occur in your data, and this can help you understand which variables are important in your research design.

We will not spend too long on this analysis because the focus of this chapter is the hierarchical regression. However, it would only be fair to let you know the outcome of this analysis and you can see the output in Figure 7.8. The first table shows that our model is significant, and it explains .072 of variance in academic achievement, which could also be described as 7.2% of the variance. Note that we reported the R^2 value, although sometimes researchers choose to report the adjusted R^2 that takes into account the number of predictors used for predicting the outcome variable. The coefficients table shows that self-oriented perfectionism, socially prescribed perfectionism, and helicopter parenting are significant individual predictors, while the first-generation student is not a significant predictor of academic achievement.

Model Summary [b]

Model	R	R Square	Adjusted R Square	Std. Error of the Estimate
1	.269[a]	.072	.060	12.04664

ANOVA[a]

Model		Sum of Squares	df	Mean Square	F	Sig.
1	Regression	3338.520	4	834.630	5.751	.000[b]
	Residual	42810.876	295	145.122		
	Total	46149.397	2.99			

Coefficients[a]

Model		Unstandardized Coefficients		Standardized Coefficients	t	Sig.
		B	Std. Error	Beta		
1	(Constant)	57.231	3.079		18.589	.000
	Perfect_self	.075	.029	.152	2.612	.009
	Perfect_society	.080	.033	.138	2.389	.018
	Heli_parent	-1.248	.600	-.117	-2.079	.039
	First_gen	1.701	1.395	.069	1.220	.224

Figure 7.8 Output from a simultaneous multiple regression

Designing a hierarchical regression

We started by presenting a very simple correlational design, whereby we correlated only two continuous variables at a time. We then moved to advanced correlational designs, where we added a couple more variables to our initial correlational design and conducted a simultaneous multiple regression analysis. Now, we want to engage with a more complex type of regression: hierarchical regression. This will require you to think about our research question, our design, and our variables a little differently.

Developing a hierarchical regression

As with other types of regression analysis, hierarchal regression involves a bunch of predictors and an outcome variable. However, what distinguishes it from other types of regression is that the predictors are entered in blocks or steps, and each block represents one model. You need to decide the order they should be entered into your analysis, and this decision must be based on previous research and theory. Typically, the predictors that are already known to be associated with your outcome variable are entered first, within the first block, and they will be your Model 1. They are sometimes referred to as 'confounds' or 'control variables'. They are entered first because you want to control for them (by removing their variance) before analysing the relationship between the remaining new predictors and your outcome variable. New predictors (these are your main predictors of interest) are entered next within a second block. This will be your Model 2. This type of model building in regression can show you whether your predictors of interest can explain a statistically significant improvement in R^2 (the amount of explained variance in your outcome variable) after accounting for control variables. See the hierarchical regression variance cake in Figure 7.6: it shows the variance explained by Models 1 and 2, as well as the remaining unexplained variance.

You can even go a step further and decide that your predictors of interest are not of equal importance, and so split them into further blocks/models. You can add multiple predictors within each block and so on. Make sure that your decisions about this are always based on previous research and theory. And, just to remind you: the final model is the one you should be most interested in.

So, let us build our hierarchical regression. For demonstration purposes, we will treat the predictors we used previously (in our simultaneous regression) as our main predictors of interest. To remind you, these were self-oriented perfectionism, socially prescribed perfectionism, helicopter parenting, and first-generation student. We will enter them in the second block (Model 2) in our analysis because they are the predictors that we are genuinely interested to learn about. In the first block (Model 1), we will include two control predictors: year of study (first versus final year of study; hence this is a binary predictor) and trait anxiety (continuous predictor). They are entered first because we want to control for them. Trait anxiety is measured with the Spielberger State-Trait Anxiety Inventory (STAI) (Spielberger, 1983). It has 20 items that are rated on a 4-point scale; higher scores indicate greater anxiety. For this fictional design, we assume that these are known and well-established correlates of academic achievement and, as such, they may influence the outcome variable. Academic achievement remains our outcome variable and is measured as a percentage mark on a scale of 0–100%.

In summary, we are interested to find out whether self-oriented perfectionism, socially prescribed perfectionism, helicopter parenting, and first-generation student (Model 2) predict academic achievement over and above any variance in academic achievement that can be explained by our two control variables, year of study and trait anxiety (Model 1). In Figure 7.9 you can see how this looks for our hierarchical regression model.

Developing hypotheses for a hierarchical regression

You have probably gathered by now that developing hypotheses for an advanced correlational design typically includes more than one hypothesis. This contrasts with a simple correlational design whereby one hypothesis would be sufficient. So, for one of our simple correlations in Figure 7.2, we could hypothesize that *self-oriented perfectionism will be positively correlated with academic achievement*. In advanced correlational designs, such as hierarchical regression, you will need one hypothesis for each relationship tested (i.e. for each predictor), and you can see an example of how this could be done in Figure 7.10. Also, you may also hypothesize about the amount of variance in your outcome variable that can be explained by each model in your analysis. Your hypotheses should be informed by past research and theory. See the various hypotheses for our hierarchical regression:

There are a few points to bear in mind when writing your hypotheses. You should use terminology that describes how two variables are associated and avoid terminology that may

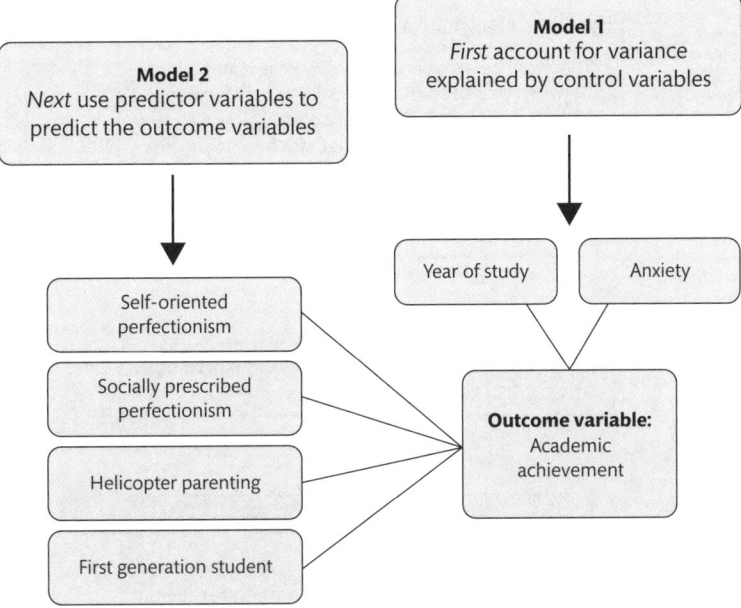

Figure 7.9 A hierarchical regression model

signal causal relationships (e.g. effect, impact). In fact, the use of causal language should be avoided whenever you are talking about correlational research unless you actually do mean to talk about a causal relationship (e.g. when discussing future research in a discussion). Your multiple hypotheses should be presented within a paragraph – listing them using bullet points or numbers is not good practice. Your hypotheses should be informed by past research and the theory that you discussed in the introduction of your research report. You will recall that in Chapter 5 we talked about HARKing (hypothesizing after data analysis; it might be worthwhile to refer back to that chapter now). This HARKing is a bad research practice, so always make sure that you generate and write your hypotheses during the design phase of your research. Do not strive to get significant results – strive to get true results! Both significant and non-significant results are useful and informative.

7.4 Designing a robust correlational study

There are several points to consider when designing and conducting correlational research. In this section, we will discuss how to ensure reliability and validity of measures (typically questionnaires) used in correlation research, assumptions of regression, and sample size.

Reliability and validity in correlational designs

Questionnaires are a common data collection tool in correlational research. You are advised to use established questionnaires, because such questionnaires have been tested for validity and reliability by previous research. This should increase your confidence in them. However,

Hypotheses for control predictor variables:

- There will be a significant positive relationship between year of study and academic achievement, with students in their final year of study having higher academic achievement than those in the first year of study.
- There will be a significant positive relationship between trait anxiety and academic achievement.

↓

After controlling for the variance explained by the control variables…

↓

Hypotheses for predictor variables:

- There will be a significant positive relationship between self-orientated perfectionism and academic achievement.
- There will be a significant positive relationship between socially prescribed perfectionism and academic achievement.
- There will be a significant positive relationship between helicopter parenting and academic achievement.
- There will be a significant positive relationship between first-generation students and academic achievement, with the first-generation students having higher academic achievement than those who are not first-generation students.

Figure 7.10 Hypotheses for each variable in a hierarchical regression

this does not mean that you should not carry out some additional checks to ensure that such tools also have good reliability in your dataset. A very common measure of reliability in questionnaire designs is internal consistency (measured with Cronbach alpha). This test ensures that all the items within a single questionnaire are answered in a similar way and are highly correlated (i.e. they measure the same concept or construct). For example, our self-oriented perfectionism scale consists of 15 items and we would expect them all to be highly correlated. This means that all 15 items measure self-oriented perfectionism, making it a reliable measure of this construct. Your Cronbach's alpha statistic (with values ranging between 0 and 1) should be .7 or higher to have good internal consistency.

If on the other hand, you decide to develop your own questionnaire, this should be done using several established steps and tests. For example, you would need to conduct a factor analysis of your new questionnaire to examine its internal structure and so on. This is outside the scope of this chapter so, for more detail, please see other resources (e.g. Bourne, James, & Wilson-Smith, 2021).

It is also important to consider validity in your correlational research. One type of validity that is very relevant to questionnaires is construct validity. This is about ensuring that your questionnaire indeed measures what it intends to measure. For example, does a self-orientated perfectionism questionnaire really measure this construct and not some other related construct – for example, socially prescribed perfectionism? You should also consider other types of validity in your correlational research, such as internal validity (are your study design, conduct, and analysis appropriate to answer the research questions?) and external validity (can your study findings be generalized to other situations?).

Assumptions of regression

There are several statistical assumptions of regression and, when they are met, you can consider your regression model robust and unbiased. We outline them briefly here, but you can find more detailed explanations in other textbooks if you want to revise the assumptions. Note that these assumptions are the same across all types of regression and they should be reported before your main regression analysis. However, there are some basic checks that you need to do on your data. First, you need to check that the relationship between the predictor and outcome variable is indeed linear, so the relationships between continuous variables are best described with a straight line. The easiest way to check this is to look at the scatterplot and see whether the line of best fit seems appropriate, or whether there seems to be a non-linear (curved) relationship between the variables. Then, you also need to make sure to check that your data for continuous variables are normally distributed. This is a basic assumption that applies to all kinds of research designs, not just correlational, and we are sure that you are already familiar with it. A test like the Kolmogorov-Smirnov can help you to assess this. You want these tests to be not significant for each variable to conclude that there is normal distribution.

There are then four key assumptions that apply specifically to regression analyses that you need to check: that there is no multicollinearity, that your residuals are normally distributed, that there is homoscedasticity in the residuals, and that you do not have too many outliers. We will go through each of these briefly now (but, if you want to revise these in more detail, take a look at Bourne, James, & Wilson-Smith, 2021).

1. *Multicollinearity*: This means that your predictors are very highly correlated. This assumption is simple to check: any Pearson correlations that are outside the ±.9 range are problematic and indicate that multicollinearity is present. We do not want our predictors to be very highly correlated because this basically means that they are extremely similar/the same and they do not uniquely predict the outcome variable. When you run the analysis, look at your table of correlations between all variables in our hierarchical regression analysis to check the *r* values. For our analysis in this chapter, all the correlations between our predictors are within the required range.

2. *Outliers*: You want no more than 5% of your sample to have outlying scores, defined by the standardized residual (the difference between their actual score and their predicted score) being greater than ±2. When you run the analysis, you can check the number of outliers in the 'Casewise Diagnostics' table. This will show you that we have 17 participants with residuals that are defined as outlying scores, which is 5.6%

of the sample. This is slightly above the required 5% but, because this is being used in an educational context, we are keeping them in for simplicity. However, if you were to encounter this situation with real data, you would want to consider removing the outliers and repeating the analysis.

3. *Residuals*: These should be normally distributed – this is about inspecting the error in your predictive model. If you look at Figure 7.11 and the line of best fit, you will see that this line is not perfect. It never is: there is always some error in how this line fits the data and this can be assessed by looking at the residuals. Residuals are the difference between a participant's actual score and the score that the model predicts they would have. The smaller the difference between these two values – the residual value – the more accurate the model is. These residuals should be normally distributed, meaning that there is a similar number of positive residuals (scores above the line of best fit, meaning our model's underestimated outcome scores) and negative residuals (scores below the line of best fit, meaning our model's overestimated outcome scores).

You can assess this by inspecting the distribution of residuals' plots like the one on the left of Figure 7.12. You can see that our residuals are normally distributed, because the peak of the distribution is centred around 0 on the X axis. If the distribution is skewed, this is most likely due to outliers in your dataset, so it might be helpful to look at the outlier statistics and consider whether you should be removing any outliers (see the previous section).

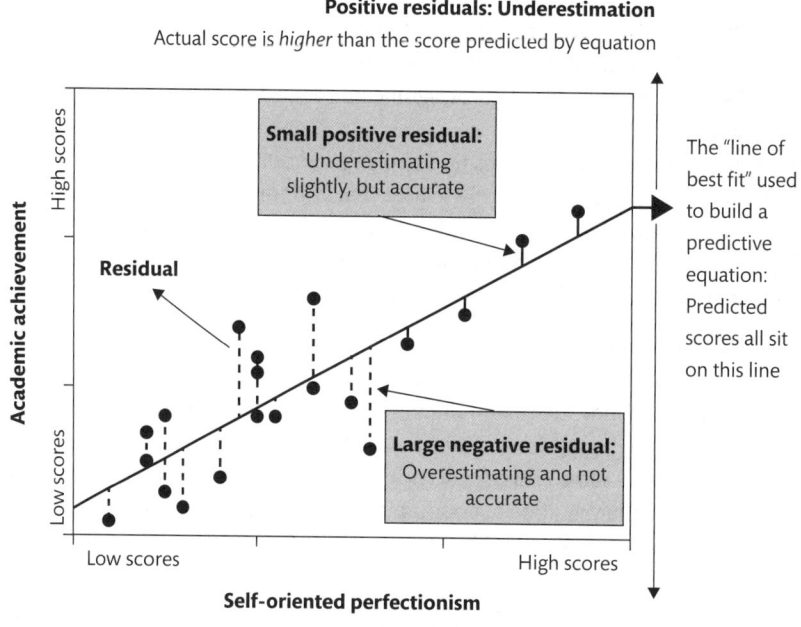

Figure 7.11 Residual values in a regression

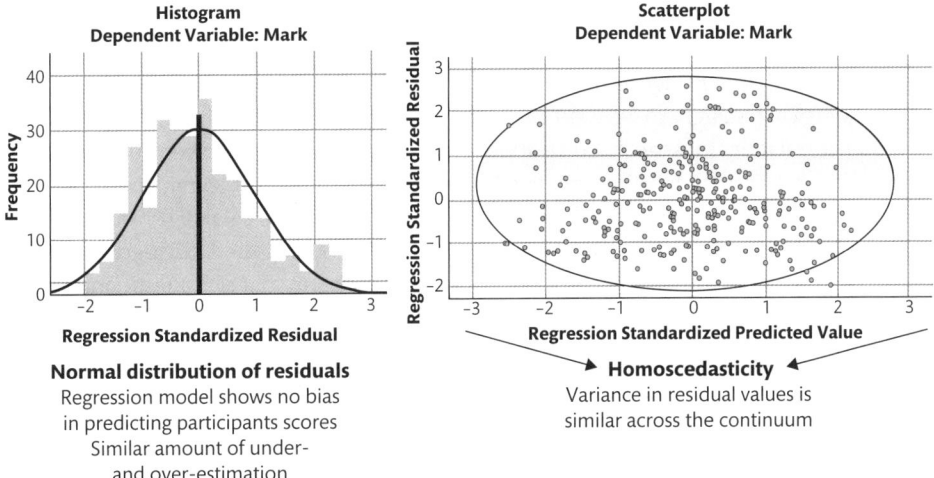

Figure 7.12 Evaluating the assumptions of normal distribution of residuals and homoscedasticity

4. *Homoscedasticity*: This means that your residuals are evenly spread across all participants. You can assess this by plotting your standardized residuals on a graph, like the one on the right of Figure 7.12. They should be evenly distributed across the graph, in a circle-like pattern rather than funnel-like pattern. This means that our model is not biased towards any particular type of error. You can see that our residuals are evenly dispersed and form a circle-like shape. As with the distribution of residuals, if there is heteroscedasticity in your dataset, then check for outliers because this is a likely explanation for violating this assumption.

Sample size

Regression analysis often involves several variables and therefore needs a lot of participants. The more variables (predictors) you have, the more participants you will need. To determine the required sample size in your design, you can use an online sample size calculator, such as the G Power calculator. You can use this to determine the minimum number of participants you will need for the study in order to have adequate power to detect an effect. To do this, you will need to know whether you expect a small, medium, or large effect size. You can find this out by checking relevant published research and identifying the effect size that is typically found when researching in this area. If you are not sure, then select the medium effect size. You will also need to know the power to find an effect (typically 80% in psychological research). See Chapter 5 for more detail on power in research and the alpha value (typically .050). For our hierarchical regression analysis, with two control variables and four predictors of interest (six predictors in total), if we expect a medium effect size with 80% power to detect it and with the alpha level of .05, we need a minimum of 85 participants.

7.5 Ethics for a correlational study

We assume that, by this stage in your studies, you are quite familiar with the ethical principles of psychological research, so we want to give you just a few reminders that are important for ethics in correlational research. Correlational research commonly involves questionnaires, whereby we ask several questions relating to our variables of interest. Often, these can contain sensitive questions – for example, questions relating to health, sexuality, self-harm, abuse, or addiction. Asking such questions can trigger distressing feelings and cause psychological harm. Therefore, it is important to consider any potential harm that our questionnaires can cause to our participants and think how to deal with this issue. It is always good to use established questionnaires, if possible, because these have been used and validated across several past studies. Wherever possible, avoid asking unnecessary personal or sensitive questions, or allow participants to not answer sensitive questions. It is important to carefully consider what data are necessary for your research.

When recruiting participants for your study, the first step of course will be to obtain informed consent from them. They will need to be told that potentially sensitive questions may be asked during the study. This will help them decide whether they want to proceed and take part in your research. If they decide to take part, they need to be told that they can withdraw at any point without providing an explanation for their withdrawal. They can also skip any questions they do not like answering. Your participants will also want to know how their data will be stored and used, so it is essential that you inform them that their data will be kept with confidentiality and anonymity. Finally, you must ensure that you debrief your participants at the end of the study. Make sure to provide information about where they can find support if they find taking part in the study upsetting in any way. Some examples of support offered include relevant support groups, NHS contacts, etc. It is the collective responsibility of all researchers to ensure that our participants are protected while involved with our study, including any possible lasting effects, so make sure to plan for this in your research protocol. Lastly, make sure to work closely with your supervisor while developing your ethics application as well as inspecting and following the British Psychological Society and American Psychological Association (APA) guidelines for ethical research.

7.6 Running a correlational study

Correlational research typically uses surveys (consisting of a lot of questionnaires) and it also needs many participants. Giving too many questionnaires will increase participant burden and may result in many incomplete surveys. This is obviously problematic because you may need to exclude participants due to missing data. This is a common issue in online data collection, which is often used in correlational research. All in all, in this type of research, participant recruitment is a balancing act whereby you need to think carefully about how to minimize participant burden while ensuring that you are collecting all the data that you need.

Running a study with others

A lot of research today is done collaboratively and this is in line with open science practices (see Chapter 5). So, you may be conducting your project with others; these are also known as 'group projects'. As discussed in Section 1 of this book, it is important to use several skills effectively to ensure a productive collaboration with your group and your supervisor to help with the smooth running of your project. At this point, it would be good to revisit those chapters. Correlational research typically requires large sample sizes, depending on the complexity of your project design. So, when running a correlational study, you may feel somewhat overwhelmed with the recruitment plans and finding enough participants to take part in your study. An advantage of group projects is that recruitment and data collection tasks can be shared. For example, if you are working in a group of five students and you need to recruit 200 participants, each group member would need to recruit only 40 participants. If all group members are using the same measures, this will be easy to do. If, however, you have different designs and measures, you will need to discuss how to combine these into one survey without increasing participant burden. You will all need to follow the same steps when doing the recruitment and data collection, and the best way to ensure this is to follow the same protocol (see below). Having a written protocol that all members can use will ensure consistency and clarity in how your study is run. It will also guarantee that all group members adhere to the ethical procedures in the same way (e.g. when obtaining informed consent and debriefing participants).

Recruitment and ways of collecting data

As with other types of research, recruitment in correlational research can be dependent on personal contacts, networking, social media, specialized recruitment platforms (your department may have one), etc. You can recruit participants and collect your correlational data either in person or online. Researchers often opt to do this online: this is perceived as an easier and more efficient method that can help them collect a lot of data quickly. It can also make the recruitment and data collection more standardized. However, there are some challenges too: for example, if your participants need to get in touch with you to ask you questions about the study, it is unlikely that they will get answers quickly. This could result in a delay in taking part in your study, or not taking part at all. We discussed this in more detail in Chapter 6, where we also talked about recruitment outside university settings (e.g. schools, hospitals). It would be helpful for you to revisit that chapter because the same points apply here.

If you are collecting your data online, you are likely to use an online research platform such as Google Forms or Qualtrics. Some of these platforms require a paid subscription, so check with the staff in your department as to which platform they use. They may also provide training on how to use it. There are advantages to online data collection. First, it enables more consistency in how data are collected across participants and can therefore help minimize researcher bias. Online participation is often anonymous, which can decrease social desirability bias (participants' tendency to respond in socially acceptable ways) because participants may feel less under pressure to provide socially acceptable answers and can therefore be more honest in their replies. They may also find it easier to answer sensitive questions when not asked in person. But, as already mentioned, with online data collection, you are likely to have a lot of missing data so make sure to factor this in when determining your sample size.

Collecting, coding, and storing data

If you are working with a group of students on your project, all members need to adhere to the same data collection, coding, and storing guidance. We recommend that you devise a study protocol that can be used by all group members. This will help ensure consistency and is relevant to both in-person and online data collection. In addition, collecting, coding, and storing your data is very much linked to ethical aspects of your study. It is important that you take good care of your participants' data and keep both their data and personal information confidential and anonymous. Having a clearly written protocol will help with that too. When transferring/downloading your online data into a statistical package, you need to handle your data carefully by ensuring that your variables are properly coded, your data are backed up and safely stored, etc. If you are collecting data in person, be very patient and pedantic with data entry because this can be a tedious and lengthy process in correlational research. Again, these tasks are likely to be shared between several group members so make sure that everyone knows what they are doing, that they are doing it in the same way, and that relevant checks are implemented as appropriate. It is always better to take the time to ensure that tasks are completed correctly the first time round, rather than having to go back and correct mistakes or misunderstandings.

7.7 Analysing correlational data

The focus of this section will be on helping you understand the key aspects of your hierarchical regression results. As in Chapter 6, we are not going to go through the steps of how to run a hierarchical regression in a statistical package. At this stage of your degree, you should already be familiar with at least one statistical package for data analysis. There are several statistics packages that can be used to run a hierarchical regression – for example, SPSS, R. We are using SPSS so, if you are not using this statistical package, don't be alarmed: they should all produce the same results although the output might look a little different.

Developing an analysis strategy

As discussed in Chapter 5, it is absolutely crucial that you develop your analysis strategy at the design phase of your research. It might be good to revisit that chapter to be reminded about bad research practices such as HARKing and how to avoid them. Make sure that you have a clear analysis strategy, that you understand all the steps within your hierarchical regression analysis, and that you know how to report and interpret your results within each step. This will make the analysis of your data far easier, quicker, and less stressful!

Preparing data for analysis

Before you start your data analysis, you need to prepare and clean your data. What do we mean by this? If you haven't already done so, you should probably start by setting up your data file and defining your variables. Your datasheets/files may have more variables than you need. This is likely to happen if you are working with other students and others are using different variables – or when using secondary data, which may contain some extra variables. One way to deal with this is to create a copy of the data file in which you can keep the variables that you need to analyse. The main aim is to make your data file manageable and clear for you to use in your analysis.

Once your data file is set up, you need to inspect it for any missing data and appropriately deal with it. You can check this by running frequency analysis. This will show you if any of your variables have missing data. If so, you will need to decide how to deal with the missing data. There are several strategies that you can use – from removing participants with missing data to replacing the missing values with an estimated value. You will have to decide about how to deal with missing data, so make sure to discuss this with your supervisor and with others in your group (if appropriate). Next, you need to inspect your variables for possible outliers. These are very high or very low scores that are outside the expected range of scores. This is also one of the regression assumptions that we mentioned earlier in this chapter. Some areas of psychological research have quite established ways of dealing with missing data or outliers, so do check for this when reading papers. You are likely to use some well-established measures in your study so, as advised earlier, you should check internal consistency of these measures in your data by running Cronbach's alpha analyses.

Checking the regression assumptions

You should inspect and report your regression assumptions before your main regression results. We have covered these assumptions earlier in the chapter so please refer back to the designing a robust research section (7.4). It showed that, overall, our predicted model was robust.

Making sense of your findings

When looking at your hierarchical regression results, it is helpful to do this in the order that you will report them in your write-up. You have already inspected your regression assumptions to see if your predicted model is robust. Now you can turn to your main regression results and inspect your models as well as individual predictors.

What are we looking for when analysing correlational data?

As explained earlier, in any multiple regression, the analysis is divided into two key stages: first, you need to analyse your model – this includes all predictors within your model. Then you need to examine individual predictors. In our hierarchical regression, we have two models. This means that our analysis will consist of four stages, which we outline in Figure 7.13.

Analysis of Model 1

This is our control block where we included predictors that we wanted to control for: year of study and trait anxiety. Here you want to examine how much unique variance is explained by the control variables and whether this variance is significant. For this and other models (see below), you will need to inspect and report the R^2 value, which represents the amount of variance explained in the outcome variable by the model – that is, all the variables within that block, taken together. You also need to report the F statistic and the associated p value to establish whether the model is significant or not. As you can see in Figure 7.14 and in the variance cake in Figure 7.6, this model explains 6.7% (R^2 = .067) of the variance in academic

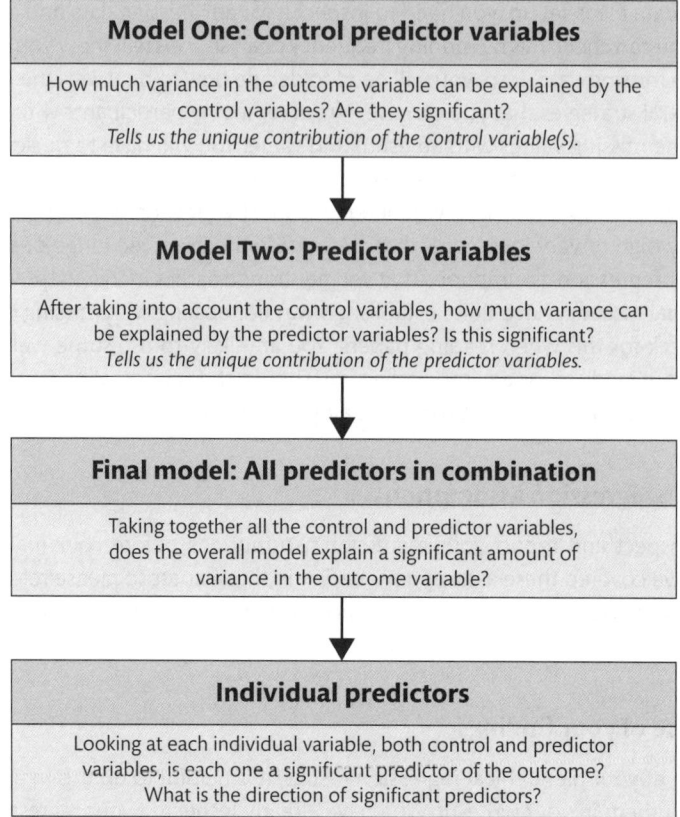

Figure 7.13 Stages of the analysis in a hierarchical regression

achievement. Year of study and trait anxiety, if combined, are significantly better predictors of academic achievement than having no predictors at all (F (2,297) = 10.74, p <.001).

Analysis of Model 2

Next, you need to examine Model 2, which includes all our predictors gathered together. It will tell you about the unique variance explained by our predictors of interest (self-oriented perfectionism, socially prescribed perfectionism, helicopter parenting, and first-generation student) while controlling for and removing the variance explained by the control variables. Figure 7.14 shows that this model explains a further 5.7% (R^2 change = .057) of the variance in academic achievement. Note that you should report the R^2 change value as this represents the change in R^2 from Model 1 to Model 2. Combined, the predictors in Model 2 significantly improve the prediction of the model over and above the Model 1 (F (4,293) = 4.76, p = .001).

Analysis of overall model

Now you need to look at the overall model (i.e. all your predictors together from both Model 1 and Model 2). You want to check how much of the variance in your outcome variable is

Model Summary[c]

Model	R	R Square	Adjusted R Square	Std. Error of the Estimate	R Square Change	F Change	df1	df2	Sig. F Change
					\multicolumn{5}{c}{Change Statistics}				
1	.260[a]	.067	.061	12.03782	.067	10.736	2	297	.000
2	.353[b]	.124	.106	11.74406	.057	4.761	4	293	.001

ANOVA[a]

Model		Sum of Squares	df	Mean Square	F	Sig.
1	Regression	3111.367	2	1555.684	10.736	.000[b]
	Residual	43038.029	297	144.909		
	Total	46149.397	299			
2	Regression	5737.989	6	956.331	6.934	.000[c]
	Residual	40411.408	293	137.923		
	Total	46149.397	299			

Figure 7.14 Output showing the model statistics for a hierarchical regression

explained by this overall model. Figure 7.14 shows that the overall model explains 12.4% (R^2 = .124) of the variance in the outcome variable. This final model is significant (F (6,293) = 6.93, p <.001).

Analysis of individual predictors

Finally, you should turn your attention to the individual predictors, both Model 1 and Model 2. You want to examine the relationship between each predictor and the outcome variable. To do this, you will need to inspect their B value, which tells you about the increase/decrease in the outcome variable for a one-point increase in the predictor variable. Don't forget to inspect the direction of any significant relationship: it can be either positive or negative. To establish whether each predictor is significant, you will need to inspect the associated t test statistic and its p value. In a hierarchical regression, you always inspect the last block within your coefficients table. As shown in Figure 7.15:

- Trait anxiety is a significant control variable of academic achievement (B = .128, t = 3.26, p = .001). A one-point increase in trait anxiety is associated with .128 increase in academic achievement.
- Year of study is also a significant control variable (B = 3.171, t = 2.31, p = .022). Being in the final year of study is associated with a 3.171 increase in academic achievement.
- Self-oriented perfectionism is a significant predictor (B = .071, t = 2.52, p = .012). A one-point increase in self-oriented perfectionism is associated with .071 increase in academic achievement.
- Socially prescribed perfectionism is a significant predictor (B = .069, t = 2.12, p = .035). A one-point increase in socially prescribed perfectionism is associated with .069 increase in academic achievement.
- Helicopter parenting is not a significant predictor (B = -1.061, t = -1.77, p = .077).
- First-generation student is not a significant predictor (B = 1.687, t = 1.24, p = .217).

Coefficients[a]

Model		Unstandardized Coefficients B	Std. Error	Standardized Coefficients Beta	t	Sig.	95.0% Confidence Interval for B Lower Bound	Upper Bound
1	(Constant)	53.673	2.174		24.683	.000	49.394	57.953
	Trait_anx	.160	.039	.230	4.091	.000	.083	.237
	Year_study	2.671	1.394	.108	1.917	.056	-.072	5.413
2	(Constant)	49.376	3.629		13.605	.000	42.234	56.519
	Trait_anx	.128	.039	.183	3.261	.001	.051	.205
	Year_study	3.171	1.373	.128	2.309	.022	.468	5.873
	Perfect_self	.071	.028	.143	2.523	.012	.016	.127
	Perfect_society	.069	.033	.120	2.120	.035	.005	.134
	Heli_parent	-1.061	.598	-.099	-1.773	.077	-2.239	.117
	First_gen	1.687	1.363	.068	1.238	.217	-.995	4.369

Figure 7.15 Analysis of individual predictor variables in a hierarchical regression

Remember that these results are based on fictional data! Also, when you write up your results, you should not use a bullet-point list. I've done it like this to be as clear as possible in this educational context, but later we will talk more about how to write up a results section.

In summary, we have four significant predictors (trait anxiety, year of study, self-oriented perfectionism, and socially prescribed perfectionism) and they are all positively associated with the outcome variable. The remining two predictors (helicopter parenting and first-generation student) are not significant. Significant predictors should be graphed as in Figure 7.3.

Effect sizes in correlational designs

A p value simply tells you if a particular relationship is significant or not, while effect size tells you how strong that relationship is. Hence, effect size indicates the magnitude and importance of the relationship, and this is obviously important for real-world application of your findings. For a reminder about why this is so important, you may find it helpful to look back at Chapter 5, where we discuss the principles behind open science practices. We divide effect sizes into small, medium, and large. A result with a small effect size has little importance in comparison with a result with a large effect size. In correlational research, the r statistic is also a measure of effect size. R values around .1 indicate a small effect size, values around .3 indicate a medium effect size, and values above .5 indicate a large effect size. An R coefficient is a standardized effect size, which means that it does not use the original unit of measurement: it is based on a standardized measure where values fall between −1.0 and +1.0. This means that it is possible to compare r results across different analyses. What about effect size in regression? In a regression analysis, you can use a standardized beta (β) as a measure of effect size, it is an equivalent to r with similar cut-off points. So far in this chapter we have mostly relied on the unstandardized beta (B), which uses raw unit of measurement for each predictor. On the other hand, the standardized beta (β) is a standardized measure which is not dependent on each predictor's unit of measure and has values ranging between −1.0 and +1.0. This means that it can be used to directly compare predictors to establish which has the strongest relationship with the outcome variable. So, as with the r coefficient, with β you do not need know how variables are measured to understand how important a result is. You can see in Figure 7.15 that effect sizes for our two significant predictors, self-oriented perfectionism (β = .143) and socially prescribed perfectionism (β = .120), are small. Another measure of effect size in regression is f^2, which is based on the R^2 value and is used for F tests in ANOVA in regression analysis. Values of f^2 that are close to .02 are considered small, those close to .15 are medium, and those above .35 are large (Cohen, 1992).

7.8 Writing up a correlational study

Your correlational study write-up should resemble your Year 1 and Year 2 lab reports. It is really just a longer and more complex version of those. Ideally, it should look much like a published psychology research paper. So, do try to find and read published papers that are relevant to your topic and design because this will be helpful to you. For each section and aspect of your report, always make sure to follow APA guidance. Having said that, you also need to consider the area of psychology your study is in. For instance, your study might be a cross of two disciplines (e.g. psychology and medicine) and this might have an impact on how information is presented within your report. It is always best to ask your supervisor about it and to follow their advice, as well as to check whether there are any institutional requirements for submitting coursework assessments. The way we write up correlational research is not very different from other research designs, so following standard research reporting rules will be sufficient. Finally, your report will have distinct sections, but you still need to make sure that it tells a story and that you bring those sections together in a coherent way.

Title

As with other types of designs, your title should be short (around 10–20 words) and focused on key aspects of your study. This means that it should mention your key variables and research question.

Abstract

Our advice is to write your abstract last. Once you have written all the other sections, you will have all the key information in place and a better idea as to which aspects to include in your abstract. Final year project abstracts are typically around 150 words or a little longer, and they should include a summary of all the key sections in your report. So, include a couple of sentences for each section of your report.

Introduction

Your introduction should set the scene for your study and include information that is directly relevant to your study's aims and design. Final year projects tend to examine several variables and relationships. Hence, it is important to carefully plan your introduction. When doing so, you could start by considering the key variables you need to talk about and the key relationships you need to discuss. I find it helpful to make a diagram of my planned structure with all key papers listed in relevant boxes of the diagram. This helps me navigate through my introduction and avoid omitting anything important or including irrelevant information. It can also help to make your introduction more integrated and coherent.

You should start your introduction with a broad overview of the topic under investigation before moving on to discuss specific variables/relationships and then presenting your hypotheses at the end. Make sure to stay focused on your study design throughout your introduction. This will help you avoid including irrelevant information and build an appropriate rationale for your study. It should be clear to the reader why your study is important and necessary. Your introduction should culminate in a set of hypotheses that are clearly backed up by your previous investigation of relevant past research.

Methods

Your method section will have several subsections – namely: participants, materials, procedure, and design and analysis. The participants' section should include information about your participants, such as participant number, gender, age, and any other relevant information. Your inclusion and exclusion criteria should also be covered in this section. If your design is complex and contains several measures, it may be helpful to include further subsections. For example, in our hierarchical regression analysis, we have six measures (one for each predictor); you may consider describing such measures under separate subheadings. Correlational research is largely reliant on questionnaires and you need to make sure to include sufficient detail about them – for example, number of items within each questionnaire; how each item is scored; total minimum/maximum scores; example items; comments on reliability and validity of each questionnaire. Next, you need to explain how the study was run. For example, explain participants' recruitment, data collection, and so on. In your design and analysis section, you need to address both your design and your planned analysis. Students sometimes omit the design part and go straight to their planned analysis. For example, our design is an advanced correlational design. Our planned analysis is hierarchical regression. You would also need to explain how many predictors you have and whether they are continuous or categorical. The same applies to the outcome variable. You must also report the required sample size for your analysis and how you established this. Lastly, don't forget to mention the statistical package you used to analyse your data.

Results

We reported results for our hierarchical regression in the previous sections of this chapter, so this is just a reminder of the order in which this should be done. As shown in Figure 7.16, you should start with reporting some basic statistics. In this case, it would be a table of correlations and relevant descriptive statistics. This table should show binary correlations between all your variables. Next, report your regression assumptions. This will show the reader how robust your analysis is. Then report your Model 1, Model 2, and the overall model results, followed by the results for individual predictors. Make sure to report results for both significant and not significant predictors, but you should only interpret further your significant predictors (you can see how we have done this earlier in this chapter). You can also graph significant

DOING A CORRELATIONAL RESEARCH PROJECT

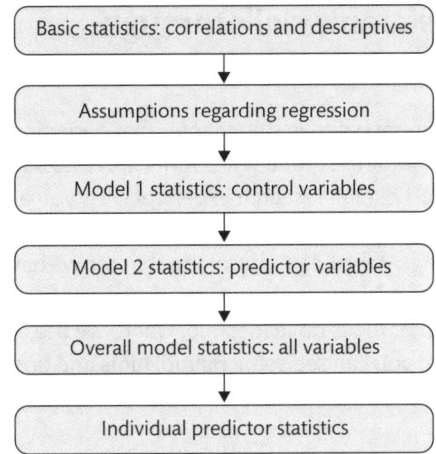

Figure 7.16 Writing up the results for a hierarchical regression

predictors, as we have done in Figure 7.3. All tables and figures should be referred to within the text and formatted according to the APA guidelines.

Discussion

Start your discussion by summarizing your key research findings. This should be a concise summary and it is not necessary to report your statistics again. Your discussion should provide a critical evaluation of your results and to do this you should consider them in relation to the relevant past research that you addressed in your introduction. When you do this, you should go beyond simply stating whether your findings support previous research or not. Instead, you should try to explain any conflicting or ambiguous findings. Might they have occurred due to methodological differences, different sampling, or other reasons? Discuss the importance of your findings but make sure not to overinterpret them – for example, avoid terminology that implies causation between your variables. The next step is to critically evaluate your study. Avoid making a long list of all possible shortcomings. Instead, focus on a few most relevant ones. For example, in our hierarchical regression, there could be other confounding factors that we did not control for (beyond trait anxiety and year of study) and which might have an impact on the relationship between our predictors and the outcome variable. In correlational research, we often need to consider operationalization of concepts and subscales within them, internal consistency of each scale, etc. If one of the scales used in your study has poor internal consistency, you need to consider the implications of this limitation for your findings. This means that it is not a reliable measure of the concept it was designed to measure in your study. Towards the end of your discussion, you should discuss what future research should be considered and how it could build on your findings. It is important to make reasonable and relevant suggestions. For example, correlational research is often a first step in addressing a research question, so you should consider the next steps you could take. You may also suggest that longitudinal, mediation, or moderation analysis might be necessary. Finally, finish your discussion with a brief concluding paragraph bringing your key points and messages together.

7.9 Building transferable skills through correlational methodology

We hope that we have demonstrated in this chapter that designing, conducting, and reporting correlational research requires several skills. Some are necessary to ensure quality in correlational study and a good overall research experience for you and those you are working with, but they can also be helpful in demonstrating your employability when you start applying for jobs after graduating. At the beginning of the chapter, we have singled out certain skills such as teamwork, leadership, independence and autonomy, initiative, critical thinking and IT skills. In Box 7.1 we further focus on leadership, where we use a brief case study to reflect on this important skill, and you can see some helpful hints and tips in Box 7.2.

> **BOX 7.1 A case study showing reflection on the leadership skills developed when conducting correlational research**
>
> **Reflecting on your transferable skills and personal attributes**
> An example – leadership
>
> **Recognize:** From the research you have conducted, what is the best example of when you have demonstrated this skill or attribute?
>
> Correlational research typically relies on questionnaires as measures. It is important to ensure that these measures are appropriate, relevant, reliable/valid, and that they are entered correctly into an online survey software, etc. When I was working on my final year project, I thought it would be helpful to have somebody in charge of this process, so I put myself forward to do it. Our group needed to work together on these tasks and I made sure that all of them were allocated to individual group members and completed in a timely manner and to a high standard.
>
> **Reflect:** What are my strengths with regard to this skill or attribute? How can I further develop or improve them?
>
> While leading this aspect of the project, I made sure that everyone was clear about what their tasks involved, and that they knew how to carry them out. I also made sure that support was provided when this was not the case. It was sometimes challenging to be absolutely fair with the delegation of the tasks because some tasks were more complex or time-consuming than others. I tried to overcome this challenge by discussing it with my group and making sure that I took into consideration their strengths and weaknesses when delegating tasks.
>
> **Relate:** Imagine you are being interviewed for your dream job or course. How would your skills in this area make you suitable for this position?
>
> I would like to teach psychology at A level/secondary school and I know that this role will present me with many opportunities to lead: for example, delegating tasks to my students when working on research projects or other teaching-related activities. Not only will I be leading them but I will also be setting an example for how to lead others. I hope to demonstrate skills and attributes such as willingness to listen, helping others to develop, strategic thinking, and honesty.

> **BOX 7.2 Hints and tips from psychology graduates and employers of psychology graduates**
>
> **The student's perspective... reflecting on IT skills**
>
> My methodology was quantitative. I collected the data using a Qualtrics survey that I had designed with pre-existing scales. I learned a lot about time management, data management, advertising... I reached over 100 participants by creating a funny poster with my cat, which I highly recommend if you need a large sample for your survey.
>
> Ines, psychology graduate
>
> **The employer's perspective... reflecting on leadership**
>
> Our team is comprised of social scientists and medics who have a passion for listening to patients and using what they hear to measure and communicate on how people experience disease and treatment. This then informs a combination of qualitative and quantitative research. This requires a person to think as well as do, showing leadership, independence, and motivation.
>
> Jeff, health psychology researcher

Wider reading

Bourne, V., James, A. I., & Wilson-Smith, K. (2021). *Understanding Quantitative and Qualitative Research in Psychology: A Practical Guide to Methods, Statistics, and Analysis.* Oxford University Press.

Section 3 of this book has a number of chapters covering different aspects of designing, analysing, and writing about correlational research. If you want to revise any of these aspects, or read more, then this would be a good place to look.

8 Doing a qualitative research project

 In this chapter you will learn . . .

- how to design robust qualitative research, specifically focusing on reflexive thematic analysis;
- how to conduct qualitative research; and
- how to report on qualitative research.

At this stage of your degree, you may have already learned about qualitative research, so we assume that you are familiar with its key principles and at least some qualitative methods. The aim of this chapter is to focus on a very popular qualitative method among both undergraduate and postgraduate students – thematic analysis. Thematic analysis is a quite simple and flexible method that involves generating themes from data. While flexibility in thematic analysis may appear to be good fortune, it can actually make it a more challenging method because you have more choices and it can be difficult to engage with this appropriately. For example, what students (as well as some researchers) often do not realize is that thematic analysis is not just one method: there are different types of thematic analysis. It is crucial for you to know which thematic analysis method you need to use, follow its steps and underlying principles, and state this clearly in your write-up. Therefore, in addition to outlining this method's key steps, we will discuss aspects that are often neglected or misunderstood by both students and experienced researchers, and we will give some hints and tips for how to do the analysis well. We will do this by using brief fictional examples as well as those from some published studies. The 'Wider reading' section at the end of the chapter contains two useful references for revising the basics of thematic analysis and qualitative methods more broadly, and there are several other relevant books in the References.

In this chapter, we will primarily focus on one popular type of thematic analysis, called 'reflexive thematic analysis'. Several topics discussed will be relevant to other qualitative methods too, so we hope that the chapter will help you to think critically about qualitative research more broadly.

8.1 Positioning qualitative research within psychology

If you are more experienced in quantitative than qualitative research, you might be tempted to observe qualitative research through a quantitative lens. However, qualitative research requires a very different approach to data and the overall research process than quantitative research. We will be highlighting the key differences between them throughout the chapter.

In the past, qualitative research has often been judged as insufficiently scientific because of its reliance on exploring meanings and producing non-quantifiable data and output. This approach is now outdated and wrong. While it cannot be denied that its role within psychology is still not as clearly established as quantitative research (e.g. it is not always equally represented across the psychology curriculum, research funding, and publishing), qualitative research is an established research methodology within today's social sciences. For example, the British Psychological Society (the accrediting body for psychology education, research, and practice) requires that both quantitative and qualitative research are sufficiently taught and examined within the psychology curriculum, indicating that qualitative research should not be viewed as less worthy or as supplemental to quantitative research. They should be treated equally. They can also work well together, as evident in an increasing use of mixed methods research whereby qualitative and quantitative techniques are combined within the same research study. You can learn about mixed methods in Bourne, James, & Wilson-Smith (2021, Chapter 29).

8.2 Skills required to be a good qualitative researcher

Like quantitative research, qualitative research requires several transferable skills, but it also requires its own very specific set of skills. For example, your participants are likely to share their personal stories with you, which means that you need to be a good listener and have excellent people and communication skills. It also requires you to have a certain degree of warmth, sensibility, and trust. Equally, qualitative data can be large in volume and consequently feel overwhelming. To be a good qualitative researcher, you will need to be able to identify and extract key aspects from your data and make sense of their meaning. Designing and conducting qualitative research will require you to interact with data with an open mind in ways that are much less constrained and formulated than in quantitative research. Therefore, it is crucial for you to be aware of your preconceived ideas and how they can have an impact on the research process and data, and to do this you will need good evaluative skills. Independence/autonomy is another key characteristic. Qualitative data collection often requires researchers to work on their own and in close contact with participants. This means that you will need to react quickly and make independent decisions. We provide an example of this in our case study (Box 8.1) at the end of the chapter. When conducting a piece of qualitative research, you will likely come across unpredictable situations and reactions from your participants, such as the sharing of sensitive information. You will need to show resilience and good judgement in dealing with such situations. We will highlight these skills as we go along, and they are also illustrated in Figure 8.1.

8.3 Key characteristics of reflexive thematic analysis

Before you start designing your reflexive thematic analysis study, it is of utter importance that you understand and take into consideration the key characteristics of this approach because they will inform and shape your study design. It is also important to understand how this approach differs from other qualitative approaches, including those based on thematic analysis.

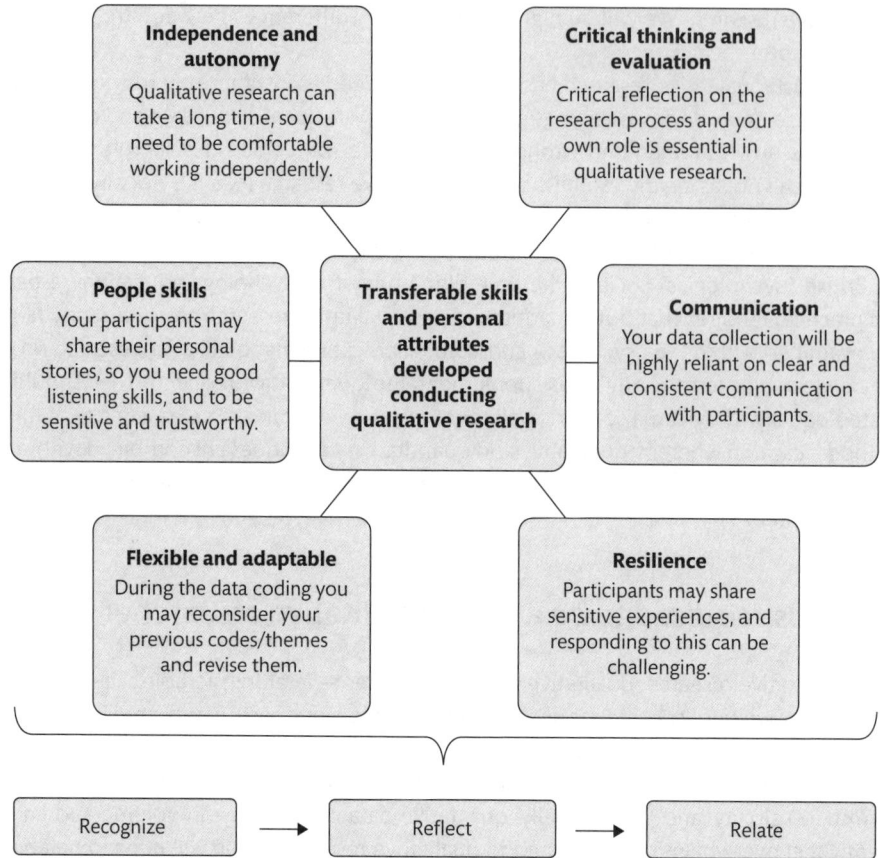

Figure 8.1 Key skills developed when conducting qualitative research

Scientific knowledge is fluid and constantly developing, and the past few years have seen a significant shift in how thematic analysis has shaped as a qualitative method. If you have engaged in thematic analysis previously, you are likely to be familiar with two prominent theorists of thematic analysis, Virginia Braun and Victoria Clarke. In 2006, they published a seminal paper where they outlined the key stages of thematic analysis. However, since then, they have considerably updated and advanced their initial position on it. Their updates have been significantly motivated by researchers not doing thematic analysis properly. A key update was coining the term 'reflexive thematic analysis' and distinguishing it from other thematic analysis approaches. We will discuss these issues and developments throughout the chapter. We highly recommend going beyond Braun and Clarke's (2006) paper and reading their more recent work, which we use throughout the chapter and include in 'Wider reading'.

What is reflexive thematic analysis?

Reflexive thematic analysis is a qualitative method that can be used to examine a range of phenomena, such as people's perceptions and subjective experiences. Its main aim is to generate, analyse, and interpret themes within qualitative data. A theme can be defined as a shared meaning within a dataset relevant to the research question. Within reflexive thematic analysis, a theme is developed by grouping codes, which are individual concepts or ideas generated from the data. We will talk about themes and codes in more detail later, but for now we would like you to pay close attention to an important distinction: theme generation versus theme extraction!

Theme generation versus theme extraction

One prominent issue within much published thematic analysis research is that researchers often say that they *extract* rather than *generate* or *develop* themes from the data, and this is a really important distinction to understand and bear in mind when doing a reflexive thematic analysis. As illustrated in Figure 8.2, theme generation recognizes the role of the researcher, meaning that themes do not sit there waiting to be discovered: they are generated by researchers. Qualitative data is rarely a summary or description of what participants say: it usually involves digging deep into their stories and the meanings behind them. It requires 'interpretation' of data, which inevitably involves a certain dose of 'subjectivity' and can never be truly objective. So, a key premise of reflexive thematic analysis is that themes do not just emerge from the data; they are created during an interactive process between the researcher (their assumptions, theoretical stance, knowledge, and experiences) and the data (Braun & Clarke, 2021a).

You will therefore be generating, creating, or developing themes rather than extracting already existing themes from your data. This is a crucial distinction that is closely related to several other key aspects, discussed later, such as how we ensure and assess quality in qualitative research, and how we communicate and write up our research. It is also linked to 'reflexivity', a key feature of reflexive thematic analysis and an important concept across much of qualitative research.

Reflexivity

A key characteristic of reflexive thematic analysis is that it recognizes that it is impossible to completely remove subjectivity (researcher's influence) from the research process. It takes a very realistic view as to what happens during the research process, and it acknowledges and embraces the researcher's role. It sees it as an integral part of research design, analysis, interpretation, and reporting of findings. Let us imagine that – for your final year project – you

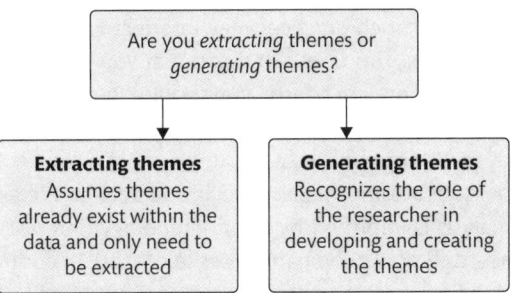

Figure 8.2 The difference between extracting and generating themes

were to conduct a study on international students' perceptions and experiences of higher education in the UK. If you, as the researcher, are an international student yourself, you may already have certain opinions about this and you will most certainly have experience of it. Moreover, these influences might be difficult to avoid or remove. In fact, avoiding them may even be unhelpful, and result in somewhat forced and unrealistic findings. So, reflexive thematic analysis advocates that they should be used instead. To address subjectivity, researchers should reflect and critically evaluate their own influence, something they can do by engaging in reflexivity. Reflexivity is at the heart of reflexive thematic analysis. It involves thinking carefully about how your thoughts, emotions, and practices may have an impact on all stages of the research process. Reflexivity means that knowledge production in reflexive thematic analysis is seen as situational and perceived as a product of the interaction between you (the researcher) and the data. Hence, it is never truly objective.

Therefore, when conducting reflexive thematic analysis, you should be constantly interrogating your own input by thinking carefully about how your preconceptions, knowledge, and experiences of the topic under investigation can influence the research process. So, you need to think carefully and fully acknowledge how you may have an impact on the questions that you ask your participants, how you communicate with them, and how you analyse and interpret participants' answers. Consequently, reflexivity relates directly to the issue of quality in qualitative research, which we discuss later.

Philosophical and theoretical approaches underpinning reflexive thematic analysis

Scientific research is usually informed by certain paradigms. A paradigm is a system of ideas underpinning knowledge generation and it incorporates certain ontological (relating to the nature of existence/reality), epistemological (relating to the theories of knowledge), and methodological assumptions. Whereas quantitative research is influenced by positivism (a paradigm concerned with generation of objective knowledge using the scientific method), qualitative research is mostly influenced by interpretivism (a paradigm concerned with the exploration and interpretation of participants' meanings). However, this does not mean that qualitative research is detached from positivist practices, nor that quantitative research is free of interpretation. For example, sometimes qualitative researchers introduce rigorous procedures (e.g. measuring interrater reliability using Cohen's kappa) to control for subjectivity and increase the objectivity of their study. However, this is not entirely compatible with qualitative approaches like reflexive thematic analysis whereby the researcher's impact on the research process is assumed and embraced, and reflexivity is a vital part of it. In fact, Braun and Clarke (2021a) argue that such practices may interfere with data analysis and result in forced and unrealistic findings. This does not mean that you should not be discussing your findings with your co-researchers – of course, you should! But this should be with the aim of discussing and getting feedback on your findings and generating fuller interpretations of your data, rather than always reaching consensus.

Some qualitative methods are informed by specific paradigms. For example, interpretative phenomenological analysis is informed by phenomenology (interest in detailed examination of lived experience, and how people make sense of that). In contrast, thematic analysis (as a broad method) is a flexible method because it does not need to be led by a particular paradigm: researchers are free to choose a position that will inform their study. However, a criticism of published thematic analysis research is that researchers often fail to make this explicit in their study. Even though thematic analysis is not underpinned by a particular paradigm, you still need to explain your position explicitly. Whichever position you take, it will inevitably influence your research procedures, data, and interpretation of those, and ultimately it will determine the type of thematic analysis you are using.

As you will see later, different thematic analysis methods are underpinned by different ideas. Therefore, it is crucial to clearly state and describe them: doing so will help the reader to understand and evaluate the study within your specific position. We will give an example of how you can do this later in the chapter when we talk about how to write up qualitative research. Braun and Clarke (2021a) recommend considering several aspects when planning to use reflexive thematic analysis, or any type of thematic analysis for that matter. Byrne (2022) nicely summarized these and used a worked example to illustrate them. We recommend reading it. Discussing these in detail is outside the scope of this chapter, but we have recapped them briefly for you below and in Figure 8.3. They can be viewed as being on a continuum rather than completely distinct categories.

Essentialist versus constructionist epistemologies: You will need to decide how you want to theoretically approach your research. If you decide to approach it from a more essentialist perspective, then you are assuming that people have an essence that determines who they are. Language is simply a carrier of those meanings and experiences, and is not involved in the production of these meanings. The opposite would be true if you decided to adopt a more constructivist approach, which assumes that meanings and experiences are socially constructed and that language is viewed as actively involved in the generation of those. Based on what we have said so far about reflexive thematic analysis, we can safely conclude that it is more of a constructivist approach.

Experiential versus critical orientation to data: An experiential orientation to data interpretation focuses on meanings as attributed by participants (i.e. you would focus on what they said and their own experiences of their reality). You would not try to interpret what they said as socially constructed, which you would do if you adopted a more critical approach to your

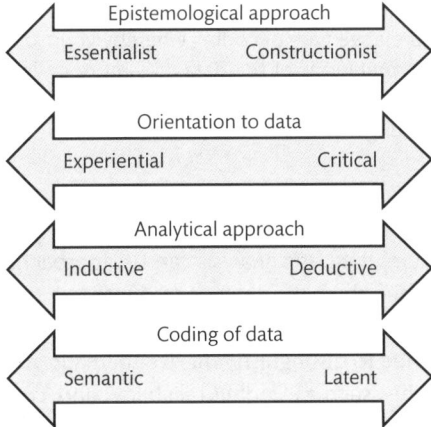

Figure 8.3 Different approaches to reflexive thematic analysis

data. Therefore, you as the researcher should clarify where on this continuum you stand, and also justify your choice. You can see an example of how this can be done in the excerpt below. Note how the researchers also included a clear explanation of why they adopted an experiential approach. The main aim of this study was to explore the impact of masculine ideologies on 26 heterosexual men's experiences of female-perpetrated intimate partner violence. Using reflexive thematic analysis and semi-structured interviews, they explored how these men made sense of themselves, their relationships, and their use of support networks.

> **An example of how to describe your orientation to data within a method section**
> (from Hogan et al., 2022, p. 126)
>
> A broadly experiential qualitative research stance was adopted in order to facilitate understanding of how participants perceived, experienced, and made sense of themselves and their relationships as well as their use of support networks (Braun & Clarke, 2013) through the use of qualitative interviews and reflexive thematic analysis (Braun & Clarke, 2006). Given the aims of this study and the focus on men's experiences, perspectives, and sense-making, an experiential qualitative design was appropriate (Braun & Clarke, 2013). Reflexive thematic analysis facilitated an exploration of the participants' contextually situated experiences, meanings, and behaviours (Braun & Clarke, 2021a).

Inductive versus deductive analysis: If you aim to analyze your data in line with a specific analytical framework that is informed by a specific conceptual framework (we will discuss some of these in the next part of this chapter), you would be using a deductive- or theory-driven analysis. On the other hand, if your analysis is purely data-driven, you would approach it inductively. Inductive analysis is more in line with the interpretative approach to data and, as such, is more suitable for reflexive thematic analysis. However, qualitative analysis is rarely purely deductive or inductive – it usually falls somewhere on the continuum.

Semantic versus latent coding of data: Another aspect you need to think about is how you will be approaching your data coding. Are you going to primarily focus on describing what your participants have said, without trying to understand why they might be saying those things? If you are, then you would be engaging in semantic coding, which is very much a descriptive type of coding. Or, are you going to engage in more in-depth coding, whereby you will also try to interpret what your participants have said? For example, you may think of underlying circumstances, assumptions, etc., having an impact on the data. This is called 'latent coding'. Latent coding is an interpretative type of coding whereby your role as a researcher is much more involved in the interpretations of the data. It is more in line with reflexive thematic analysis where, as explained earlier, you would be generating your codes and themes from the data rather than extracting them.

Comparing reflexive thematic analysis to other thematic analysis approaches

Because of its flexible nature, thematic analysis can be approached differently by different researchers, which has caused thematic analysis to become a rather undefined and messy method. As a result, different versions of thematic analysis have been developed through the years. Braun et al. (2018) tried to distinguish reflexive thematic analysis from more positivist thematic analysis approaches such as 'coding reliability' and 'codebook' thematic analysis approaches. These two approaches are more deductive and use more structured procedures for data analysis than reflexive thematic analysis.

In coding reliability approaches, researchers use a coding guide (codebook) to help them obtain objective findings from their data. If more researchers are involved in the coding of the data, they would use the measure of coding reliability to ensure a high degree of similarity in the coding process. Also, themes are informed by pre-existing theories and developed in a much more deductive way than in reflexive thematic analysis. Nonetheless, these practices would be more suitable with certain types of data that do not need much interpretation, and much qualitative research is not like that. These strategies are not really appropriate to employ in reflexive thematic analysis, which is probably the most truly qualitative approach of the three. It advocates that analysis is an interpretative process in which the impact of the researcher is inevitable and, as such, should be acknowledged, embraced, and utilized fully.

Codebook approaches (e.g. framework analysis) are somewhere between reflexive thematic analysis and coding reliability approaches. For example, they also use a codebook to analyse data but are less positivist than coding reliability approaches and recognize the value of reflexivity. Make sure to discuss with your supervisor which would be the right type of thematic analysis for your project. Be explicit about the type of thematic analysis you are using: do not just say that thematic analysis will be employed. For a helpful and in-depth comparison of the three approaches, please see Braun and Clarke (2021a).

Comparing reflexive thematic analysis to other qualitative approaches

It is important for you to know whether and why reflexive thematic analysis is the right qualitative method for your project. Differences between various qualitative methods are not always as obvious as the differences between various quantitative methods. For example, there are several overlapping concepts and procedures between different qualitative methods. When you are new to this style of research, you may feel a little lost at first and uncertain about where to start. It is crucial for you to understand the method that you are using and why you are using it. This will result in good-quality research with you feeling comfortable with the entire process. However, we understand that it might be difficult to choose the most suitable method because often the same qualitative research question and data can be addressed and analysed with more than one qualitative method.

When starting your qualitative project, you may wonder how reflexive thematic analysis may be different from other qualitative methods that also involve generation of themes. As explained earlier, many qualitative methods are underpinned by particular philosophical/theoretical approaches, so, even though they may look similar on the surface, they may differ substantially. Some qualitative methods aim to produce very specific outcomes at the end, such as theories, while others do not. To illustrate all this, we will very briefly compare reflexive thematic analysis with two methods that are in some ways similar to it: 'interpretative phenomenological analysis' and 'grounded theory'. You can see a summary of these in Figure 8.4.

Reflexive thematic analysis involves coding and categorizing data into themes, with an emphasis on patterns and connections between them, while interpretative phenomenological analysis involves a detailed examination of individual cases, often presented in very rich, narrative forms to communicate the depth of their experiences. Interpretative phenomenological analysis is specifically guided by phenomenological epistemology. This means that its primary focus is on an in-depth examination of how individuals make sense of their lived

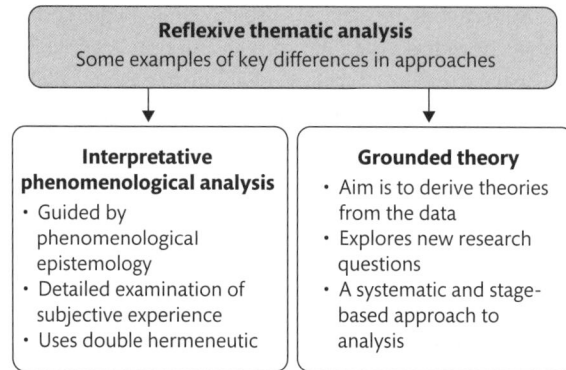

Figure 8.4 Comparing reflexive thematic analysis with interpretative phenomenological analysis and grounded theory

experiences (Smith, 2017). What we mean here is that a key aim of interpretative phenomenological analysis is to try not to just interpret participants' words but also to read between the lines. It employs the 'double hermeneutic' to do this, which involves the researcher making sense of their participant's sense-making of the phenomenon under investigation. This requires obtaining rich data from individual participants and studying each response in detail before moving on to a cross-participant examination. Because of this richness of data and depth of investigation, interpretative phenomenological analysis can be conducted with fewer participants. Research focusing on specific groups and major life events is particularly suitable for interpretative phenomenological analysis. Obtaining rich data requires careful interviewing skills, asking open questions, giving participants sufficient time to answer them, and letting them dig deep into the topic. This is likely to be more complex and potentially more challenging than reflexive thematic analysis. In light of all that, Howitt (2019) argues that it may not be the best method for projects that tend to be run by students on fellow students. If you would like to learn more about this qualitative method, you may find the paper by Smith (2017) helpful.

Both reflexive thematic analysis and grounded theory are interested in generation of themes. However, grounded theory aims higher: its ultimate goal is to derive theories from data. It is a more complex and systematic qualitative approach than reflexive thematic analysis because it involves multiple specific steps for deriving theories from data. Like many other qualitative approaches, grounded theory aims to understand lived experiences and how participants make sense of those experiences. But grounded theory is in particular useful for research questions that have not been examined much by previous research and generating new theories from those. Grounded theory is an inductive approach and, to avoid bringing preconceived ideas to the research, a detailed literature review is usually conducted after the data analysis. However, this might be unrealistic to expect because researchers need to start from somewhere, so at least some reading and planning around existing literature is usually inevitable at early stages of the research process. Grounded theory is definitely a more complex and systematic type of analysis. If used, it will require appropriate training in order for you to do it properly. If you would like to learn more about grounded theory, we suggest that you read work by Glaser and Strauss (e.g. Glaser & Strauss, 2017).

8.4 Designing a reflexive thematic analysis study

Now that you have learned about the key features of reflexive thematic analysis, you can start designing your study. However, the aim of this section is not to design a complete fictional study (like we did in Chapters 6 and 7) because that would be a little challenging with qualitative data. Instead, we will focus and provide guidance for some important and unique aspects that you should consider when designing your own reflexive thematic analysis study.

Developing a suitable qualitative research question

In contrast to quantitative research, qualitative research does not test hypotheses or predictions: it explores and seeks answers to research questions. These questions are typically open-ended and seek to explore people's perceptions and experiences rather than confirm a specific hypothesis. Qualitative research is often used to gain an in-depth understanding of a certain phenomenon. This can stem from some previous research findings (either qualitative or quantitative) that need greater understanding, or it could be a new or under-researched topic that requires exploration. Findings from such research can serve as a basis for generating future research hypotheses and theories. Your research question should indicate whether you are interested in examining relationships (quantitative research questions) or in exploring participants' experiences and opinions (qualitative research questions). As you can see in Figure 8.5, a quantitative piece of research may hypothesize that high levels of perfectionism in university students are associated with high levels of anxiety while a qualitative piece of research may want to explore how striving for perfectionism may influence university students' mental health and well-being. So, in the first example, we want to test a very specific relationship and predict a certain outcome, while in the second example we are interested in participants' thoughts and experiences and we do not know or predict the outcome in advance.

Reflexive thematic analysis is relatively flexible with the type of question being asked. Research questions interested in experiences, perceptions, and views of participants are suitable for it. So, the second question within Figure 8.5 could be addressed with reflexive thematic analysis. As noted earlier, it is interesting that the same research question could

Figure 8.5 Contrasting quantitative and qualitative research questions

be answered with more than one qualitative method. This will depend on a number of factors such as your research aims, the paradigm/s underpinning your research, and your approach to data. Therefore, by just looking at qualitative research questions, you may not always be able to place them under a certain qualitative method immediately. Once you have your research question, you will need to design an interview schedule and think of suitable questions to ask your participants. These questions should be clearly linked to your overall research question and the aims of your research. They are typically open-ended questions, which allow participants to provide answers in their own words.

Type and size of sample in reflexive thematic analysis

Purposive sampling is a common type of sampling in qualitative research. It is a type of non-probability sampling whereby researchers use their own judgement to select the most suitable participants to take part in their research. This is not the same as convenience sampling whereby participants are recruited out of convenience – for example, recruiting your fellow students or friends and family. Purposive sampling involves careful planning to decide who the most suitable participants would be for the purpose of your research, and then proactively recruiting those specific participants. It enables researchers to target specific groups. For example, in one of the previous examples, Hogan et al. (2022) used purposive sampling to recruit 26 men who self-identified as victims of female-perpetrated intimate partner violence.

It is more difficult to determine an appropriate sample size in qualitative than in quantitative research and there is no huge clarity among the research community on this. But you can be sure about one thing at least – you will need substantially fewer participants in a qualitative study than a quantitative study. A key reason for this is that qualitative data is rich: a single data transcript can typically be pages and pages long. Different qualitative methods will often have different guidance about the ideal sample size. Data saturation is a common guiding principle in qualitative research, which has also been applied in thematic analysis. It refers to the point in data collection when no new meaningful information relating to the research question is discovered during data analysis, and this serves as an indication that the data collection can stop. However, lately, data saturation has become a somewhat controversial concept and practice, which is why we want to tell you about it.

Braun and Clarke have questioned whether data saturation is the most appropriate practice in qualitative research and it seems to be particularly problematic in reflexive thematic analysis. They provide an excellent discussion of this in their paper (Braun & Clarke, 2021b) and we highly recommend that you read it. They argue that, while it may be appropriate for some other qualitative methods and types of thematic analysis (e.g. where the research question is interested in fairly superficial and concrete topics within a homogenous sample), it is not appropriate for reflexive thematic analysis where, in essence, data analysis is never truly finished and there is always more to develop from the data. Hence, deciding that new participants cannot add much to our data makes little sense in reflexive thematic analysis. Braun and Clarke also advise against having in mind a specific ideal sample size for reflexive thematic analysis. Instead, they recommend the approach shown in the excerpt that follows. This also means that determining your sample size in advance might be difficult, even though you may be required to do it as part of your project proposal and in line with open science practices. Exact sample sizes are more appropriate in quantitative research and this requirement cannot be easily applied in qualitative research.

> **Recommended approach for determining sample size in reflexive thematic analysis** (Braun & Clarke, 2021b, p. 211)
>
> ... researchers reflect on the following intersecting aspects of their research: the breadth and focus of the research question; the methods and modes of data collection to be used; identity-based diversity within the population or the desired diversity of the sample; likely experiential or perspectival diversity in the data; the demands placed on participants; the depth of data likely generated from each participant or data item; the expectations of the local context including discipline; the scope and purpose of the project; the pragmatic constraints of the project; and the analytic goals and purpose of their reflexive TA.

Designing a robust qualitative study

As with quantitative research, it should be every qualitative researcher's imperative to ensure rigour in their research and credibility of their findings. However, qualitative research has often been portrayed as overly subjective and missing scientific rigour. This view can sometimes result from directly comparing qualitative and quantitative research. Although quality in qualitative research cannot be applied and assessed in the exact same way as in quantitative research, that does not mean that qualitative research cannot be robust and rigorous.

Reliability and validity in qualitative research

In contrast to quantitative research, which uses numbers as data and statistically analyses them, qualitative research mostly uses words as data to capture the lived experiences of people, and it employs qualitative techniques to understand their meaning. Hence, qualitative research requires a different approach to data and to the overall research process than quantitative research. For instance, the reliability and validity tests we use in quantitative research, such as Cronbach's alpha, cannot be applied in qualitative research. In fact, many researchers argue that the terms 'reliability' and 'validity' are not appropriate to use in qualitative research, and they suggest using different terms, such as 'scientific rigour' and 'credibility'. This means that a qualitative piece of research should be designed and conducted in a rigorous way and should be trustworthy. This has a lot to do with the concepts of subjectivity and reflexivity mentioned earlier. We will now explore this in more detail.

Subjectivity and reflexivity

You already know about the importance of objectivity in research and have learned to judge its opposite, 'subjectivity' (researcher bias), as potentially problematic. In qualitative research, this concept is slightly more complicated. It is difficult to control for subjectivity in qualitative research when the researcher's interpretation of the data is at the very heart of it. Braun & Clarke (2021) argue that subjectivity is inevitable in qualitative research; hence it is better to acknowledge and embrace it, and to deal with it properly through reflexivity. As discussed earlier, because themes are generated, it is the researcher's perceptions, knowledge, and experiences that unavoidably have an impact on how they interpret the data. So, if you are doing reflexive thematic analysis, make sure that you engage in a reflexive practice by questioning your approach and assumptions, and recording and reporting on them. One way to monitor your input is to keep a self-reflective log. This may help you produce a good self-reflective account in your research write-up, and we have given you some prompt questions below. By doing this, you are being a responsible and truthful researcher.

Example questions to prompt self-reflection throughout conducting a qualitative research project:

Developing the study

- Why were you motivated to study this research question and what influenced your choices?
- Why did you make certain design choices, such as the development of interview questions?

Running the study

- What influenced your decisions about the participants you selected (or chose not to)?
- What influenced your decisions about how to communicate with your participants?

Analysing the data

- Were there any influences on how you extracted codes from the data?
- Were there any influences on how you interpreted the data?

Writing up the study

- Were there any influences on your selection of key messages to present from your findings?
- Were there any influences on your critical evaluation of your research project?

Making your philosophical/theoretical position clear

We discussed earlier how qualitative research is commonly underpinned by different paradigms and that these will also have an impact on how quality is perceived, dealt with, and assessed within qualitative research. Make sure to explain and justify the position you are taking. It is also important that you ensure that your position is clearly reflected in your research design, data collection, data analysis, and the reporting of your research. We expand on this in the writing-up section and provide an example.

Transparency in qualitative research

The open science principles outlined in Chapter 5 can help you think about how to improve the quality of the qualitative research that you conduct. In particular, you should think about improving transparency in your research process. By this, we mean ensuring that you include detailed and clear information about the entire research process. This will also help other researchers replicate your research, although replication is a lot more challenging in qualitative research. Can we really replicate people's unique experiences, opinions, and meanings? Sharing data with other researchers so that they can replicate it is another key aspect of open science. However, qualitative data normally involves personal accounts by participants. Anonymizing data might not always work in such situations. Even when anonymized, it might not be acceptable for participants to have their stories shared with everyone. So, you need to consider this carefully and discuss it with your supervisor. There are potential solutions, such as sharing partial stories, but this is not without limitations and challenges either, such as your data being incomplete and less replicable.

Finally, there are checklists available for assessing qualitative research. A popular checklist is the Consolidated Criteria for Reporting Qualitative Research (COREQ; Tong et al., 2007), which is sometimes required to complete and submit when submitting a qualitative manuscript to a journal. A checklist can be helpful in that it informs you as to whether your research is meeting appropriate quality criteria and thresholds. However, they should also be used with caution because they differ substantially, so using a generic checklist may not be entirely appropriate for every qualitative method.

Ethics in qualitative research

We assume you have existing knowledge of ethics in research, so this is just a reminder of some key ethical issues in qualitative research. As in quantitative research, key ethical aspects need to be carefully considered in qualitative research, such as issues surrounding anonymity, confidentiality, and informed consent. However, when it comes to ethics, qualitative research is more challenging than quantitative research. You are likely to encounter ethical challenges at every stage of your study. A key characteristic of qualitative research is participants sharing their personal stories with the researcher. This makes ethics in qualitative research complicated and challenging. You might need to carefully consider the impact of your research on your participants, as well as their impact on you. Qualitative research often examines sensitive questions and this can be difficult for both your participants and you. It can also be both emotionally and ethically challenging, so you will need to use the best of your people and communication skills. It is important to think ahead and plan very carefully how to deal with potential distress and issues. Have clear procedures in place to deal with them. Discuss these with your supervisor because they will be more experienced and knowledgeable about the issues you may encounter and how to address them. They will also provide or direct you to appropriate training for dealing with upsetting data and sharing your experiences within a safe and supportive environment. You also need to think ethically when analysing data – for example, by making sure that your analysis (i.e. your generated themes) is fair, inclusive, and representative of the participants' stories. Reflexivity will be important here as well: by interrogating your research practices, you can produce an ethically sound study. Finally, we would recommend reading the British Psychological Society (BPS) Code of Ethics and Conduct and the BPS Code of Human Research Ethics before embarking on your research. We come back to some specific ethical issues in the next section of the chapter.

8.5 Running a qualitative study

In this section, we assume that you already know the basics of qualitative research but we will consider a few key issues that are worthwhile as a reminder. When running a qualitative study, your communication with your participants is one of the most important aspects to think about. Qualitative research usually involves lengthy conversations about private and/or sensitive topics with participants. Your participants are more likely to relax, trust you, and share their perceptions and experiences if they feel you have provided a safe space for them to do so. Good communication will make your study more ethically sound and will also help you obtain quality and rich data.

Running a study with others

We have covered key aspects of how to run your study with others in previous chapters: in Chapter 3, we discussed how to work with your supervisor; in Chapter 4, we talked about managing your research and working with other students; in Chapters 6 and 7, we discussed how to run an experimental/correlational study with others. Generally, a lot of the points we raised in those chapters apply to qualitative research too. If you are working in a group, ensure that you work collaboratively with your fellow students and follow the same study protocol. Within a qualitative study, you are likely to be involved in the analysis of the same data (e.g. interview transcripts) and providing feedback on each other's codes. Your critical evaluation and teamwork skills will be fully used here. This can be a little challenging if you are new to doing reflexive thematic analysis, because you will not be following a pre-existing codebook when carrying out coding and generating themes (see Section 8.6, 'Analysing qualitative data' for more detail). If you do disagree with someone else on the research team, try to be constructive in the way you approach this, and think about how you would receive similar comments. It is totally fine to disagree with people, but this should be done in a respectful manner. So, try and be helpful, kind, and supportive of your fellow students.

Recruiting participants and collecting data

Recruiting participants for a reflexive thematic analysis study is not very different from many other qualitative methods, but doing so for any qualitative study can be challenging for novice researchers. You may need fewer participants than in quantitative research, but participants' involvement is likely to be greater and more demanding on both them and you. For example, to take part in your interviews or focus groups, participants will need to dedicate quite a lot of their time. If you are targeting specific types of participants (e.g. disadvantaged groups or those with particular health conditions or engaging in illegal activities), this can be challenging for both you and them because your study will involve direct interactions and discussions surrounding private and sensitive issues. You may struggle to find and recruit eligible participants willing to take part in your study. Therefore, don't underestimate the time and preparation needed for recruitment. What approaches can you use to recruit participants? The simplest way would be to ask people you know: for example, your fellow students or family and friends. But this will also depend on your research topic. If your topic is sensitive and interviews are to be conducted in person, it may be more difficult to recruit and interview people you know than people you do not know. As mentioned previously, you may use various online platforms or your institution may have a recruitment platform. If you are targeting specific groups, you may need to find contacts and establish communication within relevant services, support groups, etc. This can be challenging for a student researcher so make sure to seek support from your supervisor.

When it comes to data collection, reflexive thematic analysis is a flexible method. It usually involves analysing text that can come from several sources and take several forms, such as in-depth interviews, focus groups, diary entries, media and internet data. This also means that your data can be collected by you, or you can use existing data. As a project student, you are likely to be involved in the data collection and its transcription too. This will be very useful to you because it will help you become familiar with the data (the first step in your data analysis, see Figure 8.6). Today, qualitative researchers benefit from developments in technology and can use various gadgets and online platforms to collect data. For example, you could interview your participants in person, but doing it online or via the phone may be an equally suitable option. This will often depend on how much time and resources are available to you. If you decide to collect your data online, then you may find the BPS Ethics Guidelines for Internet-Mediated Research[1] helpful.

When conducting your study, think carefully about potential ethical issues, such as asking sensitive questions, respecting participants' privacy, and your overall communication with your participants. We have discussed some of these issues in previous sections of this chapter. Before you start collecting data, make sure that you are trained in your data collection method and able to conduct yourself in a professional manner. Your interpersonal skills will be of high importance here, as well as several other skills that we have discussed earlier.

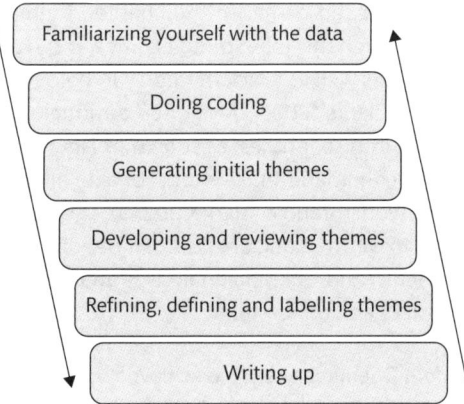

Figure 8.6 Six stages of (reflexive) thematic analysis (Braun & Clarke, 2021a)

---

[1] https://www.bps.org.uk/guideline/ethics-guidelines-internet-mediated-research

Storing data

You will need to follow your university's guidelines for safely storing data. These will be in accordance with the General Data Protection Regulation (GDPR), which regulates how entities protect personal data. Make sure to also check the BPS guidelines, which we mentioned earlier. Protection of data in qualitative research is extremely important for both ethical and legal reasons. You must protect participants' anonymity and have procedures in place to keep their data confidential. However, bear in mind that anonymity cannot be fully guaranteed if you collect any personally identifiable information – anonymity assumes that the participant is not known by anyone conducting the research. Confidentiality, on the other hand, means that, even though the participant's identity is known by the researcher, great care is taken that their identity is not revealed to anyone outside the research team. In contrast to quantitative research, where a lot of data consists of single figures that will not mean much without wider context, qualitative data usually contains lengthy records of participants' experiences and thoughts. These data are of a personal and sensitive nature. Qualitative research is often based on data from interviews that are audio- or video-recorded so take care to keep these safely stored at all times. Do not reveal participants' identity when using quotations in your write-up: use an ID instead. Make sure that the quotations do not contain information that might reveal participants' identity, such as place of work or the street where they live. Earlier, we discussed the sharing of data (as part of open science practices). This, of course, would need to be approved by your participants and their data would need to be anonymized and checked for any identity-revealing information.

8.6 Analysing qualitative data

Here we outline key stages in a reflexive thematic analysis. If you decide to conduct it for your project, we recommend that you do some further reading in order to gain an in-depth understanding of it. As we discussed earlier in the chapter, thematic analysis is a flexible method in many respects. Although this may sound positive, it can also contribute to inconsistent and unclear procedures as well as a lack of rigour. To help researchers to avoid this in their data analysis, Braun and Clarke (2006) developed a model that outlines the thematic analysis process and breaks it into six phases, as shown in Figure 8.6 and described below. This process applies to reflexive thematic analysis too. For a detailed account of all six phases, see the authors' more recent work (Braun & Clarke, 2021a). They describe it as a guide rather than rigid rules. Because reflexive thematic analysis can be informed by a variety of philosophical/theoretical approaches and the data analysis is an interpretative process, creating strict rules would be impossible and unhelpful.

Familiarization with the data: Thematic analysis is achieved by first familiarizing yourself with the data, a process that starts during data collection and transcription. Your aim should be to gain a deep understanding of your data by reading your data transcripts and listening to recordings of them several times.

Data coding: Developing codes is a crucial step in thematic analysis and codes can be defined as elementary ingredients in your analysis. Within reflexive thematic analysis, coding is very much an interactive process between the data and the researcher. They should be systematically developed from the data during the coding process when you read your data transcripts very carefully and try to identify relevant codes that represent the data and relate to your research question. As you progress and spot something relevant in your data, try and think whether an existing code applies to it. If it does not, create a new code. Codes can be simple and descriptive as well as rich and analytical. Therefore, when coding, you can already start thinking about the data in a more analytical way. There is no strict rule for how you should do this and how many codes you should extract. The overall aim should be to be thorough and prepare your data analysis for the next stage, which is theme extraction. Also, some segments of your data may have many codes while some may have none. This will largely depend on the research question and how much of your data relates to it. You will need to move back and forth between your codes and data in order to refine your codes and ensure rigour in the coding process. Braun and Clarke (2021a) suggest that you do at least two rounds of coding. As with other aspects of reflexive thematic analysis, coding is an interpretative and subjective process for which no preparation is needed. For example, you would not use a pre-prepared codebook, like you would with some other types of thematic analysis. This means that you may derive codes that are somewhat different from those of your co-researchers. As discussed earlier, it is understood that different researchers may develop different codes and there is no need to seek agreement between them because this may result in shaping codes into something they are not. After all, coding is a reflexive exercise that should involve a reflexive engagement with the data. If you are conducting a group project where more than one person is involved in the coding of the data, you can engage in discussing and challenging each other's codes and different interpretations of them. However, the aim of this is not to produce exactly the same codes but thoughtful and more developed interpretations of the data.

You can do your coding by hand or rely on specialized software such as NVivo, especially if you have lots of data. However, you do need to consider the advantages and disadvantages of using such software in relation to reflexive thematic analysis, which requires an in-depth engagement with the data during the coding process.

Researchers do not usually report their initial coding in their published papers, so in Table 8.1 we have some fictional data and codes for our above-mentioned fictional study of international students' perceptions and experiences of higher education in the UK. We suggest that you cover up the column on the right with our codes and try to generate your own codes to see how similar or different they are from ours. What do you think of the codes we generated? Are they representative of the data? Are they clear? Do you think we could have extracted more or fewer codes? Notice that certain codes were generated from both excerpts, e.g. 'Teachers are supportive' and 'Easier to communicate with teachers than fellow students'.

Generating initial themes: The next step is for you to classify (or group) your codes into themes that represent shared meaning. Try and visualize codes as the building blocks of themes. Your codes will represent single ideas while your themes will represent shared meaning across several codes. To be able to generate themes, you need to look for patterns in your codes. This means that themes are broader patterns that emerge repeatedly from your data and they attach meaning to your data. These are more abstract conceptualizations of data. You may also end up with some subthemes – for example, a theme can be categorized or broken down further. This process will require a lot of going back and forth from one code to another until you are able to sort them and categorize them into themes.

Table 8.1 Generating codes from qualitative data

	Data	Codes
Participant 1	Some people think that being an international student means you will only stick with students who know you, students from your own or similar culture. I mean, this is true to an extent, but I feel that this misconception itself prevents me from socializing with students who are not from my culture. I sometimes feel forced into this, if you know what I mean. I have met several UK students who were totally open-minded and I felt they approached me as if I was a UK student. This made me instantly relaxed and I became chatty. Maybe it's just me but I do feel self-conscious and worry that I won't fit, like the way I speak, my manners, even the way I dress . . . so I guess I'm instantly drawn towards people who are more like me. It's just easier. With teachers it is a bit easier: they are all very supportive and professional. I guess they are used to international students so actually it's funny that I often feel more relaxed and myself when talking with them.	• Misconceptions about who you socialize with • Living up to misconception about who you socialize with • Forced into socializing with students from own culture • Being around open-minded students helps with being yourself • Worrying about not being able to fit in • Easier to socialize with people like yourself • Teachers are supportive • Easier to communicate with teachers than fellow students
Participant 2	Lecturers are very friendly here. We can call them by their first name . . . umm . . . I still can't get my head around it as back in my country we wouldn't do that, we look at our professors as gods, ha-ha. But I love that and it's really nice being able to informally chat with lecturers here as they are approachable. I don't think they treat international students differently. I feel comfortable approaching them, well most of them. It's a bit different with fellow students though, I mean most of them are really nice to me, but I do feel cultural difference between us, like simple things, like communication, for instance . . . umm . . . I sometimes need to stop myself from being direct and speaking my mind and try to wrap up things a little.	• Teachers are supportive • Different relationship with teachers compared to own country • Teachers are approachable • Feeling comfortable around teachers • Easier to communicate with teachers than fellow students • Cultural differences noticeable in communication with other students • Adjusting behaviour due to perceived cultural differences

Looking back at Table 8.1, can you see any potential themes emerging? For example, across both excerpts there seems to be the following:

1. A theme emerging about the importance of being able to fit in.
2. A second potential theme around how others' approachability seems to make a lot of difference about how they feel as an international student.
3. A third potential theme is about the difference in how they communicate with fellow students versus teachers.

What do you think of these themes? Did you generate different or additional themes?

Developing and reviewing your themes: This involves checking your themes against your data. You want to make sure that your themes represent your codes and the data well. During this process, you can look for supporting evidence in your data for each of your themes and organize your data in that way. You may find that some of your themes have very little or no support in your data and that you need to exclude or revise those themes. One way to revise a theme is to divide it into subthemes or combine themes. Also, think how they relate to each other and to existing research and practice. There are no specific rules about this and you will need to decide what works best for your data. Important to remember, though, is that you should not be rushing this process and you should take time to review your themes.

With regard to our examples in Table 8.1, it is a little hard to develop our initial themes because we do not have enough data. It may also be a little early to think about splitting themes or combining them, but, hopefully, you will agree that there is evidence for our initial three themes in both excerpts.

Refining, defining, and labelling themes: Some of your themes might be easy to name and define, but there will always be those that will need more thinking when deciding on a label that represents them accurately. During this process, you may realize that certain themes actually represent similar or the same things and can be excluded, combined, and split further. There is no prescribed number of themes that you should develop. As an example, Hogan et al. (2022) developed these four final themes:

1. Feeling shame and embarrassment for not having met masculine expectations.
2. Perceptions of violence shaped by masculine norms.
3. 'It's the shame of it': shame and gender norms as barriers to seeking help.
4. The importance of having a safe space to talk without fear of judgement.

Going back to the initial three themes generated from Table 8.1, how would you label them? Again, we do not have enough data and these are not our final themes. But try to imagine they are and see if this would be a suitable label for our first theme: 'The importance of fitting in'. How would you name the remaining two themes? How about this for our second theme: 'Approachability of others matters'? And this for our third theme: 'Teachers versus students: differences in communication'? Do these three labels represent our themes well? Try to think how they could be improved!

Note that you need to be flexible with the above stages and you may need to go back and forth between them. For example, while doing Step 4 (review of themes), you may need to go back to Step 3 and even Step 2 to examine the codes and themes you initially generated. While this stage in the analysis may be time-consuming, try to persist with the process and ensure that you leave plenty of time for this analysis. At this point, we recommend that you look at a couple of published reflexive thematic analysis studies and inspect their analysis (i.e. the themes they generated and how they did that). You can start with the study we mentioned earlier by Hogan et al. (2022).

8.7 Writing up a qualitative study

When it comes to writing up a qualitative report, the same general principles apply as when writing up a quantitative report. But, as demonstrated earlier in the chapter, qualitative research is quite different from quantitative research and this is also reflected in the way it is written up.

In this section, we provide some guidance on the key elements and aspects of reporting qualitative research, but of course with a more specific focus on reflexive thematic analysis.

Embedding reflexivity

As you have gathered already, a major element of reflexive thematic analysis is reflexivity. In contrast to quantitative research, this means that the researcher will readily dwell on how their own emotions, perceptions, and knowledge may have influenced the research process and outcomes. For example, I (Danijela) was an international student here in the UK, so this may have had an impact on our fictional example in several ways. It may be hard to keep an open mind about the topics that we already know a lot about, or have experience of. So, I would need to consider that carefully. Writing in the first person ('I' or 'We') is commonly seen in qualitative publications, in contrast to quantitative ones. Reflexivity can be embedded throughout the report or it can be addressed within a separate section, placed in either the method or the results/discussion section. It may come as no surprise to you that, where reflexivity plays a major role in qualitative methods, it tends to be embedded throughout the report. This means that the researcher discusses their involvement in the research process at each stage of their research, from their initial ideas to their conclusions. Make sure to discuss with your supervisor which approach would be the best in the context of your study.

Start writing up early

We advise you to start writing up early and as you are developing your study. You can start writing up all sections of your report in the early stages of your research: you do not need to wait to finish your analysis of data in order to write it up (like you would normally do in a quantitative study). This does mean that you may need to rewrite a lot as you go along, but this should not put you off because it may actually help you develop and evaluate your ideas. As explained in the analysis section earlier, your themes will be developing and changing throughout your analysis and you want to capture this process. It is extremely important for you to reflect on the process and to explain how you generated themes from the data. Remember, themes do not emerge from the data – hence, it is crucial to record how you generated them. Your writing needs to be informed by your chosen philosophical/theoretical approach. Outlining it early in your report will help guide your reader through your ideas and your research aims.

Finally, think carefully about how your report flows and the big picture or story that you want to tell. Your report will have separate sections, but they need to tell a story. Before you start, it will be helpful to look at key journals in your area of research. Ask your supervisor and look for resources that will provide the best source of expertise and guidance.

Key sections within a qualitative report

Title

Your title should emphasize your research question (i.e. it should be clear from your title what your study examined). As with other types of research, you may also specify the qualitative method used in your study, although this is not a requirement. Here is an example: *Self-ascribed paranormal ability: reflexive thematic analysis* (Drinkwater et al., 2022). Another interesting feature of qualitative research titles is that researchers sometimes include a short quotation from a participant that represents the key findings.

Abstract

As with other types of research, your abstract should include the main features of your report and include a sentence or two about each key section of your report. You should state the main aims of the study/research question, study design, participants or some other source of information, type of analysis, significant findings, and implications. It might be best to write this section last, once you have completed and written up your study.

Introduction

You can follow the same principles and structure as in quantitative research – starting from the broad topic and gradually narrowing it down to your research question. There could be numerous reasons for doing your research and you need to provide a clear explanation and justification for it. During this process, you need to review relevant past research and provide a clear rationale for your study. Your rationale is likely to stem from some gap in past relevant research, or you may seek to understand current topics and issues. You may also want to introduce your qualitative method as well as your philosophical/theoretical approach, but this is something you would elaborate on in the method. Your study aims and research questions should be presented at the end.

Methods

The method section in a qualitative report may differ from that in a quantitative report. It is common to include different subsections (e.g. an ethical considerations subsection; a reflexivity subsection). Their order may differ too. It is best to discuss this with your supervisor and check relevant guidance. However, every qualitative study is different so you will need to be flexible and adapt your structure and writing to the needs of your study. The method section commonly starts with Design, where you describe and justify your chosen qualitative method. Make sure to describe and justify your philosophical/theoretical position and analytical strategy. When doing this, avoid generic statements. Instead, tailor this information and explain it in the context of your research aims and needs. For example, Drinkwater et al. (2022) explored personal perceptions of self-ascribed paranormal abilities in 12 participants with supposed supernatural powers, using semi-structured interviews. They employed reflexive thematic analysis and started their method section by explaining why they had used it. They also explained their philosophical/theoretical position. They tried to relate this information to their research aims and needs rather than merely providing a generic description of reflexive thematic analysis and what it does. You can see a brief excerpt below of how they did this in their method section.

An example of how to justify your choice of qualitative method, philosophical/theoretical position, and analytical strategy in your report (Drinkwater et al., 2022, p. 3)

Within the present study, the authors viewed self-processed paranormal ability as a "psychological" rather than parapsychological process, analysis was broadly informed by an attributional approach (Drinkwater et al., 2019; O'Keeffe et al., 2019; Laythe et al., 2021). This acknowledges how the social perceiver uses information to construct and rationalize deterministic inferences and explanations (see D'Souza et al., 2020). Central to this, is how participants collate and integrate information to produce causal judgements, which shape and structure ability-related experience, meanings, and assumptions (Braun & Clarke, 2013). From this perspective, RTA enables assessment of personal psychic abilities from a psychological, social, and cultural perspective rooted in social constructionism (Braun & Clarke, 2019). This is commensurate with Braun and Clarke (2020), who emphasize the need for researcher transparency regarding paradigmatic, epistemological, and ontological assumptions. Thus, use of RTA enabled detailed investigation of the impact and significance of self-ascribed paranormal abilities from the individual's viewpoint (Murray & Wooffitt, 2010).

Next, you need to describe your source of data (i.e. your participants, materials, and procedure). You do not need to include your interview schedule (your interview questions) within the method section – place it in the appendices – but you still need to describe it and introduce the key areas it assesses. If you used some quantitative measures (e.g. to collect demographic data in order to describe your participants), describe them too or place them within a table. Next, describe your study procedure (e.g. how the study was conducted, how interviews were conducted). You will also need to have a section on ethical considerations. Apart from standard information (ethical approval, informed consent, anonymity, etc.), you should address additional ethical issues and how you dealt with them (e.g. discussing sensitive issues with your participants). Finally, describe your data analysis approach. For instance, describe your stages of reflexive thematic analysis and make sure you explain them in the context of your research and how you applied them.

Results and discussion

You need to report your results (i.e. your developed themes and relationships between them). It is common practice (although not a requirement) to combine results with the discussion section. Results can also be referred to as 'findings' or 'analysis' within qualitative research reports. Studies that involve a more constructivist approach (such as reflexive thematic analysis) are likely to combine these sections because it is hard to separate reporting of study findings from the interpretation of the same – reporting them separately can be repetitive and less coherent.

Your results need to be supported with data so if, for example, your study involved interviews with participants, you should include some appropriate quotations to support your key findings. These can either be interjected in your writing or presented within a table (although it may be more challenging to link them to your interpretations of data when they are within a table). Participants' quotations should be sufficient and representative of your findings, and they should justify your themes and key points. One quotation per theme will not be sufficient: include a range of quotations that represent your data well. Include interpretation/analysis of your data in relation to your key findings. If you are a novice qualitative researcher, it may be hard to strike the right balance and know how to engage in the interpretation of this kind. Braun and Clarke (2021a) provide helpful examples in their book and we recommend that you read relevant published papers and discuss these with your supervisor. Make sure to check the American Psychological Association guidance on how you should present your quotations. This will be dictated, too, by the journal that you may submit your report to. You also need to anonymize your selected quotations by creating IDs for them. This is in order to protect participants' anonymity.

You may find that your themes and the relationships between them can be best depicted within a table or as a thematic map/diagram. If so, make sure that these are clear and informative and support your in-text explanations. If you are combining your results and discussion, then present an interpretation of your results here too and discuss them in relation to the relevant literature. Finally, do not forget your reflexive analysis.

Compare your findings to relevant past research and theory, discussing any limitations and implications. When discussing limitations, it may not be entirely appropriate to discuss issues that are common in quantitative research and that you are probably used to criticizing (e.g. sample size). Consider what is important to your study. At the end, you should present your conclusions. Sometimes it is appropriate to include a separate general discussion or conclusions section. You should discuss this with your supervisor because presentation of findings will vary from one qualitative study to another (due to different types of data and analytical strategies).

8.8 Building transferable skills through qualitative methodology

In this chapter, we have discussed how to design, run, analyse, and write up qualitative research with a specific focus on reflexive thematic analysis. We have also tried to encourage you to think critically about it and about thematic analysis more broadly. Doing qualitative research requires a number of skills and we hope that we have managed to show you why they matter. We finish the chapter by reflecting on one of them – independence and autonomy (see Box 8.1) and giving you some hints and tips from graduates and employers in Box 8.2.

BOX 8.1 A case study showing reflection on the independence and autonomy developed with conducting qualitative research

Reflecting on your transferable skills and personal attributes
An example – independence and autonomy

Recognize: From the research you have conducted, what is the best example of when you have demonstrated this skill or attribute?

My qualitative research project meant that I worked independently at various stages in the project. For example, I ran semi-structured interviews to collect the data. During these, I had to work independently and rapidly to develop the follow-up questions within each interview, responding to each individual participant and the responses they gave.

Reflect: What are my strengths with regard to this skill or attribute? How can I further develop or improve them?

At the beginning of the project, I found it a little difficult to get the right balance between working independently and working as part of a research team with my supervisor and the other student researchers in the group. But, being involved in a qualitative research project has allowed me to develop my skills and my own confidence in running semi-structured interviews. Now I feel far more confident in communicating with the research team and participants.

Relate: Imagine you are being interviewed for your dream job or course. How would your skills in this area make you suitable for this position?

I'd like to work in market research, so my experience in running interviews and working with qualitative data will be invaluable in my career development. By independently running semi-structured interviews, I feel that I have developed a good insight into how to work independently and adapt to a participant's responses during an interview, while still keeping the broader research question and aims of the project in mind.

BOX 8.2 Hints and tips from psychology graduates and employers of psychology graduates

The student's perspective . . . reflecting on teamwork

As a research group, it is important to plan in advance as much as possible. Ensure to communicate any questions or concerns you might think of from the start with your supervisor and group (as they tend to creep up afterwards when it is harder to fix) and learn to adapt plans when needed.

Katie, psychology graduate

The employer's perspective . . . reflecting on communication skills

Good communication skills are very important for building and maintaining internal and external networks. In policy research, we have regular meetings with a diverse range of external experts such as researchers, funding bodies, think tanks, industry professionals. We also keep in touch with research teams across parliament and collaboratively work on documents together. We ask applicants to demonstrate times when they have worked in a team, and how they adapt their working style to meet the needs of others.

Anwar, parliamentary advisor

Wider reading

Braun, V., & Clarke, V. (2019). Reflecting on reflexive thematic analysis. *Qualitative Research in Sport, Exercise and Health*, 11(4), 589–597.

Braun, V., & Clarke, V. (2022). Conceptual and design thinking for thematic analysis. *Qualitative Psychology*, 9(1), 3–26. https://doi.org/10.1037/qup0000196

Doing a systematic review

 In this chapter you will learn . . .

- what systematic reviews are and why we need them;
- how to plan and design a systematic review; and
- how to conduct and report a systematic review.

Systematic review methodology is not commonly taught at undergraduate level, and even postgraduate Master's courses may not cover it in depth. There is therefore a lot of new ground to cover in this chapter. There is not going to be a comprehensive guide to systematic review methodology in this short chapter, but we hope that what we do provide will be a good starting point for you and help you understand the fundamentals of this methodology. We start by explaining what systematic reviews are and how they differ from other types of reviews. We then introduce you step-by-step to the key components and stages in a systematic review. It is extremely important to document how you have designed and conducted your review so, throughout the chapter, we highlight which aspects need to be reported in your write-up. We address reporting of a systematic review more broadly in Section 9.6 of this chapter, 'Writing up a systematic review'.

We use a combination of published systematic reviews and brief fictional examples to illustrate specific aspects of this methodology. For example, I (Danijela) will occasionally refer to one of my systematic reviews (Serbic et al., 2023), which examined psychological, social, and academic functioning in university students with chronic pain, so I hope you will find this topic interesting and relevant. Although this is my own research, it is far from a perfect systematic review – remember that no piece of research is ever 'perfect' – so we will also look at what I could have done better.

Finally, a note about terminology used in this chapter. The following terms are used interchangeably, mean the same thing, and relate to systematic review results and outputs: study, paper, article, reference, record, and publication.

9.1 What are systematic reviews and why do we need them?

Types of systematic reviews: qualitative, quantitative, and mixed

Systematic reviews are reviews of literature that involve the systematic searching, identifying, evaluating, and synthesizing of existing research evidence relating to a particular research question. It is possible to conduct systematic reviews of both quantitative and qualitative studies, as well as mixed methods reviews (which include both quantitative

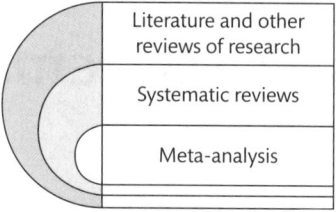

Figure 9.1 Different types of review papers

and qualitative studies). They all follow the same basic underlying systematic review processes and structure. Because systematic reviews are most common in quantitative research, we will focus on quantitative systematic reviews.

Systematic reviews with and without meta-analysis

You may have heard of meta-analysis, which is a statistical method for combining results from individual quantitative studies sometimes included within a systematic review. Even though meta-analysis may be employed in a lot of systematic reviews, for reasons discussed later in the chapter and as illustrated in Figure 9.1, most systematic reviews do not actually include it. As an undergraduate (and even Master's) student, you will more likely conduct a systematic review without meta-analysis and synthesize your review results in a more descriptive way, known as 'narrative synthesis'. For this reason, we only provide a brief discussion of meta-analysis and teaching you how to conduct it is outside the scope of this chapter.

How do systematic reviews differ from other types of reviews?

Before starting a systematic review, it is crucial to check what type of review you need to conduct to meet the needs and requirements of your research project or module. The term 'systematic' is really important here because this is what distinguishes systematic reviews from other types of reviews, such as literature reviews. To illustrate this, as an undergraduate or Master's student, you are likely to be asked to do a literature review on a topic, often as part of your lab or scientific reports. For example, as part of your final year project, you might be expected to conduct a literature review of studies relevant to your topic. This review would not usually involve a 'systematic' search of literature and methodology to carry out your search. As such, it would not present all available evidence for the question under investigation, and would not assess and analyse this evidence systematically and thoroughly. Contrary to this, systematic reviews use rigorous and transparent methodology to systematically search all available literature relating to a well-defined research question, critically appraising that literature and systematically synthesizing the findings. There are also other types of reviews, such as scoping and rapid reviews, but none of these enable a systematic review of literature using a very clear and stringent methodology, like systematic reviews do. A systematic review process consists of several stages that we have outlined for you in Figure 9.2 and described in more detail below, under relevant sections.

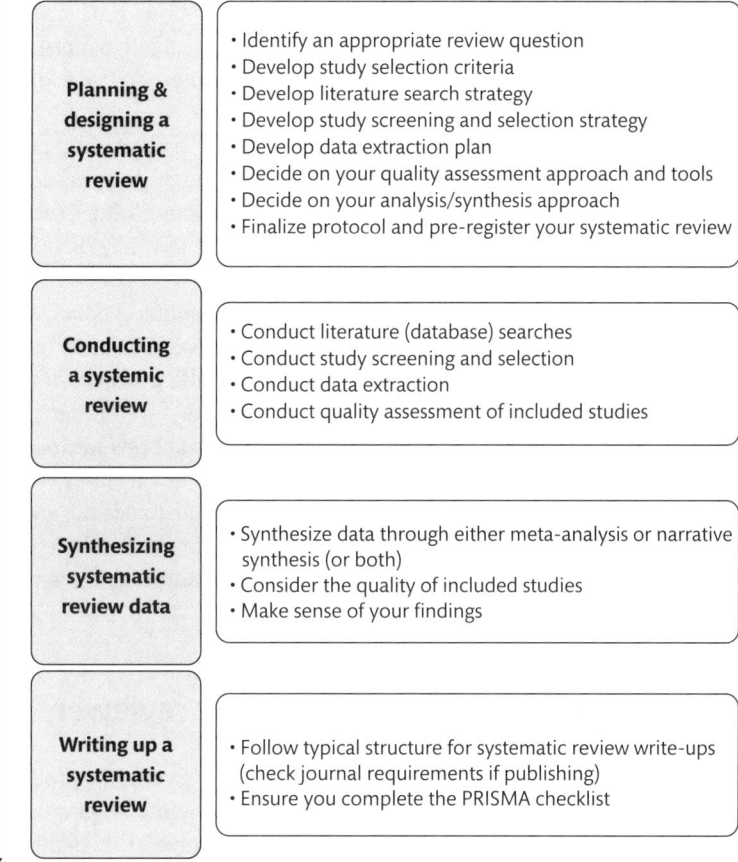

Figure 9.2 Key stages in a systematic review

Why do we need systematic reviews?

With the advancement of science and knowledge, it can be difficult for researchers, practitioners, and policy-makers to keep up with all research developments. For example, if you wanted to understand the effectiveness of cognitive behavioural therapy (CBT) for depression, you would need to read multiple (potentially hundreds) of published studies and find a way of establishing what they collectively show us about it. Without using a well-defined review methodology, such as systematic reviews, this would be an impossible task for you. Systematic reviews can be particularly beneficial when used by non-academic users, who are aiming to apply the research that psychologists conduct. By having an unbiased summary of the research findings, it may be easier to apply findings within a real-world context and to have a positive impact on society.

While a systematic review can lead to dealing with an overwhelming number of papers, it is important to ensure that all evidence is reviewed rather than cherry-picking findings that support the conclusions that you wish to draw. Systematic reviews are regarded as the 'gold standard' of research evidence, meaning that they have a reputation for being a very reliable research methodology. However, to meet this high standard, you need to make sure that you minimize bias in your review every step of the way. In this chapter, we talk a lot about minimizing bias in systematic reviews.

Systematic reviews are often used to inform future research, practice, and policy. For this reason, they are often commissioned by various bodies although, as an undergraduate or Master's student, you are more likely to carry out an independent (rather than a commissioned) review for your project. Systematic reviews are used in many disciplines but are particularly popular in health research where they often provide a concise evidence base for implementing and delivering health interventions and developing policy. As a psychology student, you may have heard of Cochrane systematic reviews. Cochrane[1] is a non-profit global organization that works collaboratively with various health practitioners, researchers, patients, policy-makers, and health organizations to enable the development of evidence-informed health-related guidelines and policy. Cochrane systematic reviews follow very strict and structured research processes and, because of their high quality, they help to inform many health policies and guidelines, such as the National Institute for Health and Care Excellence guidelines in the UK. They are published within the Cochrane Database of Systematic Reviews. If you would like to find out more about Cochrane and their systematic reviews, there are two useful links where you can read about them.[2]

9.2 Skills required to be a good systematic reviewer

Designing, conducting, and writing up a systematic review is a complex process. Hence it requires several transferable skills, some of which are highlighted in Figure 9.3. It is also a lengthy process, which is likely to take longer than a quantitative or qualitative study that involves data collection. For many of you, this is probably the first time that you are learning about or carrying out a systematic review. Due to their complexity, good planning and organizational skills are really important in systematic reviews. Below, we provide advice on how to use some of these skills in your systematic review.

Organizing your time, tasks, and resources

Designing and running a systematic review requires a high level of organization, planning, and time management. Systematic review methodology consists of many steps. It usually requires the use of specialist software and generates a lot of references to go through, categorize, and analyse. Therefore, as illustrated in Figure 9.4, it is important to plan carefully before you embark on your systematic review, by familiarizing yourself with all necessary research steps, estimating how long they will take, knowing which resources will be required to do them, and organizing your time and tasks accordingly.

Unfortunately, we cannot tell you how long each step will take. This will depend on several factors such as the scope of your review, availability of resources, your preparedness, and organizational skills. But do not underestimate the time required for each stage of your

---

[1] www.cochrane.org
[2] https://consumers.cochrane.org/cochrane-and-systematic-reviews; https://training.cochrane.org/handbook

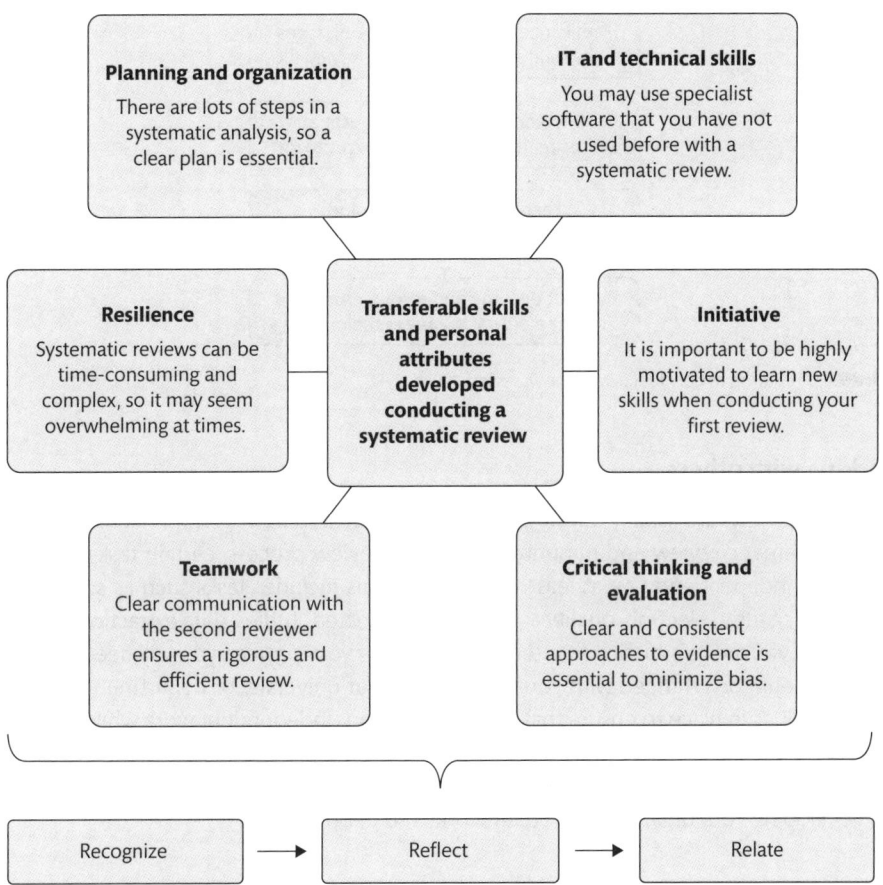

Figure 9.3 Key skills developed when conducting a systematic review

systematic review – plan carefully and as a precaution be generous with the time allocated for each stage and task.

Systematic reviews usually require using numerous files, such as research papers, reports, and records of how selection and quality assessment of papers were conducted. Managing and storing these files in an organized manner will be of huge help to you. We advise you not to delete or overwrite files but to keep all versions of your files in a chronological order because you may need to come back to earlier versions later. It is also important to manage your numerous references and it is highly recommended that you use a reference manager program, such as EndNote or Mendeley. You may also consider using other specialized systematic review software such as EPPI-Reviewer or Rayyan, which can help you with various stages of your systematic review, such as study selection. We will explain this in more detail in later sections of the chapter. All in all, conducting a systematic review requires excellent organizational, planning, and timekeeping skills, and keeping a record of your activities (e.g. by timeline or Gantt chart) will also be immensely helpful to you.

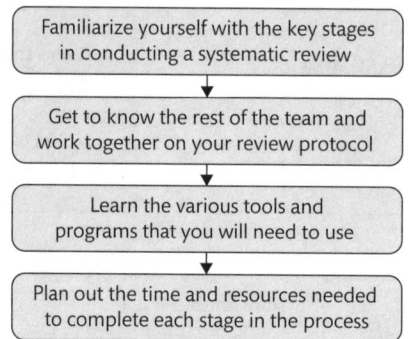

Figure 9.4 Preparing to conduct a systematic review

Working with others

Systematic reviews are usually developed and conducted as part of a team. To ensure a good-quality systematic review and minimize bias in the review process, certain tasks should be conducted independently by at least two people. This includes tasks such as screening of publications, study selection, quality assessment of selected studies, data extraction, and data synthesis. If you are conducting a systematic review for your project, you will need to discuss how this should be arranged with your supervisor. Your university or department is likely to have guidelines in place to ensure that the review is your independent work while still fulfilling necessary requirements for producing a good-quality review, such as working collaboratively on certain aspects of it. In addition, while working with other people, you will be using and developing your organizational, teamwork, and people skills.

9.3 Designing a systematic review

Checking whether your systematic review is necessary

Before we talk in detail about how you should go about developing a systematic research question, it is important for you to know that, if you plan to conduct a systematic review, the first step should be to check whether there are already recently published or ongoing reviews on your research question. If there is an existing or ongoing review, this would make your own review somewhat redundant and unwarranted unless there was enough newer primary research to review that has been published since the last relevant systematic review, thereby making an update of that research necessary. You can check this on a prospective register of systematic reviews such as PROSPERO.[3] This is an international database of prospectively registered systematic reviews, based at the University of York, UK. It reviews and stores systematic review protocols that involve a health outcome. If your systematic review does not involve a health outcome, then you may want to look for another suitable register. In recent years, there has been an increase in published systematic reviews examining the same question without clear need or justification. Systematic reviews are complex and costly to carry out, so one key role of systematic review registers like PROSPERO is that they help to prevent unnecessary duplication of reviews.

[3] https://www.crd.york.ac.uk/prospero

Preparing a review protocol and pre-registering a systematic review

If your research question is not being examined by another researcher or a research team, then you can proceed and start working on your own research protocol (plan). As you have probably already gathered, all systematic reviews should be pre-registered by developing a research protocol and submitting it for approval on a prospective register of systematic reviews such as PROSPERO. Once your protocol is checked and approved, it will be publicly available, and you can then start conducting your review.

Pre-registration of your review protocol is in line with the open science practices (see Chapter 5). By pre-registering your protocol, you can follow a clear and pre-established plan for your research. This will prevent you from altering your research aims and methodology when conducting your review. As you have learned in Chapter 5, this helps to minimize bias in the research process. Some changes to already published protocols are possible, so long as they are clearly described, justified, and approved by the prospective register where the protocol is published. You will need to disclose and justify any such changes in your systematic review report as well.

A typical systematic review protocol will include questions about all aspects of your systematic review design. At this point, it would be good for you to inspect a couple of published protocols, so we would suggest that you visit the PROSPERO website (see footnote 3) and search for a topic that interests you by entering a few search words. Alternatively, you could use our fictional example: effectiveness of CBT for depression. Upon inspection of one or more published protocols, you will notice that published protocols cover all systematic review key stages presented in Figure 9.2 (apart from the actual review results and discussion of those). Therefore, you are expected to plan for every stage of your systematic review and include sufficient detail about it in the protocol. We will be referring to the protocol throughout the chapter and reminding you of things you need to include in it.

Developing a systematic review question

Typically, systematic review questions are very specific and focused. For example, our fictional review question on the effectiveness of CBT for depression is quite specific, but consider how we might make it more focused. Here are two examples from published research that also examined CBT and depression: *Effectiveness of CBT for children and adolescents with depression: A systematic review and meta-regression analysis* (Oud et al., 2019); and *Effectiveness and Acceptability of Cognitive Behavior Therapy Delivery Formats in Adults With Depression A Network Meta-analysis* (Cuijpers et al., 2019).

These two systematic reviews focused on specific age groups, while the following systematic review focused on different modes of CBT delivery: *A comparison of electronically-delivered and face to face cognitive behavioural therapies in depressive disorders: A systematic review and meta-analysis* (Luo et al., 2020). Nevertheless, there are instances where broad questions are suitable for systematic reviews. Just be aware that this may lead to a very large number of papers that you will need to review. Our systematic review on psychological, social, and academic functioning in university students with chronic pain (Serbic et al., 2023) is an example of this. It encompasses three broad areas of functioning in university students with chronic pain. Functioning of university students with chronic pain is poorly researched, so we were able to address psychological, social, and academic functioning within a single review. We broke down our objectives according to those three broad outcomes and analysed them separately. This allowed us to draw some wider and more general conclusions at the end. However, our population of interest (university students with chronic pain) was specific, so, in terms of population examined, our review was focused. It is important to note that no matter how focused a systematic review question is, it is still not a hypothesis because it does not propose and test relationships: it examines what previous research has found.

Developing a good and appropriate research question for your systematic review is very important because it will have an impact on several key aspects of your review, including its scope (i.e. the amount of research available to review). This could range from zero studies to hundreds and thousands of them. If there are no existing studies on your research question, then it would be impossible to conduct a systematic review. Having many studies to review is perfectly fine, but the more studies you need to review, the more time-consuming your review will be, and this may be somewhat problematic for students who need to work within strict and relatively short deadlines. It is therefore always best to discuss the scope of your review with your supervisor.

Conducting a preliminary literature search to check suitability of a review question

To ensure that your research question (and subsequently your entire review) is manageable, it is recommended that you carry out a preliminary literature search of available studies: this will give you an idea of the amount of research that is available on your review question. Although this preliminary search does not need to be comprehensive, try to search several databases. If you realize that there are too many studies and that you may not be able to accomplish your review before the set deadline, then you could try to narrow down certain aspects of your question, such as your population or outcomes. For the previously mentioned example of the effectiveness of CBT in depression, you might consider narrowing down your question by focusing on a particular age group such as adolescents, or a particular depressive disorder such as Major Depressive Disorder. Then again, you may discover that there are no published studies addressing your research question. Although there is no established minimum number of studies to be included within a systematic review, you will still need at least some to be able to synthesize them. Furthermore, preliminary searches will help you establish other important aspects such as the type of available existing research. For example, if you plan to conduct a review of randomized controlled trials (RCTs) only, but your preliminary search shows that no such studies are available, this will be a good indicator that your research question is probably not suitable for such a review and that it may be necessary to modify it.

Using PICOS to formulate a systematic review question

It is really important that your systematic review question is clear and specifies the following aspects (widely known as PICOS, see Figure 9.5):

- The population you want to study (P). In our fictional example, this would be adolescents who experience depression.

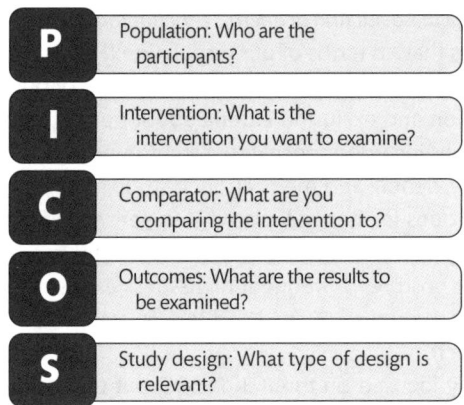

Figure 9.5 Using PICOS to formulate an appropriate research question

- Intervention or exposure (I). If you are interested in examining this, in our example it would be CBT. Note that this does not just mean health interventions: it could be a process of care, social intervention, educational intervention, experimental manipulation, etc.
- Comparator (C). You would need to decide what you want to compare CBT to. In our example, this could be, for instance, placebo, pharmacological treatment, waiting list, etc.
- Outcomes (O). The outcomes and/or results you plan to examine. In our example, this would be depression scores.
- Study design (S). In our example, we may want to examine RCTs or include other designs too.

Note that not all components of PICOS are always needed and relevant. For example, the study design element is sometimes omitted because it may not be important for the review. Also, not all systematic reviews examine intervention and have a comparator. Instead of intervention, we could be interested in processes, mechanisms, exposure to something, etc. This would depend on your review question of course. For example, our systematic review (Serbic et al., 2023) did not really examine effectiveness of any interventions: we simply wanted to examine psychological, social, and academic functioning. The PICOS is not just important for formulating your review question: it will also help guide your inclusion and exclusion criteria, which we discuss next.

Developing systematic review study selection criteria

Developing selection criteria is all about setting clear inclusion and exclusion criteria for your systematic review. You need to specify detailed inclusion and exclusion criteria for all (relevant) elements of the PICOS, and report them in the method section of your report. This should be carefully tailored to enable you to find all relevant studies. By this, we mean that these criteria will further inform your literature search, which we will discuss shortly. Your inclusion and exclusion criteria should also be very clearly stated in your published study protocol and reflected in your research question. Consider our review (Serbic et al., 2023) research topic: *Psychological, social and academic functioning in university students with chronic pain*. This clearly states that, in terms of our population (P), we are interested in university students who experience chronic pain. In the method section of our paper, we included further very specific inclusion and exclusion criteria about our population. One exclusion criterion was whether studies included specific student groups such as music, athletics, dance, nursing, physical therapy, dental, and medical. Such studies were excluded from our review because pain in these groups is often associated with very specific demands attributable to their studies and training, such as the use of frequent repetitive movements of a particular body part, specific body posture, or frequent high-stress exposure. We were not interested in such special cases and, if you read our method section, you will see that we also supported these criteria with research.

So far, we have mostly focused on the P in PICOS, but the same principles apply to the other elements of PICOS, so you will need to specify your inclusion and exclusion criteria for all of them. If you take a look at our paper or find some other published systematic reviews, you will see how this can be done.

Concepts within a systematic review can be defined differently by different researchers, and it is therefore important to operationalize them. For example, in our systematic review, we provided a clear definition of chronic pain, and specified that we were interested in both primary and secondary chronic pain, and that we operationalized both.

In addition to ensuring that all relevant elements of the PICOS are addressed in your inclusion criteria, it is also necessary to specify language, time, and publication type. Ideally, all published studies should be included because otherwise your review might produce biased findings. However, it is often impractical and costly to get papers professionally translated, so often researchers limit their search to studies published in the English language. However, note that, just because research is published in English, it was not necessarily conducted in an English-speaking country. For example, in our systematic review on chronic pain in students (Serbic et al., 2023), 18 studies were included in our synthesis that were published in 10 different countries: the United Kingdom (n = 1), Portugal (n = 1), Singapore (n = 1), Turkey (n = 1), Slovenia (n =1), Japan (n = 1), Brazil (n = 2), Germany (n = 2), China (n = 2), Canada (n = 3), and the United States (n = 3).

You will also need to decide whether you want to search 'grey literature' or not. This term is used to describe any evidence sources that are not produced within traditional publishing, such as unpublished papers, internet sources, conference proceedings, legislation, and unpublished dissertations and theses. Because grey literature may not have received the same level of academic review, researchers often exclude it, but it is important to remember that the peer-review process does not guarantee validity of published studies. You can find more about research publication and review process in Chapter 11. Including grey literature in your search strategy will also depend on available time and resources. Finally, you should specify whether any time limits apply to when the studies were published. For example, you might want to look for studies published since the last relevant systematic review was published, or you may not have any time limits imposed at all. Many of these decisions will depend on your research question and resources, and you will need to discuss them with your supervisor.

It is crucial to get your inclusion and exclusion criteria right before you start your literature searches and your study selection process. These are time-consuming exercises, so redoing them because your inclusion and exclusion criteria have changed is not a wise thing to do.

It is really important to take your time when designing your review question and inclusion and exclusion criteria, and not get carried away with the excitement of starting your first systematic review!

Developing a literature search strategy for a systematic review

Once you have clear inclusion and exclusion criteria, you can start developing your literature search strategy. By this, we mean that you can identify the most appropriate databases to be searched and develop key search terms (words) to be used when searching those databases.

Deciding which databases to search

Normally, researchers search several bibliographical databases, so you will also need to decide how many and which electronic databases to search. This will largely depend on your research question because different databases cover different areas of research. For example, after consulting with our university library services, we searched the following databases for our review (Serbic et al., 2023): PsycINFO, PubMed/MEDLINE, Scopus, and Web of Science. Our review was in health psychology so it is no surprise that we used PsycINFO, which mostly contains psychological papers, and PubMed, which contains medical and health research papers. Web of Science and Scopus were used as two generic databases. Your supervisor is likely to be familiar with most relevant databases in your discipline, and your university library will be able to help with this as well.

If you decide to include grey literature, you might resort to additional search strategies such as contacting relevant people and/or institutions in order to obtain these sources because they are not always readily available. For our fictional review on the effectiveness of CBT for depression, we would not have included grey literature if we had wanted all our studies to have been through peer review.

Planning additional searches

It is unlikely that your database searches will find every study published on your review question, so it is usually necessary to plan some additional manual searching of literature. There are different ways of doing this. One is to inspect reference lists of key studies published on your research question to see if any additional relevant studies can be identified. This is called 'backward searching'. Another way is to look for studies that cited those key studies. This is called 'forward searching'.

Finally, you will need to include a description of your planned search strategy in your protocol. This will involve stating the databases that will be searched and including your key search terms.

Developing and perfecting key search terms

Your search terms should be guided by PICOS and your inclusion and exclusion criteria. Your main aim should be to identify all relevant studies because this will help minimize bias in your research and accidentally omitting relevant studies may have an impact on your synthesis and findings. However, this is not a straightforward process: it is likely to take several attempts at running the search with your key terms in slightly different ways until you design your final search terms, which will enable you to find as many relevant studies as possible. Your aim should be to design a sensible search strategy that optimizes your chances of accessing as many relevant studies as possible.

Make sure that you do this carefully and thoroughly. For example, in our review (Serbic et al., 2023), we developed an initial list of search terms and then carried out initial searches of our databases. This enabled us to learn which terms and combinations of those produced the best results, so that we could then amend and finalize our search terms. Our resulting terms were: student, pain, chronic pain, functioning, social, academic, psychological, quality of life, and well-being. Our list of key terms was relatively short, which might have been because our research question was broad. Many systematic reviews have far lengthier and more complex lists of search terms. For example, you can see a particularly lengthy search string in the previously mentioned review by Cuijpers et al. (2019).

When developing your key search terms, consider whether you need to include all possible terms representing the same concept. For example, if one of your key concepts is psychological treatment, then you should also consider including terms such as therapy and intervention. Also, the same search terms should be used in all databases, but they will need to be adapted to each database and formatted accordingly (this will also take some time to figure out). When searching in bibliographical databases, you can use several strategies to make your search more precise (databases will usually have online guidance to help you with this). For example, Figure 9.6 shows how our search terms were adapted to each of the four databases

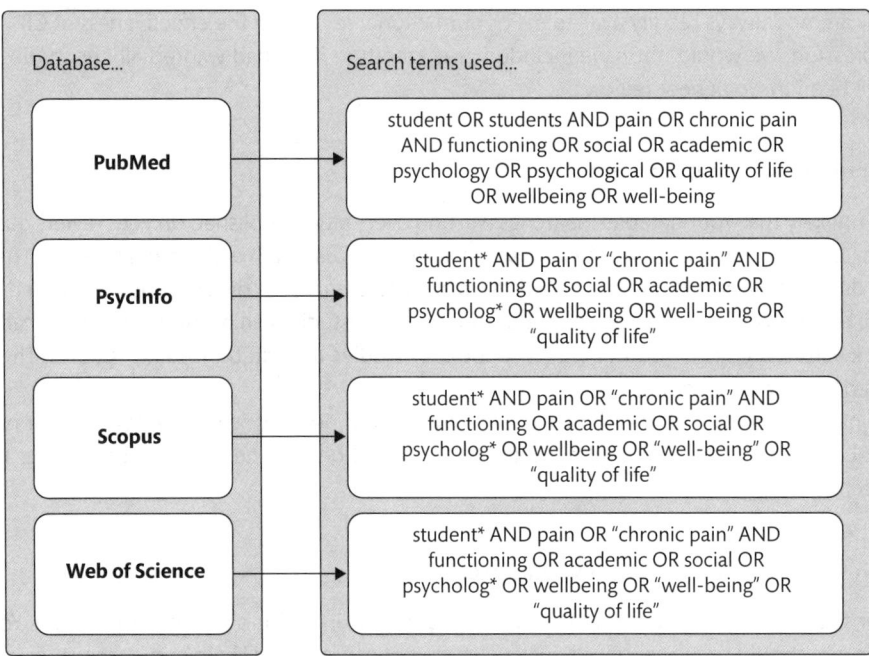

Figure 9.6 Using search terms in different databases

we searched. Try not to forget to save this information because you will need to include it in your report and may also need to re-run your searches later. You would need to re-run your searches if there were a long time-gap between your first search and submission of your review report for publication. Re-running searches ensures that any relevant studies published since the first search was conducted are identified and included.

Making your search more precise

Databases offer handy options to help you make your search more precise. You will notice that all four versions in Figure 9.6 contain AND and OR. These are Boolean operators that help to navigate your search and make it more precise. Including AND between two terms (e.g. pain AND students) means that you can identify papers that mention both of those terms rather than just one of them. Including OR between them will return papers that contain at least one of those two terms. NOT is another Boolean operator. Using it before a term will exclude any papers containing that term. You may recall that, as part of our population exclusion criteria, we said that we excluded papers that examined certain student groups, such as medical, nursing, and dance. We chose not to specify this within our search strategy using NOT. This was because some studies had mixed samples (students with different academic degrees) and we decided to include them as long as no more than 50% of the sample related to one or more of these excluded groups or degrees. Using NOT to exclude such studies might have resulted in missing potentially useful papers for our review.

When searching, you can use whole words such as 'psychology' or 'psychological' (as in our PubMed example earlier), but some databases allow you to use 'truncation' and 'wildcards' that will ensure that different variations of a word are searched. These are usually represented with one of these symbols: * ? #. Typically, truncation (*) is added to the end of the root of a word, while wildcards (* ? #) can be used at the end of a word or within a word. Different databases have different rules for using them. If you inspect our Scopus, Web of Science, and PsycInfo searches and compare them to our PubMed search in Figure 9.6, they contain the term 'psycholog*' to cover all possible ending variations of that word. Another example is that they are also used to search for plural forms of a word and variations of words that may have different spelling (e.g. 'behavi*r' would be used for both UK spelling 'behaviour' and US spelling 'behavior').

Databases may offer other useful options that will make your search more precise. We cannot provide an exhaustive list of these, but here is an example: you can select various restrictions when searching databases, such as the time that the paper was published, the language it was published in, etc. These of course will be informed by your research question and inclusion and exclusion criteria. Furthermore, most databases allow you to limit your search to titles, abstracts, or full texts of papers. You are most likely to search titles and abstracts of papers only. Options like these can make your search more accurate. Despite this, you can expect your search to return a lot of papers that are not relevant. At this point, it would be wise to seek help from your university library services because they may have staff trained in literature searching. Further advice and examples on how to do this effectively can be found in various systematic review guides, such as those written by the Centre for Review and Dissemination (CRD, 2009).

Developing study screening and selection strategy

Study screening and selection are typically conducted in two stages. The first involves an initial screening of all titles and abstracts against your inclusion and exclusion criteria. This will help you identify potentially relevant papers that you will need to read fully at the second stage. Your search strategy will never be precise enough to identify all relevant studies and avoid irrelevant studies. In fact, it will most likely identify a huge number of irrelevant studies. Study screening and selection is a lengthy and time-consuming process, so make sure that you plan ahead and are well prepared for it. This process should involve at least two researchers who should conduct the screening of papers independently, and any disagreements should be resolved by consulting a third reviewer.

You should also decide how to code and store your decisions. If your searches return hundreds and thousands of papers, it is best to use software to help you handle the screening and selection of studies. You will be able to save all your studies there and record your decisions. This is where you can also store full text papers. This will help you speed up the process of screening and study selection. One such software is EPPI-Reviewer.[4] Unfortunately, you will need to pay to use this software (or you may be able to get access to it via your supervisor, research group, or department that already has a subscription), but a free alternative is Rayyan.[5]

These programs are helpful because they help you to streamline this process; Figure 9.7 shows how you can label each paper for inclusion and exclusion. If excluded, you can include a reason for this by selecting one of the existing categories within the software that best reflects your judgement, or, alternatively, insert your own reason. There are many useful options that you can use within such programs, so we highly recommend that you familiarize yourself with one of them when planning your review.

Your published protocol should state how study selection will be conducted, how decisions about studies' eligibility will be made, and how any disagreements will be resolved.

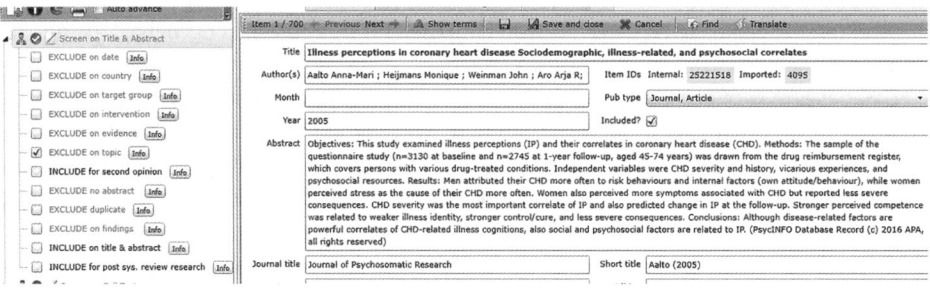

Figure 9.7 Using EPPI-Reviewer to do screening and select studies

---

[4] https://eppi.ioe.ac.uk/CMS/Default.aspx?alias=eppi.ioe.ac.uk/cms/er4&
[5] https://www.rayyan.ai

Finally, when you write up your report, remember to provide enough detail in your method section about how you developed your search strategy, and your plan for conducting your searches and your screening and selection of papers. At this point, it would be useful to find one or two published systematic reviews in an area of research that you like and have a look at how the researchers did this. We will ask you to do this throughout the chapter, so this is a good time to search for them.

Developing a data extraction plan

Data extraction involves extracting key information and results from the studies included in your review. This will include information relating to the study and the participants' characteristics (e.g. authors, year of publication, country, study design, participant number, age, gender) as well as data needed for your analysis and synthesis, such as study outcomes. However, you need to think carefully about the information that needs to be extracted for the purpose of your review. This will depend on the review question as well as on information available in the published studies. You also need to consider the format of extracted information, in particular relating to the key outcomes that you will analyse or synthesize later. For example, in our fictional review of the effectiveness of CBT in depression, a key outcome would be depression scores. It is likely that this would be measured using different depression scales across studies and/or reported using different statistics, and you and your supervisor and/or co-reviewers will need to discuss how to approach this. The best way to extract data is to create extraction tables. There is no single way of reporting results in your table – for example, they often include confidence intervals and effect sizes. Often reviewers need to convert statistical results from different studies into a single format. Make sure to discuss how to approach this with your supervisor.

Your protocol, as well as the method section, should outline the data-extraction process – for example, how many researchers will be involved (ideally two) and what information will be extracted. As previously mentioned, it would be best for you to inspect a couple of published protocols on PROSPERO and also published reviews to see the level of detail that needs to be included in the protocol and method section of your report.

Developing a synthesis strategy

The next step is to develop a synthesis strategy and report it in your protocol. There are two main ways of synthesizing evidence from systematic reviews: quantitative synthesis, using meta-analysis, or narrative synthesis.

Meta-analysis

Meta-analysis involves statistically combining results from individual studies to examine whether an overall effect exists and how large it is. Meta-analysis is commonly used in RCTs, but it is not exclusive to them.

Meta-analysing results from non-randomized studies, poor-quality studies and those that include diverse designs is much more tricky, and not always possible or recommended.

Therefore, systematic reviews do not always involve meta-analysis. In fact, in most systematic reviews, meta-analysis is neither possible nor sensible. So, it is important for you to consider whether your data are suitable for meta-analysis and to discuss this with your supervisor. In some cases, you may not be entirely sure whether meta-analysis will be possible until you inspect the results sections of the studies included in your review. In our review (Serbic et al., 2023), based on a preliminary inspection of available evidence, we realized that meta-analysis was unsuitable because our research question was very broad and relevant studies used different designs and measures, making the findings difficult to combine. As a result, we proposed to carry out a narrative synthesis of evidence in our protocol.

Meta-analysis is a more precise way of synthesizing data than doing it narratively. For example, one advantage of meta-analysis is that combining results from several studies will increase sample size and subsequently increase statistical power. This is particularly important when synthesizing results from interventions that inform practice and policy, such as health interventions, but these are used in other disciplines too. However, not all systematic reviews require meta-analysis, and it should only be conducted when the design and results from included studies are similar and it makes sense to synthesize them that way. For guidance on how to conduct and interpret meta-analysis, please see other resources (e.g. CRD, 2009) and speak to your supervisor. If your systematic review needs to include meta-analysis, it would also be worthwhile talking to a statistician who could help you with it.

When using meta-analysis to synthesize evidence from included studies, it is still necessary to describe and interpret findings in a narrative format. Also, it is possible to use meta-analysis and narrative synthesis within a single systematic review – for example, a narrative synthesis can include statistical pooling of some results. But, when studies are too varied methodologically, it may be best to synthesize them entirely narratively using narrative synthesis.

Narrative synthesis

First, we should make it clear that narrative synthesis is not a narrative review, which we addressed earlier in the chapter. Narrative synthesis involves a systematic analysis by a way of describing, comparing, assessing, and summarizing findings from included studies, following some pre-established steps. There are different guidelines on how to do this, so at the design stage of your review make sure that you consider which approach would be best to use. One approach is to employ an overarching general framework for narrative synthesis (Popay et al., 2006; CRD, 2009), which we describe and provide some brief examples of in Section 9.5, 'Synthesizing systematic review data'.

In terms of reporting this information in your review report, you will have to provide sufficient detail about your synthesis strategy in the method, including information about who will be conducting the synthesis. As with some other aspects of this methodology, two reviewers should synthesize the results independently.

Planning quality assessment of included studies

No research is perfect and the purpose of assessing quality of included studies is to check for methodological rigour. Note that different terms can be used to describe this, such as 'critical appraisal', 'quality assessment', and 'risk of bias'. Many systematic reviews are used to inform treatment and policy. Therefore, it is essential to assess risk of bias, which is the possibility that certain aspects of the study design, conduct, analysis, interpretation, and reporting can produce false results. Identifying bias in studies included in a systematic review will enable an understanding of the differences in findings. We are interested in a number of factors when assessing quality, but this is largely dependent on the systematic review question and needs. In general, this assessment may include assessment of study design, appropriateness of measures, statistical analysis, reporting of findings, etc. Two reviewers need to conduct quality assessment, so discuss with your supervisor how to arrange this.

There are numerous 'risk of bias' or 'quality assessment' measures and you will need to select the most appropriate one for your research. This will largely depend on the design of studies included in your review. For example, RCTs are regarded as the most suitable design for studying effects of interventions and there are different assessment tools specifically designed for the quality assessment of these. One of them is the Cochrane Handbook[6] assessment tool for assessing risk of bias. Another example is observational studies, whereby an effect is studied without manipulating who is exposed to it. As such, these are more prone to bias than RCTs and therefore require a specially tailored quality assessment tool. There are many such tools available: for example, the Joanna Briggs Institute[7] has several tools suitable for different study designs. We used one of their tools in our review (Serbic et al., 2023) and you can see the checklist in Figure 9.8, and our use of it in Figure 9.12. You will notice that this tool, like other quality assessment tools, contains a checklist that indicates whether a particular criterion has been met or not.

For other research designs, including qualitative, you may need to use a different specialized tool, so make sure to spend time identifying the most suitable one for your review. One way to go about this is to inspect other systematic reviews published in your research area or topic and see which tools were used. And, of course, discuss this with your supervisor who will be able to provide advice.

As with the previous aspects, your protocol should explain how the quality of the studies included in your review will be assessed. This should describe the quality assessment tool and criteria, as well as how many researchers will be involved and how disagreements in quality assessment will be resolved. You will need to do the same in the method section of your report, and here you can provide further detail – for example, information about how each criterion was interpreted will be helpful to report. You can inspect a couple of published reviews to see how much detail is required. If you look at our published review (Serbic et al, 2023), you will see that we could have done this better: we described the tool but did not elaborate on how we interpreted each item in the context of our review.

Developing a robust systematic review study

As you can see, the systematic review process consists of several stages and, to minimize error and bias in your review, it is crucial to ensure that you have planned each stage, considered potential issues and taken necessary steps to avoid or minimize them. A good-quality review starts with a carefully developed review protocol and pre-registering it. This will contribute

---

[6] https://training.cochrane.org/handbook/current
[7] https://jbi.global/critical-appraisal-tools

JBI CRITICAL APPRAISAL CHECKLIST FOR ANALYTICAL CROSS SECTIONAL STUDIES

Reviewer_____ Date_____

Author_____ Year_____ Record Number_____

	Yes	No	Unclear	Not applicable
1. Were the criteria for inclusion in the sample clearly defined?	☐	☐	☐	☐
2. Were the study subjects and the setting described in detail?	☐	☐	☐	☐
3. Was the exposure measured in a valid and reliable way?	☐	☐	☐	☐
4. Were objective, standard criteria used for measurement of the condition?	☐	☐	☐	☐
5. Were confounding factors identified?	☐	☐	☐	☐
6. Were strategies to deal with confounding factors stated?	☐	☐	☐	☐
7. Were the outcomes measured in a valid and reliable way?	☐	☐	☐	☐
8. Was appropriate statistical analysis used?	☐	☐	☐	☐

Overall appraisal: Include ☐   Exclude ☐   Seek further info ☐

Comments (Including reason for exclusion) _____
_____
_____

Figure 9.8 A checklist for analytical cross-sectional studies

Source: Joanna Briggs Institute (2020), https://jbi.global/critical-appraisal-tools
(*Note:* Each type of research design has a different checklist).

to the robustness of your systematic review. As mentioned earlier, one way to minimize error and bias in the review process is to involve a second independent reviewer in the selection and quality assessment of studies as well as in the extraction and synthesis of data. Also, you can use various tools to help you assess the methodological quality of your systematic review such as AMSTAR (A MeaSurement Tool to Assess systematic Reviews).[8] The AMSTAR checklist

---

[8] https://amstar.ca/index.php

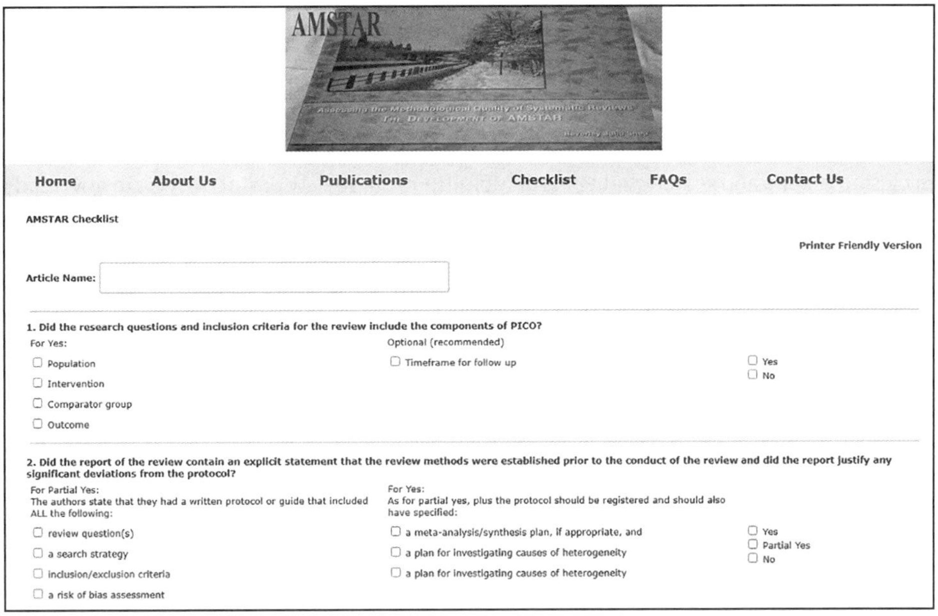

Figure 9.9 Two items (from 16) from the AMSTAR checklist
Source: AMSTAR (2017), https://amstar.ca/Amstar_Checklist.php

not only assesses the methodological quality of systematic reviews, it can also be used as a useful guide to conducting a systematic review. Figure 9.9 shows the first two items from the AMSTAR checklist.

Furthermore, your report should be written with the PRISMA (Preferred Reporting Items for Systematic Reviews and Meta-Analyses; Moher et al., 2009) statement in mind. PRISMA has established standards for how systematic reviews should be reported and it helps promote the transparency of systematic reviews. Like AMSTAR, it can also be used as a guide to conducting your review. The inclusion of a PRISMA checklist is usually required by journals. We will come back to this later, when we discuss how to write up your systematic review.

Finally, developing and following a good review plan that will allow you to spend sufficient time on each review task and to be meticulous will minimize errors in your review. To avoid bias in it, try to be as rigorous and objective as possible in your synthesis, evaluations, and interpretations of studies and data, and in your overall decision-making.

Ethics for a systematic review

Systematic reviews typically do not need ethical approval because they involve already published studies. However, it is always good for project students to learn and engage with ethical procedures, even though they may not be needed. You are likely to be required to do some form of ethics application and submit it through an ethical approval process. Your supervisor will discuss this with you, and your institution or department may have relevant guidelines in place. Not needing to obtain full ethical approval for your systematic review may seem as if systematic reviews are easier to conduct than other types of research that require one. This is not strictly the case because other aspects of systematic review methodology can be very demanding and time-consuming.

9.4 Conducting a systematic review

Conducting literature searches

So, you have designed a suitable systematic review question, developed your inclusion and exclusion criteria and search strategy, and submitted your review protocol. You are now ready to run your systematic review and the first step is to conduct your literature searches. Now you simply need to input your search terms into databases such as Scopus or PsycInfo (which you also formatted appropriately to suit each database) and run searches.

Organizing records

You are likely to get a great number of references or records after you finish searching databases, and it is important to organize and process them efficiently. First, you will need to extract them from individual databases into one place, typically using a referencing manager software such as EndNote. Extracting them usually requires just a few simple steps, which you can find within the guidance information in each database. Before you do that, be sure to write down how many records were found in each database because you may need to include this information in your report.

De-duplicating records

Your literature search will result in a number of duplicate references because the same references are obtained via different databases. Once you have downloaded all your references into referencing manager software, you will need to remove the duplicates (i.e. any additional copies). If there are not many of them, this can be done manually; otherwise, this is best done by using referencing manager software such as EndNote or specialized software such as EPPI-Reviewer. The steps for doing this can be found in their guidance or a simple Google search will show you how. Finally, the above information should be reported in the results section of your write-up. For example, you should specify how many duplicates were identified and removed.

Refreshing literature searches

As mentioned earlier, if your search was conducted several months ago, it is highly recommended that you repeat your search before finalizing your review report. This is to ensure that your literature search includes any more recently published papers that are relevant. If you are submitting your review to a journal, you are likely to be asked to do this. When doing it, you should search databases from the date that your last search was conducted. Alternatively, in some databases, you can set up alerts (at the start of your review) whereby you will receive regular notifications about new published studies that relate to your search terms.

Conducting study screening and selection

You will begin this process by looking through all the titles and abstracts and screening them against your inclusion and exclusion criteria. This is the first stage of study screening and selection, and it is intended to exclude studies that are obviously irrelevant to the review. There are usually a lot of them! If you are unsure about whether a paper should be included based on its title and abstract, then it is best to include it for the full text to be read at the second stage, because you do not want to exclude a potentially relevant paper. Potentially relevant papers will then be read in full at the second stage. When screening the papers, you need to think how they fit within all your inclusion and exclusion criteria. Ideally two researchers should independently conduct study screening and selection. To ensure consistency and accuracy of the selection, we suggest a pilot run of this process by selecting a few papers and screening them independently. You can then discuss your outcomes with your co-reviewers and supervisor. Consider providing a clear list of your inclusion and exclusion criteria for yourself and your co-reviewer/s as a guide.

At the second stage, you will need to download full-text papers that passed the first stage. Some of these papers might not be available to you, in which case you can contact the authors directly and ask for a copy, or you can contact your university library and request an inter-library loan. Make sure you include this in the planning of your review because it might take several days (even weeks) to obtain these papers. Do not be surprised if most of the papers do not make it to the second stage: this is a common occurrence. For example, see Figure 9.10, which shows a PRISMA flow diagram of our Serbic et al., 2023 screening and selection process. You will see that, after having screened 8,183 titles and abstracts (first stage), only 127 were read full text (second stage). In addition, of those 127 that

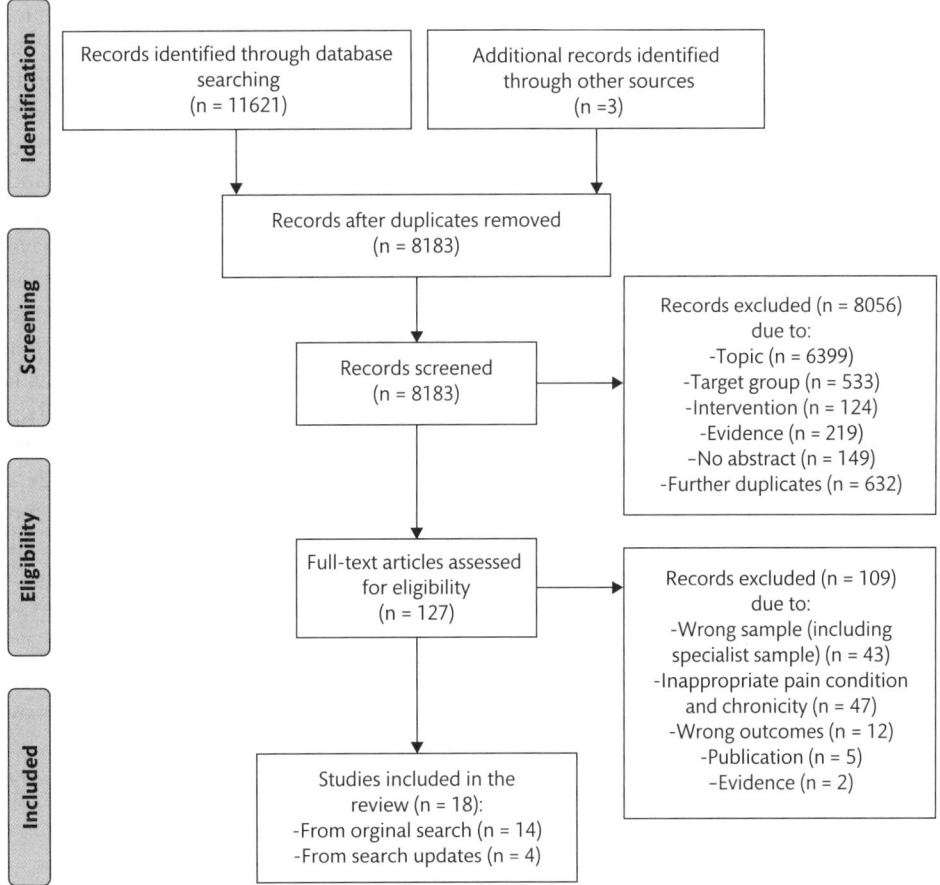

Figure 9.10 Example of a PRISMA flow diagram

Source: Serbic et al. (2023: 2902).

were read full text, only 18 were included in the review. So, try not to worry if your initial search does give you a huge number of papers, and allow enough time for the screening process!

Finally, in your report, you will have to describe all the steps you have taken during your study screening and selection in the results section of your report by making a PRISMA flow diagram, similar to Figure 9.10. This will include the number of papers (records) identified, de-duplicated, and selected at the first and second stages of screening, and the number of excluded studies and the reasons for their exclusion.

Conducting data extraction

The next step is to extract relevant data from the papers that passed the second stage and will be included in your review. When extracting results from studies, it is always better to extract original information and organize and manipulate it later. Extracting information is a laborious process, so you do not want to go back to studies to look for information that you did not extract the first time round.

As with the previous steps, preferably two reviewers should extract data independently. This will minimize bias and error in the data-extraction process. While it is advised that two reviewers do this, it might not always be easy and possible to have a second independent reviewer due to limited time and resources. In such circumstances, one reviewer can extract all the data and a second reviewer should inspect the accuracy of the data-extraction process and resulting information. Any disagreements should be resolved by discussing them and/or consulting a third reviewer. A lot of information might be open to interpretation and it may be difficult for you to reach an objective solution. Make sure that you keep a record of disagreements because you may need to revisit them at a later stage. To avoid bias and error during data extraction, all the researchers involved in must use the same extraction tables and agree on how to conduct the data extraction. For example, they should have clear instructions as to how to extract and code data – in particular, ambiguous information. This will improve the reliability and validity of the review. It is good practice to pilot the extraction tables before starting the data extraction: this will help you to identify whether all the necessary data can be extracted, as well as potential discrepancies and issues with data, and, overall, this will save you time in the long run. After all, you do not want to end up extracting unnecessary data or missing important information during the extraction process. Data extraction tables should be reported in the results section of your report, alongside a descriptive summary of the data, and, while the categories used can differ in the column headings, you can see an example of how this might look in Figure 9.11. This table contains information related to the study and participant characteristics. Please note that the study outcomes needed for our synthesis were reported in a different table, which you can find in our published paper (Serbic et al., 2023).

During the extraction of data, you need to read included papers very carefully and to look for specific information, so attention to detail is essential. While already doing this, you may also decide to extract the information needed for the quality assessment of the included studies, discussed next. However, whether you extract information necessary for the quality assessment before, during, or after your data extraction is up to you.

DOING A SYSTEMATIC REVIEW

Table 1. Summary of study and participant characteristics of included studies.

Author/year/ country	N/sex (F)/age Total sample (pain groups)	Health issue (HI)/pain duration (PD)/ pain intensity (PI)[a]	Setting/degree	Design	Analysis	Measured variables[b]
Bottos and Dewey (2004)[48] Canada	N: 291 (CP: 18; frequent pain: 179; infrequent pain: 69; incomplete data for pain frequency: 25) F: 85% (CP: 83.3%; frequent pain: 87.2%; infrequent pain: 82.6%) Age: $M = 22$, SD = 5.32 (CP: $M = 20.89$, SD = 2.74; frequent pain: $M = 21.58$, SD = 4.20; infrequent pain: $M = 23.45$, SD = 7.05)	HI: chronic headache PD: CP: $M = 7.67$, SD = 1.38; frequent pain: $M = 6.47$, SD = 10.75; infrequent pain: $M = 7.40$, SD = 11.43 PI: CP: $M = 7.67$, SD = 1.38; frequent pain: $M = 6.69$, SD = 1.32; infrequent pain: $M = 6.35$, SD = 1.40	University undergraduate psychology students; data collected in person	Cross sectional; questionnaire study	ANOVA	Headache frequency and intensity (Headache Assessment Questionnaire); college student daily hassles (BCSHS); perfectionism (MPS)
Feldman et al. (2020)[50] USA	N: 121 (CP: 45) F: 78.5% (no information for groups) Age: $M = 19.6$, SD = 1.5 (no information for groups)	HI: variety of chronic health conditions with CP and without CP PD: not reported PI: not reported	University undergraduate students (variety of courses); data collected in person and online	Longitudinal design; questionnaire daily diary study	Correlations; regression	Symptoms of CP (medical providers independently classified chronic health conditions into two categories: chronic conditions with pain as a symptom and conditions without pain as a symptom); perceived social support (MSPSS); illness-related social support (number of friends to whom they disclosed their condition and how supportive their friends had been)
Furtado et al. (2014)[46] Brazil	N: 198 (CP: 58) F: 65.2% (CP: 81%; no CP: 58.6%) Age: $M = 22.9$ (CP: $M = 22.2$; no CP: $M = 23.1$)	HI: chronic nonspecific LBP PD: not reported PI: CP: $M = 2.85$, SD = 3.13; no CP: $M = 1.80$, SD = 2.31	University students (degree level and course and reported); data collected in person	Cross sectional; questionnaire; observation	Correlations; t test; Chi-square	Presence of chronic nonspecific LBP (persistence of pain over a period of 3 months); pain severity (visual analogue scale for LBP 0–10 cm); self-rated quality of life (SF-36 Health Survey); self-rated social functioning, mental health, social functioning and role-emotional (these are the domains of SF-36 that are relevant to this review); self-rated anxiety (self-assessment form, no further information provided by authors)

Figure 9.11 Example of an extraction table

Source: Serbic et al. (2023: 2897).

Conducting quality assessment of included studies

You have already planned your quality assessment (see earlier), so now you need to conduct it in accordance with that plan. You have selected the most suitable quality assessment tool for your review. Now it would be good to pilot it on a few studies to ensure that all reviewers (at least two) involved in the process use it in the same way. All reviewers need to agree on each criterion and any disagreements should be resolved by discussing them with a third reviewer. Sometimes, researchers compare their assessment scores by calculating an inter-rater agreement score, such as a Kappa statistic.

You are likely to report your quality assessment results within a table, like the one in Figure 9.12, where you will report which criteria were met. You will also need to include a brief narrative summary of this in your report. You may decide to exclude poor-quality

Study	External validity			Internal validity					
	Inclusion criteria clearly defined	Subjects and setting clearly described	Exposure/ predictor variable valid and reliable	Objective, standard criteria used for condition measurement	Confounding factors identified	Confounding factors dealt with	Outcomes measured reliably and validly	Appropriate use of statistical analysis	Study summary score
Bottos and Dewey (2004)[48]	✓	✓	✓	✓	✓	✗	✓	✓	7/8
Feldman et al. (2020)[50]	✓	✓	✓	✓	✓	✓	✓	✓	8/8
Furtado et al. (2014)[46]	✓	✓	✓	✓	✗	✗	✓	✓	6/8
Graham and Streitel (2010)[39]	✓	✓	✓	✓	✓	✓	✓	✓	8/8
Gulewitsch et al. (2011)[52]	unclear	✓	✓	✓	✓	✓	✓	✓	7/8
Gulewitsch et al. (2013)[47]	unclear	✓	✓	✓	✓	✓	✓	✓	7/8
Jiang et al. (2019)[43]	✓	✓	✓	✓	✓	✓	✓	✓	8/8
Karoly and Lecci (1997)[37]	✓	✓	✓	✓	✓	✓	✓	✓	8/8
Kato (2020)[35]	✓	Unclear	✓	✓	✓	✓	✓	✓	7/8
Klemenc-Ketis et al. (2011)[51]	✗	✓	✓	✓	Unclear	Unclear	✓	✓	5/8
Minghelli et al. (2014)[44]	✓	✓	✓	✓	✓	Unclear	✓	✓	7/8
Natu et al. (2018)[40]	✓	✓	✓	✓	✗	✗	✓	✓	6/8
Pesqueira et al. (2010)[45]	✗	✗	✓	✓	Unclear	✗	✓	✓	4/8
Rachor and Penney (2020)[36]	✓	✓	✓	✓	✗	✗	✓	✓	6/8
Serbic et al. (2020)[42]	✓	✓	✓	✓	✓	✓	✓	✓	8/8
Shen et al. (2009)[38]	✓	✓	✓	✓	Unclear	Unclear	✓	✓	6/8
Soyuer et al. (2012)[41]	✓	✓	✓	✓	Unclear	✗	✓	✓	6/8
Thomas et al. (1992)[49]	unclear	✓	✓	✓	✓	✗	✓	✓	6/8

Figure 9.12 Section of a table showing the use of the checklist

Source: Serbic et al. (2023: 2901).

studies from your review, or you may decide to include them and then consider the impact of this decision on your findings in your discussion.

9.5 Synthesizing systematic review data

At this point, you should already know how you are going to synthesize your data – remember that you planned it all at the design stage of your review and described it in your protocol! Here we will focus on how to conduct the narrative synthesis. By now, you have also extracted relevant information (results) from included studies and organized them within a table or tables. Now you need to combine or synthesize them in some way.

Narrative synthesis

One possible way to synthesize your data narratively is by employing an overarching general framework for narrative synthesis (Popay et al., 2006), which consists of four key steps (see the next section). It is important to note that these four steps can interact and do not need to be carried out in this order. They can also be broken down further. For further guidance on this, please see the Popay et al. (2006) paper. It describes a range of tools and techniques that you can use to conduct your narrative synthesis. Which ones you choose to use will depend on the nature and needs of your review. Note that Popay et al.'s guidance is mostly based on systematic reviews examining effects of interventions. However, they can be used with a variety of systematic review questions. Furthermore, we also recommend a paper by Campbell et al. (2020), which provides a reporting guideline for synthesis without meta-analysis.

1. *Developing a theory of how the intervention works, why, and for whom.* You will need to consider whether it is possible to develop a theory or a theoretical model based on the available evidence. A developed theory can enhance the interpretation and application of your review findings. However, it may not always be easy or even possible to develop a theory, and this will largely depend on your review findings, study design, study quality, etc.

2. *Developing a preliminary synthesis of findings of included studies.* This means that you need to find a suitable way to collate your results in a meaningful way. There is a range of ways and tools to do this and the paper by Popay et al. (2006) elaborates nicely on these. How you do it will depend on your review question and its goals. For example, one way is to group results according to certain characteristics. Obviously, this should be in line with your research question and goals. In our review (Serbic et al., 2023), we grouped studies and their findings according to the broad outcomes we were interested in – psychological, social, academic, and quality of life – and then narrowed these down according to specific outcomes, such as depression and anxiety. When reporting results for your narrative synthesis, it is also important to include relevant statistics (e.g. effect sizes) because these can be used to support your narrative synthesis.

3. *Exploring relationships within and between studies.* As you are doing your preliminary synthesis, you will be able to monitor whether any particular patterns in the data are emerging that may help you to interpret similarities and, in particular, differences in findings. One way of doing this is to do some subgroup comparisons. For instance, you

could subgroup your findings according to features of your population. In our review (Serbic et al., 2023), we planned to do this for specific pain conditions but the results from individual studies were insufficient to do this. For further strategies that you can use for exploring relationships within and between studies, we would recommend reading the Popay et al. (2006) paper.

4. *Assessing the robustness of the synthesis*. Finally, it is important to assess the robustness of your synthesis – for example, by considering the quality and potential risk of bias in the included studies. It is also important to reflect critically on your synthesis process – for example, by being clear about any assumptions made and any inconsistencies in the synthesis process.

Making sense of your findings

As you will have gathered, your synthesis should not involve mere reporting of findings from individual studies: you should try to interpret them and build a bigger picture, and, in some cases, they may even allow you to build a theoretic model. For instance, you could examine whether your synthesis findings are consistent across individual studies and, if they are not, explore potential reasons for this. Interpreting your findings in this way will make them more reliable. The above framework provides a clear structure for doing this.

9.6 Writing up a systematic review

It is extremely important to document in detail how you have designed and conducted your systematic review. As we have worked through this chapter, we have already covered several aspects of systematic review reporting, so in this section we address some general aspects related to writing up your systematic review. In a systematic review report, you will find standard sections: abstract, introduction, method, results, and discussion. However, the contents of these sections, in particular method and results, will be quite different from previous research reports that you have written. We highly recommend that you look at some published systematic reviews before you embark on writing up your systematic review. And, of course, ask your supervisor for advice. If you intend to publish your systematic review, then you should also check the requirements of the journal that you plan to submit your review to. Different journals and commissioning organizations may have specific requirements for writing up systematic reviews.

PRISMA Statement/Checklist

As discussed earlier in the chapter, your report should be written with the PRISMA statement in mind (or some other similar systematic review checklist). In fact, each section of your report should correspond with the PRISMA checklist. If you plan to submit your review to a journal, you will be requested to include a PRISMA checklist within your submission to demonstrate that you have followed its standards. You can see the first page of the PRISMA checklist in Figure 9.13 and the full checklist includes 27 points. Notice how detailed it is: it covers every aspect of a systematic review process and also requires you to report page

Section/topic	#	Checklist item	Reported on page #
TITLE			
Title	1	Identify the report as a systematic review, meta-analysis, or both.	1
ABSTRACT			
Structured summary	2	Provide a structured summary including, as applicable: background; objectives; data sources; study eligibility criteria, participants, and interventions; study appraisal and synthesis methods; results; limitations; conclusions and implications of key findings; systematic review registration number.	2
INTRODUCTION			
Rationale	3	Describe the rationale for the review in the context of what is already known.	4 to 6
Objectives	4	Provide an explicit statement of questions being addressed with reference to participants, interventions, comparisons, outcomes, and study design (PICOS).	5/6
METHODS			
Protocol and registration	5	Indicate if a review protocol exists, if and where it can be accessed (e.g., Web address), and, if available, provide registration information including registration number.	6 (PROSPERO registration)
Eligibility criteria	6	Specify study characteristics (e.g., PICOS, length of follow-up) and report characteristics (e.g., years considered, language, publication status) used as criteria for eligibility, giving rationale.	6 to 8
Information sources	7	Describe all information sources (e.g., databases with dates of coverage, contact with study authors to identify additional studies) in the search and date last searched.	8
Search	8	Present full electronic search strategy for at least one database, including any limits used, such that it could be repeated.	Uploaded as supporting document
Study selection	9	State the process for selecting studies (i.e., screening, eligibility, included in systematic review, and, if applicable, included in the meta-analysis).	8/9

Figure 9.13 Example of a PRISMA checklist

Source: Serbic et al. (2021), https://doi.org/10.1111/bjhp.12529
(Note: You can find the PRISMA checklist in the supporting information at the bottom of the webpage).

numbers where you covered those aspects in your report. You should inspect this checklist before you start your review because it can be a useful guide when planning, designing, and conducting your review.

Structure and sections of a systematic review

At the beginning of the chapter in Figure 9.2, we listed all key steps in a systematic review. Your report should, more or less, follow this structure too. You should report on each stage and task within your review. Broadly speaking, your report should include the following sections:

Title

As with other research designs, your title should be clear and to the point, ideally around 10 to 20 words long, and it is very helpful to indicate that the study is a systematic review.

Abstract

This should cover all key aspects of the report and it is probably best to write it last. You should make sure that you cover the study: background, aims and objectives, methods (e.g. data/study sources, selection, extraction, quality assessment, and analysis/synthesis), results, and conclusions.

Introduction

This section should contain a background of your review. It should describe the topic under investigation, its importance and relevance. Make sure to explain why your systematic review is necessary. If there have been previous systematic review/s, include a clear justification for your review. Your introduction should not be too long, and it should end with a clear statement of the aims and objectives of your review. Remember that systematic reviews do not state hypotheses.

Methods

This section of your report will differ considerably from the method sections for other research designs, such as the experimental or correlational research outlined in our previous chapters. This section should follow the steps taken in the review because you need to explain how you carried those out. While we have already explained much of this in previous sections (mostly in the designing of a systematic review section), Figure 9.14 below outlines key aspects that need to be included in a method section.

- Review protocol – explain where this has been submitted and provide the protocol number.
- Sources of information (databases, etc.) – which database was searched and when. Include detail about any additional manual searches.
- Study inclusion and exclusion criteria – these should be clearly explained and justified.
- Screening and selection of studies plan – explain how this will be carried out, how many researchers will be involved and their roles.
- Quality assessment of studies plan – explain how this will be carried out, how many researchers will be involved and their roles, what tools will be used and how they will be used in your review.
- Data extraction plan – outline your data extraction plan, how many researchers will be involved, their roles, and which information will be extracted from studies.
- Data synthesis plan – explain how the data will be analysed and synthesized, how many researchers will be involved and their roles.

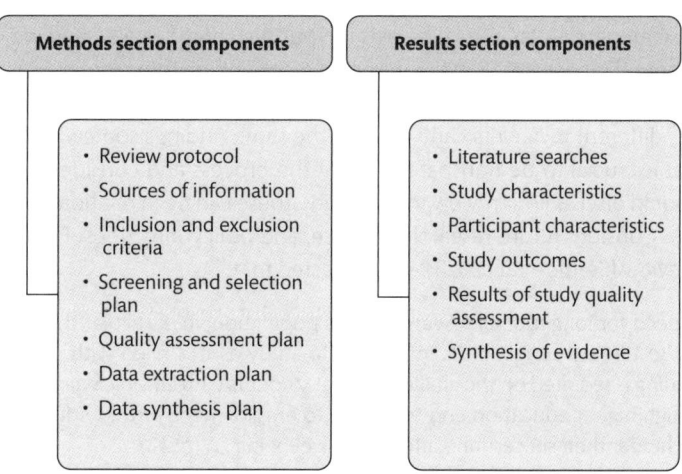

Figure 9.14 Information to include in the Methods and Results sections of a systematic review

Method subsections may vary slightly across reviews and journals. For instance, you may need to have additional subsections in your methods section, so make sure to discuss this with your supervisor. We recommend that you inspect several published systematic reviews to understand how much detail is necessary to include in your method section, because it may be more detailed than you are used to seeing or writing about.

Results

As with the method section, we addressed how to report your results throughout this chapter. As illustrated in Figure 9.14, you will first need to report on extracted data from included studies (both in tables and summarizing key information narratively). This will be followed by reporting on results of your quality assessment, including relevant table/s and a narrative summary of this. Then you will report on your main analysis and synthesis of findings.

Make sure that your data extraction tables contain sufficient information to enable readers to assess your interpretation of the results and understand them. However, they should not include unnecessary information. The quality assessment table/s and summary should be clear and, as discussed earlier, this information should be considered in your synthesis of results. Sometimes these tables can become very large, but this is not unusual in systematic reviews and it might be helpful to look at some published reviews to see how they formatted and organized their tables.

Discussion

As with other types of research, in your discussion, you need to summarize and interpret the results of your review. You should discuss the results in relation to the existing evidence and knowledge – for example, how your review results compare with those of other relevant published reviews. You should also take into consideration the quality assessment of studies included in the review – for example, results from studies that you included that were of lower quality should be interpreted with caution. Discussing the strengths and shortcomings of your systematic review is your next step. You should consider how any limitations of the review might have influenced your findings and the interpretation of those. There are a lot of different ways to introduce bias in your systematic review and we would advise that, throughout the review process, you keep a record of anything that may have an impact on your findings. Despite its structured approach, systematic reviews are still prone to bias. For example, different reviewers can interpret the same findings somewhat differently. This means that it is crucial to be transparent about the process and consider its shortcomings. Next, you should discuss your review implications: these can be in relation to practice, policy, and research. Consider future research, practice, and policy directions. For example, in our systematic review (Serbic et al., 2023), we suggested that:

> there is a need for longitudinal research in this population, in particular the transition from secondary to tertiary education is important to study as it is filled with challenges. More understanding is required on the challenges that students with chronic pain face as they progress through higher education and transition to employment/further education, and how this might hinder their success and affect their wellbeing . . . (p. 13)

Finally, finish your discussion by presenting clear and balanced conclusions at the end.

9.7 Building transferable skills through systematic review methodology

We hope that this chapter has illustrated how working on a systematic review requires the use of several transferable skills. Good organizational and teamwork skills are particularly important and in Box 9.1 we reflect on the latter using a brief case study; you can see some hints and tips in Box 9.2.

BOX 9.1 A case study showing reflection on teamwork when conducting a systematic review

Reflecting on your transferable skills and personal attributes
An example – teamwork

Recognize: From the research you have conducted, what is the best example of when you have demonstrated this skill or attribute?

As part of my systematic review project, I had to work closely with the second reviewer, who was another student. This involved planning out the review process together, agreeing on the appropriate method, and piloting various steps within the process to come up with the best and most consistent approach that would reduce any possible sources of bias.

Reflect: What are my strengths with regard to this skill or attribute? How can I further develop or improve them?

Agreeing on the process involved a fair amount of discussion with the second reviewer. I was able to listen to the other person's ideas and take into account their views when we worked out how to divide up the various tasks that needed to be completed. I feel that my listening skills really helped to ensure that the review ran smoothly and any possible bias reduced.

Relate: Imagine you are being interviewed for your dream job or course. How would your skills in this area make you suitable for this position?

While I feel I am good at listening and taking on board another person's views, I am not quite so good at clearly communicating my own views. I find it difficult to explain my views in a conversation, but find it far easier in writing.

BOX 9.2 Hints and tips from psychology graduates and employers of psychology graduates

The student perspective . . . reflecting on taking the initiative.

> My advice would be to have a conversation with your supervisor before planning your literature review and search terms. Arrange a time to go to their office and take a list of questions with you. In that conversation, ensure you fully understand the scope of the review and agree on the next steps.
>
> Kenji, psychology graduate

The employer perspective . . . reflecting on critical thinking

> One of the core activities for anyone I employ is the ability to review, understand and evaluate prior research. It is essential that my team have the skills to sense check and validate anything they find. For graduates I expect this to be something they have learned to do as part of their degrees, however in the commercial world it takes on new importance because the insights we pass on to clients can affect our recommendations.
>
> Sophia, human factors researcher

# Presenting your research

 In this chapter you will learn . . .

- about the range of different ways in which we can present our research projects;
- how to create and give good research presentations; and
- how to share your research more broadly, within both academic and non-academic communities.

So far, much of this book has focused on you conducting a research project. However, it is important to also share your research findings. While you will spend lots of time thinking about how to write up your research project for your assessment, you will hopefully feel proud of the work you have done and you may want to share your research beyond your studies. It is important that research is shared among the academic community because every finding helps us to build our understanding of how people think, feel, and behave. Sharing our work can foster research collaborations across different universities and may also have more real-world benefits when shared outside the academic community. The experience will also allow you to develop additional skills that are likely to put you in a stronger position for whatever you choose to do next in life. Until now, you will mainly have seen research disseminated through published articles, but there are other possible ways to share your work. In this chapter, I (Victoria) will discuss some of the potential avenues for sharing and publicizing the research that you have done.

If you are considering presenting your research beyond your assessed work, it is vital that you start by discussing your ideas with your supervisor, and with your collaborators if you conducted a group project. For any way of disseminating your research, it is important to credit all the people who were involved in the project, so it is likely that your supervisor and potentially other students from your research group will also be co-authors on any work that you present. Your supervisor will be able to talk to you through who should be involved, how the group should collaborate to ensure that everyone is happy with the work being presented, and how to agree on authorship (i.e. who is included and in what order). Just because you graduate doesn't mean that you can no longer communicate with your supervisor and with any other students and researchers involved in the project, so try to keep in touch with them.

As I mentioned, most of the research that you will have seen will have been in the form of published research articles. You may also have had some experience through your studies of presenting your research orally to an audience, or perhaps through poster presentations. In academia, these are two very frequently used ways to present our research, whether at a conference or when invited to give a research talk to academics from other institutions. Increasingly, academics are engaging in communicating their research to the general public, often using social media to help disseminate their work. These various ways of communicating science may also be helpful in your preparing for your next steps in your career. In addition to building your CV, you may also be asked to give a presentation as part of an interview. While giving a presentation can be nerve-racking, the information in this chapter will be helpful when preparing for job applications and interviews, and hopefully also with calming any anxiety you may experience. If your research project was more applied in nature, you may also have the opportunity to share your work with non-academic audiences, such as schoolteachers or health professionals. So, being able to present your research clearly and in different formats can be beneficial for yourself and wider society. In this chapter I will talk through each method of sharing your research with others, giving you lots of hints and tips for how to do this well.

10.1 Developing research skills through presenting your project

Through conducting your research project, you will have developed a wide range of skills, and you can continue this skill development if you choose to present your research in other contexts. You can see some of these skills in Figure 10.1. A presentation is often a solo endeavour, allowing you to demonstrate your independence, but it is always the end result of working with others. This is relevant not just in conducting the research itself but also in preparing and practising for your presentation, and you may need to show leadership in putting all this together. When writing your presentation, you may also be using new IT packages and putting information into formats that are unfamiliar to you. To select the information that you want to present, you will need to apply your critical thinking skills and communicate with others about the best way to approach the task. During and after the presentation itself, you will also need to practise and develop your people skills, thinking about how to respond to any questions that you may be asked.

10.2 Research articles

You are probably quite used to reading research articles now (also sometimes called 'papers' or 'reports'), and you have probably written a few too. There is a standard format recommended by the American Psychological Association (APA) that is used to structure most research articles, following the usual Abstract, Introduction, Methods, Results, Discussion, and References format. In Section 2 we went through how this is typically applied across different methods used within psychological research, so please do take a look back there for guidance on writing up your research project. If you are considering writing up your project for publication, then it is important that you first discuss this with your supervisor. Then take a look at Chapter 11, which goes through the whole process of publication in considerable detail.

10.3 Presentations

In addition to writing about our projects in traditional research reports, there are many contexts in which we may need to present our findings in other ways. If you are a student, there is a good chance that you will have been asked to give an oral presentation about your research

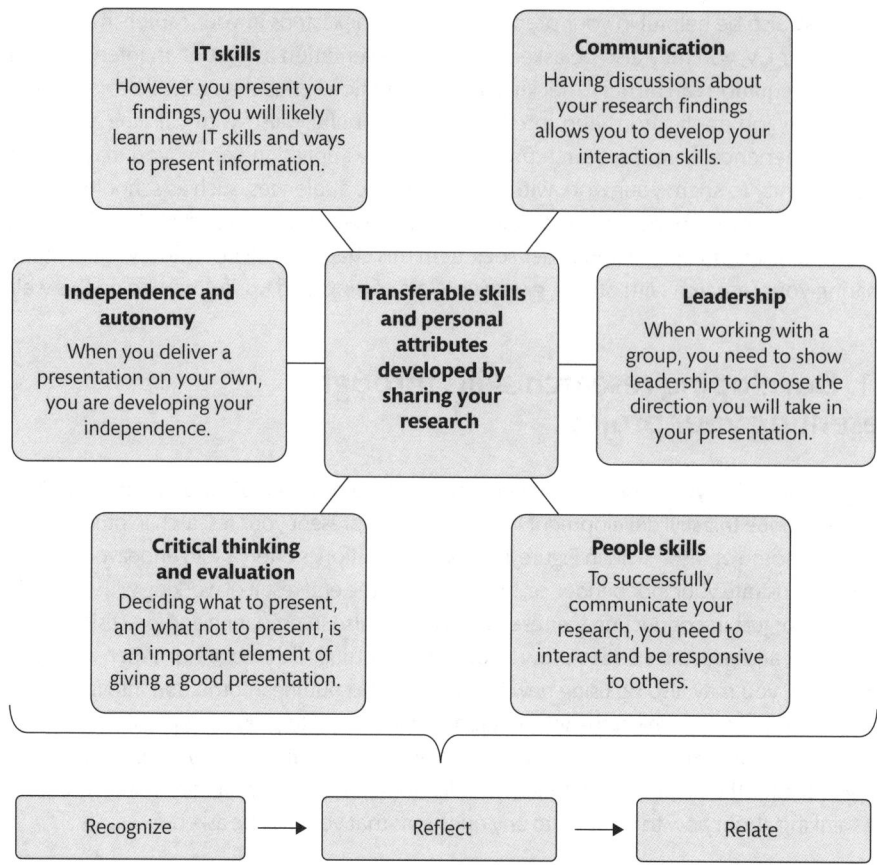

Figure 10.1 The key skills developed through presenting your research

at some point during your studies. Thinking beyond your studies, you may also be asked to present your work at research meetings, such as lab group meetings run by your supervisor or at conferences. Here, I will outline different ways that we can present our research. It is natural to feel a little nervous about giving a presentation, but this section contains many hints and tips to hopefully make your presentation a more enjoyable and rewarding experience.

Broadly speaking, there are two types of presentation that you can give: oral or poster presentations. With oral presentations, we typically create slides (such as in PowerPoint or Prezi), and then talk through these slides in front of an audience, usually followed by answering questions from the audience. With poster presentations, we create a single page poster that summarizes our study so that other people can view the poster and ask questions in a more informal and relaxed setting.

If you are giving either an oral or a poster presentation as part of the assessment on your degree course, then it is important to follow the guidelines given to you by your department, such as how long the presentation should be, and their expectations as to how to prepare your presentation and present your work. It is very important that you follow these requirements because they may form part of the marking criteria that are used to award you a mark for your presentation.

If you are considering presenting at a conference, then the first step is working out which conference to go to. For this, it is best to start by speaking with your supervisor because there are likely to be a few key conferences that are relevant to the area of research you are working in. Almost all conferences require a registration fee; however, be careful of conferences where there is a large fee to attend because there are some illegitimate conferences that are unlikely to reach the academic audience that you want to be presenting to. If in doubt, check with your supervisor. You will probably need to apply in advance for any conference that you want to attend and present at. The submission deadline for conferences can be quite a few months before the conference is due to take place, so, if you are considering attending and presenting at a conference, it is good to be thinking ahead and using the organizational skills that you developed through your research project. For most conferences, presenters effectively have to apply to be allowed to present. This usually takes the form of submitting an abstract that summarizes the content of your research study. While you may have written an abstract already for your project, pay close attention to the requirements for your conference submission, because they are often longer than a research report abstract and they may require subsections within the abstract or additional information that is not typically included. For most conferences, the submissions undergo a process of peer review, whereby academics read through the abstracts and decide whether the research fits within the remit of the conference topic and is of sufficient quality to include (you can find out much more about the peer review process in Chapter 11 of this book). Occasionally, an abstract will not be accepted for a conference, particularly if there are space or time restrictions – there may not be space to accept every submission. If your abstract is not accepted, this will understandably be disappointing. Please do talk to your supervisor if this happens because rejections are part of academic life, and we have all had to deal with them many times. If your abstract is accepted, congratulations – you will be presenting your research at a conference!

Oral presentations

There are many different styles of oral presentation that you can give, so the first step is to understand the exact format and requirements of yours. Some of the more frequently occurring formats are as follows:

- Standard presentations: These are typically presentations of 15-20 minutes, followed by a few minutes where members of the audience can ask the presenter questions about their research presentation.
- Quick-fire presentations: These are far shorter presentations, sometimes even as short as 5 minutes. When people give quick-fire presentations, there are often a few short talks in a row, followed by questions for all the presenters in one open discussion session.
- Workshops: These are usually interactive, combining elements of an oral presentation with discussions and exercises based around a particular topic or theme. They may be longer, taking around 45–60 minutes.
- Symposium: This is a collection of oral presentations that all focus on a particular topic, often with four to six different presenters giving talks. It will be organized by an academic

who will give a short presentation to open the session, providing an overview of the topic and how the different talks fit together. The talks are then followed by a discussion to bring together the different aspects raised and to take questions on the talks. This is led by a 'discussant' who is usually a more senior academic who has expertise in the area.

- Keynote talk: This is often the highlight of a conference, whereby a very accomplished academic will give a longer talk that gives an overview of their research and their expertise. It is not unusual for a keynote talk to be an hour long.
- Online talks: Some conferences are online, or there is sometimes the option to present online at an in-person conference. When you present online, this is typically done in one of two ways. Sometimes you give your presentation live, through a platform such as Zoom or Teams, sharing your presentation slides with the online audience, and the presentation is followed by taking questions from the audience. Alternatively, for some conferences, online presenters are asked to pre-record their presentation, which is then shown to the audience whose questions are then taken live. This way of presenting online can avoid some of the technical challenges experienced with online conferences, but it still allows for live discussion after the talk.

Preparing your oral presentation

Before starting to prepare your presentation, it is important to find out the format of your talk and how long it should be. Make sure to check separately on the length of the presentation and the time allowed for questions. For example, if your talk is 20 minutes long, should you talk for 15 minutes and allow 5 minutes for questions, or is the talk 20 minutes long followed by additional time for questions?

Once you know the length of your talk, you can start structuring it. Broadly speaking, the presentation should follow the same structure as your written report (i.e. Introduction, Methods, Results, Discussion), but you will probably need to be more concise, deciding on what essential information needs to be presented and what information can be left out. I tend to start with the number of slides that I can present in the time I have, and then work out the appropriate level of detail from that. A good guide for the number of slides would be 2 minutes per slide, plus a title slide and a closing slide. So, if you are giving a 20-minute talk, I would recommend 10 slides of content, plus the title and closing slides. In Figure 10.2, you can see an example of how you might structure a 10-minute presentation and distribute the content across the 7 slides. You can then work out how to distribute the content appropriately across the number of slides that you have.

The next step is to format your slides and set up your title and closing slides. Often, universities will have branded templates for giving talks, and it is good to use these. Alternatively, ask your supervisor because they may have templates for the department or lab that you are working in. If you do not use a branded template, then you should include the logos for your institution, department, and/or lab on your title slide. Remember also to include the title of your talk, your name, and the name of any other authors on your title slide. It is also helpful to share your (or your lab's) social media information on the title slide, because sometimes people in the audience will share social media posts about the talks they attend and, if they have your social media information, they can tag you in their posts.

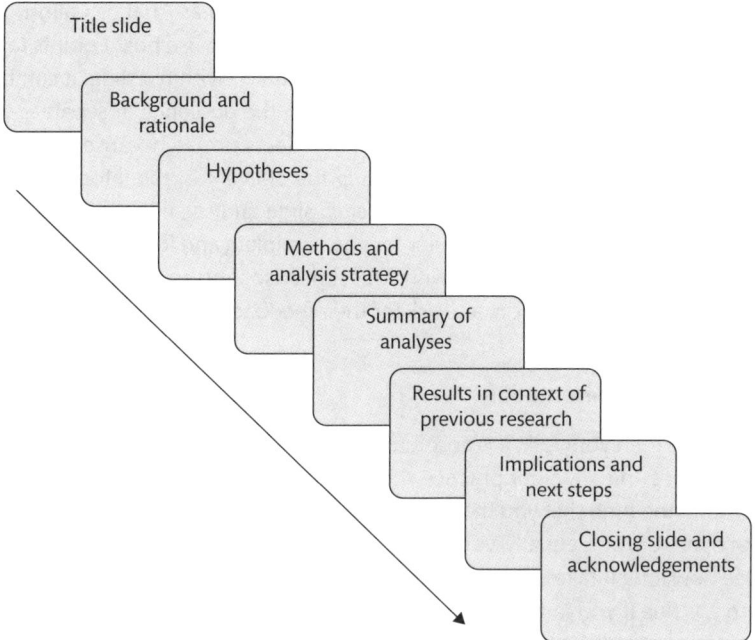

Figure 10.2 Example of the structure of a 10-minute presentation

Your closing slide is where you can acknowledge and thank people who contributed to the successful delivery of your research project and presentation – for example, if there was any funding for the research, if others contributed to collecting data, or perhaps colleagues helped you prepare and practise your talk. This is also a good place to share your email address and any relevant social media links in case people wish to follow up with you after the presentation. Finally, it is nice on this closing slide to also thank the audience for their attention and to invite questions from them.

Now that you know how many slides you have and what they look like, it is time to start adding the information that you want to present on them. It is sometimes tempting to write out what you want to say on your slides, but this is not necessarily a good way to approach writing a talk. Try to avoid using too much text on your slides and also reading out loud the exact wording that is written on your slides. When I'm writing a talk, I try to think about it as two parallel streams of information that are presented together to form a clear and engaging presentation. First, you need to write the spoken information that you want to present, and then you need to create the visual information that you will present to the audience in your slides. While these may overlap in places, they should not be identical.

In PowerPoint, I like to use the 'Notes' area to help me prepare my talk. I start by 'writing' the spoken part of my talk, dividing the relevant sections across the number of slides that I have. I tend to practise on individual slides to make sure that the amount of information I have can be delivered in the time that I have. I then look at the points I want to make and I pick out the key information to show to the audience on each slide. As much as possible, try to use visual information rather than plain text. Particularly for the Methods and Results sections, try to rely on figures rather than written summaries. If you do include text, try to keep it to a minimum and ensure that you pick a simple font (such as Arial or Calibri) that is no smaller than 18-point. Where text is appropriate, it is helpful to use bullet points to break up the information into smaller and more manageable chunks. Within a slide, it can be helpful to use the animation function to reveal the content to the audience in separate segments. Try to use animations sparingly and keep animation effects simple because they can end up being distracting when they should be facilitating the delivery of the information. Go back to the points that you want to talk through for each slide and see if there is a natural way to divide up the information so that it is easier for you to explain and for the audience to digest. Don't forget to share your presentation with your supervisor and any other co-authors well in advance of giving the presentation, and ask for their feedback.

Delivering your oral presentation

Once you have written your talk, it is absolutely essential for you to practise it, and to practise it quite a few times. Initially, your practice should focus on whether your talk can feasibly be delivered within the time that you have. Conferences have to run to very strict timetables, so you cannot over-run, but, equally, you do not want to finish too soon. Practise your talk a few times to see how long it takes. The more you practise it, the smoother your presentation will become, so it is fine if you initially run over by a minute or two. However, roughly speaking, your presentation should be the length of time you have. If your first couple of practices seem too long or too short, then go back to your slides and edit them accordingly.

Once you are happy with the length and the structure of your talk, try presenting it a few times to people so that you can focus more on your manner of presenting. While you may need notes the first few times that you practise, ideally you can put your notes to one side when you get to doing the actual presentation. Not relying on notes often makes a presentation feel more natural and relaxed. We all sometimes make a mistake or need to pause to gather our thoughts in the middle of a presentation. While having notes may feel reassuring, they can sometimes cause more anxiety as we try to find the right place in our notes or to read out the relevant section.

If you are presenting and you lose track of what you are saying, you feel you missed something or were not clear, then try not to panic. First, we all have moments like that when giving talks, so every single person in the audience will know exactly how it feels. Second, when we have these moments, it can feel like time is going incredibly slowly and as if we are standing in silence for a long time. I can tell you with absolute certainty that what feels like hours to you will look like a moment of contemplation and reflection to the audience. If that happens, take a deep breath, look at your slides, and pick back up again where you left off. When you are practising your talk and you make a mistake, it can be tempting to stop and start again from the beginning. Try not to do this, and instead practise pausing and picking back up again. This way, if it does happen during your actual presentation, you have experienced continuing with the talk and it will feel more natural and less stressful.

It is important to practise your talk enough so that you can give your presentation within the time allowed, being comfortable enough with the content that you do not need any notes and confident enough to manage any nerves that you may experience when standing in front of the audience. When you practise, make sure that you are standing up and try to walk around a little because this can help to manage your nerves. Also practise making eye contact with people in the audience. At every conference, you will find a few kind people in the audience who will actively try to make eye contact with the presenter, and who will smile and nod reassuringly in the right places. Look for these people and, if you have a moment where you need some reassurance, try to make eye contact with them during your presentation! Try not to over-practise though. Once you have a couple of practise runs that have gone well, stop practising and try to relax a little.

Once you have finished your presentation, the audience is usually invited to ask you questions about your talk. Some people find the questions more nerve-racking than the actual presentation because it is not as easy to prepare for and you don't necessarily know what questions will be asked. While being nervous about the questions from the audience is natural, there are quite a few things that you can do to help prepare for these. Also, remember that you are the expert – no one knows your research project better than you do!

First, remember that you probably had to cut parts of your full research report to fit your talk into the time allowed. Very often, the questions asked are seeking more detail on particular aspects of the presentation. Don't be afraid to move back in your slides to the relevant section of your talk to help you answer the question. Doing this gives you the information on the slide to help you with your explanation, but it also gives you a few moments to gather your thoughts before answering the question. Another strategy that many people adopt is to include additional slides after their closing slide that they can then use during the discussion. For example, if you needed to cut some of the methodology or analysis to fit within the time allowed, you can still make a slide that summarizes these and introduce it after your closing slide. Then, when an audience member asks you to clarify a particular point around your methodological choices or analyses, you can magically present a slide with all the relevant information on it.

Second, you do not need to know the answer to every possible question. It is absolutely fine to say that you need a moment to think about something, or to say that you are not sure about the answer to a question. Try to keep your answers as focused as possible, and try not to feel under pressure to give a really long and elaborate answer. You've just finished giving a talk, so your brain is likely to be very tired and may not work at full capacity! If someone pushes for further elaboration or raises a particularly complex point, it is fine to suggest catching up after the talk to discuss the issues further. Most people are genuinely excited and interested in research, and will ask questions because they want to know the answer. However, occasionally, there will be a difficult person who relishes the opportunity to 'look smarter' than others. If you are unfortunate enough to be in this position, try not to let it throw your confidence. Everyone else in the audience will be able to see it and they will be on your side. I had an experience like this at the first conference I ever presented at, and it dented my confidence for a long time. In hindsight, I wish I had paid less attention to that person and been able to see that they were just unpleasant, and that the interaction reflected more on them than it did on me and my research. Often, people will ask a question based on their own experience and expertise, and this may be in a very different research area from your own. So, it may feel as though some questions are tricky to answer, but that is not due to your not knowing the 'right' answer. Often discussions focus on new research findings and we are all trying to work out how various findings and areas of psychological research fit together to tell us something meaningful about how people think, feel, and behave. Try to think about the time after your talk as more like a discussion and less like an interrogation, and it can sometimes be quite fun!

Poster presentations

An alternative way of presenting your research within a conference setting is a poster presentation, and some universities use posters as a form of authentic assessment (an assessment that develops 'real life skills'), so you may already have some experience in creating a poster. For a conference, you make up a poster to summarize your research study (more on this in a bit), which you then put up in a room at some point during a conference for people to look at. Typically, there are a large number of posters presented within a session, and they may be left up for a while, but usually with a specified time when the authors are available to discuss their poster. In some conferences, this may be done during a break between the oral presentations, and there may be drinks during the poster session. It is usually intended to be quite a relaxed and informal way to present your research at a conference, and often early-career researchers will do a few poster presentations before doing an oral one. However, bear in mind that you can be discussing your work and answering questions for quite a long time with a poster, so make sure you have eaten and have plenty of water with you! Presenting a poster can be a nice way to start attending conferences and sharing your research with others.

Formatting and structuring a poster presentation

When you do a poster presentation, much of the work happens well in advance of the conference itself because you will need to create your poster and get it printed up in time to travel to the conference. Alternatively, you may be presenting at an online conference, so you would need to check on the digital formatting requirements. Before even starting to think about how you will put your poster together, first check on the conference's formatting requirements. Usually, they will have some kind of guidance document, and this will include the dimensions of the poster boards at the conference. It is important that you design your poster with these dimensions in mind so that the presentation itself goes smoothly and so makes the whole process as stress-free as possible for you!

For example, are the poster boards in portrait or landscape format, and what size are they? You need to start your poster design with these two facts in mind. Otherwise, your poster may not fit onto the boards that are available! Most often, posters are printed on large pieces of strong paper or cardboard, which means that you will need to get yours printed up before you leave. Check with your department or university library as to whether they have poster-printing facilities. Alternatively, there are several companies online whereby you can send a PDF of your poster and they will print it and post it back to you. Leave a couple of weeks for this, just in case of any printing delays. You will also need a poster tube to safely transport your poster to the conference. If your poster has been printed and sent to you by a company, it will probably come in a poster tube, but, if you are getting it printed at the university, you will need to either buy a poster tube or ask your supervisor if they have one you can borrow. Some conferences are now running poster sessions using large monitors where presenters can show their poster and, for this style of presentation, you would just need your poster digitally to share in the session or they may ask you to submit it in advance.

But, back to actually creating your poster! In many ways, it is just creating a very concise version of your research paper, and most posters follow the usual structure of Abstract,

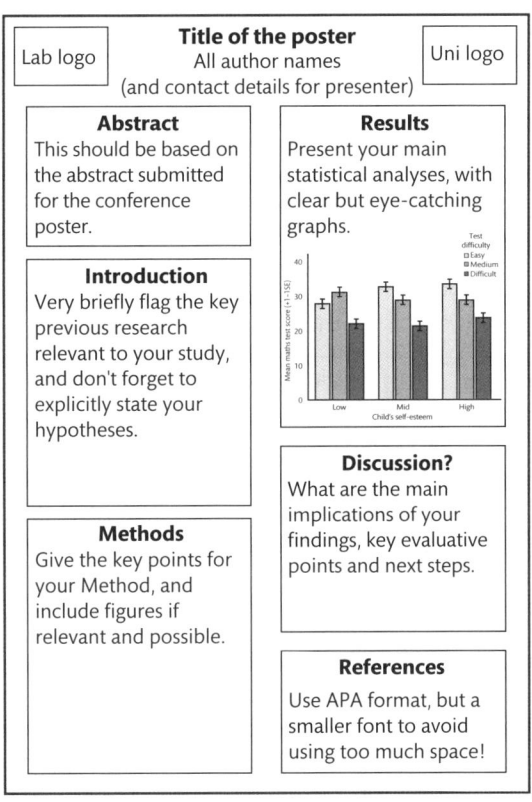

Figure 10.3 Example template for a simple format portrait orientation poster

Introduction, Methods, Results, Discussion, and References, with each of these presented within self-contained boxes on the poster. Sometimes, you will see sections broken into smaller ones to make the information easier to digest quickly. Two examples of how a poster may be presented are shown in Figure 10.3 and Figure 10.4. In Figure 10.3, you can see that the format is portrait and the sections adhere to the standard APA article sections, whereas in Figure 10.4 the format is landscape and I've broken down the main sections into smaller parts. There isn't a single 'right' way to put a poster together, so chat through your ideas with your supervisor when planning out how to structure yours. Depending on your area of research, you may need a larger 'block' for one particular part of the poster, so try not to stick too rigidly to any examples you might see – instead, think about how to most clearly present your research and what works for you. There are editable PowerPoint files with each of these templates in the online resources for this book, so you can download these and play with how they look, if that would be helpful to you.

How you actually create your poster depends on what packages you are most used to and prefer, but many people use PowerPoint because it is flexible and easy to use. Simply make the size of the page appropriate for the poster you need (do this by customizing the slide size in the 'Design' template) and put the various components in place. You will also need to pick a theme or colour scheme for your poster. Some institutions have recommended colour

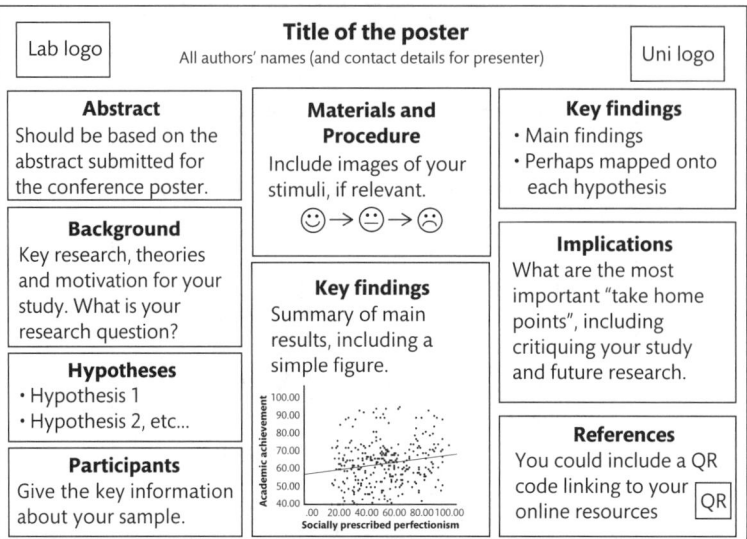

Figure 10.4 Example template for a more detailed format landscape orientation poster

schemes, formatting, and logos for people to use, so look through your university's website to see whether there is helpful material that you can use. It can also be useful to consider how the colour scheme you choose might look to someone who is colour-blind, and there are various websites where you can upload a document to simulate how it would look and to ensure that it will be fully accessible to all. Your supervisor may have templates that are used for research presentations by people working in their lab, so it is worth asking what they already have available.

However you choose to format your poster, it is important to acknowledge all the relevant people and groups who have supported the research you are to present. You should identify both your institution and the department and/or lab that you have been working in. This is most easily done by using the relevant logos and including them at the top of your poster. If the research was funded, then this also needs to be acknowledged on the poster. Finally, you should name all the researchers involved in the project who are co-authors and clearly identify who is the presenting author. It is also important to provide contact details, either for yourself or for your supervisor, so that anyone interested in your research knows who to go to with further questions. This should include an email address as a minimum, but links to social media accounts can also be a helpful way of developing research links with others.

Developing the content of your poster

When you have set up the overall structure and format of your poster, the next step is to think about the content. In many ways, a poster is a very condensed version of your full paper. Each section of a standard research report should be reflected in a poster, but with a focus on highlighting the key points. You will probably need to decide on certain details to leave out of the poster itself, so try to think carefully about the most important theoretical and methodological points you need to establish, and then what are the most important findings and implications. With a poster, it is often better to avoid using too much text and to use figures as much as possible. So, try to think about how best to communicate your methods and findings through images. When text is necessary, such as in explaining the theoretical background, hypotheses, and implications, using bullet point lists can help to break up information for the reader. Finally, think carefully about the font style and size that you use. Remember that most people will be looking at your poster from a short distance away, so try standing back from your draft poster to make sure that the font is simple and large enough to be read. When looking at your poster, it is important that it is eye-catching because you want people to notice it, but you also need it to convey your research project clearly so try not to make it too busy or distracting. Simple and straightforward is best, and remember that people are there to ask you more about your research – you do not need to include too much detail on the poster. Save some of the exciting and more nuanced aspects for your discussions with other people attending the poster session of the conference. The first time you create a poster, try to leave plenty of time to work on it, because it can be quite challenging and different from other pieces of work you may have done (see Box 10.1 for an example of this).

Presenting your poster at a conference

Once you are at the conference, you also want to think about how you will attach your poster to the poster board. Often the conference will provide each presenter with some pins, blue tack or Velcro dots, but it can be a good idea to take some with you, just in case! Arrive at the poster session with plenty of time to find the board that you have been allocated (each poster board is usually numbered and the number is included in the conference programme), put your poster up, and get comfortable for the session. Have a bottle of water handy as you will probably end up chatting a lot about your research project during the poster session.

During the discussion time, people are likely to approach you and ask questions about your study. Mainly, people will just ask for more detail about your project and this is likely to relate to the full information in the write-up that you had to cut for the poster. Make sure that you read through your full project a couple of times before the poster session so that the details are fresh in your mind, and you may want to have a copy with you in case you need to double-check something. Occasionally, people will ask you to summarize your poster to avoid their having to read it, so it can be helpful to prepare and practise a two-minute summary of the key points that you want to make.

The moment everyone dreads is when someone asks an awkward question! You don't need to know the answer to every question and to have considered every implication of your study. It is totally fine to say that you don't know the answer to something, or to say that a particular issue hadn't occurred to you before. If this does happen, maybe ask the person to email you with their thoughts so that you can get back to them with a more considered option. Or, if they are not the friendliest communicator, you can always suggest that they get in touch with your supervisor for a more in-depth conversation about the issues they have raised!

The final aspect to think about is what happens after the conference, and how you can facilitate people getting in touch with you if they want to find out more about your project. It can be helpful for people to be able to go away from the session with a copy of your poster. This could be as simple as you having some printed A4 copies of the poster with you as handouts. Alternatively, you could create a QR code online, embed that into your poster and have this link to a webpage where you can have a copy of your poster. Within this link, you might also want to think about alternative ways of presenting your poster so that it is more accessible. For example, you may want to create a version that is compatible with screen readers, or perhaps make a short video of you talking through the poster. You can also include your contact details and social media accounts, which may help with building networks, either for research or for your career development. The ideal poster presentation is one that leads to further conversations.

10.4 Sharing your research

While much research is shared through journals and conferences, it is important to share your work as widely as you can so that it gets seen by others and hopefully cited by researchers in subsequent publications and conferences. Many academics are very active on various social media platforms, and this can be a great way to share your research as well as becoming part of the wider academic community. Make sure that you follow the key researchers in the area you are interested in, and be active in replying to posts and sharing content from others. Not only will this allow you to have a better understanding of the current research that is being done, it will also give you a wider platform for sharing your own research. Also think about non-academic communities that may be interested in your research, and consider how to promote the potential application and impact of the work you have done.

If you get a paper published in a journal, this is a big achievement and something to share as widely as you can. Post about your publication; share a link to where the paper can be found; give some of the key highlights; maybe include a figure from the paper. If you are presenting at a conference, post about it, include pictures from your poster session, and also share information about other talks that you attend and which you find interesting.

Building your academic profile on social media can also be beneficial when you start applying for jobs. Nowadays, many people include their social media accounts in their job applications, and potential employers may look through your posts to get a feel for your research interests and the kind of work that you do. So use your social media to create a good impression of who you are as a researcher.

Sometimes we focus so much on the academic community that it is easy to forget that there is a whole world outside academia, but, as researchers, we also have a social responsibility to share our research findings and expertise with the general public. If we embed social responsibility into our academic practice, sharing research with and involving the public in research is an incredibly valuable, and often incredibly rewarding, action that we can take. There are many ways that we can share our research more widely, whether that is online through blogs and videos shared in places like YouTube, or in-person through Science Festivals or initiatives such as Pint of Science, whereby academics discuss their research in pubs across the UK. It is always important to remember that research is never about doing a single study. We only get a broader understanding of how people think, feel, and behave when we draw together findings from different studies, different research groups, and different communities. By sharing our research with academic and wider public audiences, we all contribute to the broader development of our understanding of psychology. You can see some further hints and tips in Box 10.2.

PRESENTING YOUR RESEARCH

BOX 10.1 An example of how to recognize, reflect, and relate your IT skill development

Reflecting on your transferable skills and personal attributes
An example – IT skills

Recognize: From the research you have conducted, what is the best example of when you have demonstrated this skill or attribute?

At the end of our degree, the department ran a conference where students could give poster presentations about their research project. I decided to do this, even though I was quite nervous about it. I made my poster in PowerPoint and, although I had used it before, the way that I needed to structure the poster and present lots of information on one page pushed me to learn new functions in PowerPoint and to take a different approach to visualizing information.

Reflect: What are my strengths with regard to this skill or attribute? How can I further develop or improve them?

I feel that I was good at creating images to represent different elements of my research project. For example, I created a figure showing the timeline of one trial within the experiment that we ran.

Relate: Imagine you are being interviewed for your dream job or course. How would your skills in this area make you suitable for this position?

In my first attempt at creating the poster, I tried to squeeze too much information in. I had to rethink what information was essential and the best way to present it clearly.

BOX 10.2 Hints and tips from psychology graduates and employers of psychology graduates

The student's perspective . . . reflecting on people skills

Although I wasn't able to attend the conference, our group worked really well together and we knew we had complementary skills. Through supporting each other we were able to create an additional paper together. This was then accepted at a conference. It increased the level of work and responsibility, but allowed me to write a better final year project.

Martha, psychology graduate

The employer's perspective . . . reflecting on communication

We require people that communicate complex scientific information in an accessible way for a non-specialist audience. This relies on strong oral and written communication skills. We produce research briefings, which must be concise and also impartial. We often ask applicants to write a sample briefing, or to give us a link to published work. We often ask applicants when they have had to communicate something to a non-specialist audience, so practising communication in different settings is helpful.

Johann, psychological science writer

11 Publishing your research

 In this chapter you will learn . . .
- the process of publishing research papers;
- how to prepare a paper for submission to a journal; and
- about the revisions process and how to respond to reviewers.

Once you have finished your research project, you may well be wondering what comes next. You have completed a research project that is well designed and appropriately analysed, so maybe it could be shared more widely with the world. In Chapter 10, we talked about different ways of sharing your research with others and, in this chapter, we will talk more about the processes of trying to publish your work in a journal. Students' research projects can be publishable, and the best starting point is to discuss this with your supervisor. Publishing can be a long, complicated, and sometimes stressful process. However, publishing research is a huge achievement for any researcher and, as an early career researcher, it is a valuable opportunity to share your hard work with others, both within academia and beyond. Your supervisor will be very experienced in publishing, so they will be an invaluable source of support and information.

It is important to bear in mind that you wrote your research project for educational purposes and, no matter how good it is, you will probably need to make some changes before the manuscript (which is how papers are often referred to during the publication process) can be submitted to a journal. For example, the Introduction may be reduced, or you may need to add some further analyses. Your supervisor may also suggest that your study is combined with other studies, making the paper more substantial and potentially far stronger. When publishing, your paper is likely to become more of a collaborative piece of work, so it can be quite a different writing experience. You will get to further develop some of the skills you gained during your studies, such as planning your work and thinking critically about your research, but you may need guidance from your supervisor to help you develop the resilience and communication skills that are needed through the publication process. In Figure 11.1, you can see a summary of some of the key skills that you will develop and need when publishing your research.

11.1 Pre-registration and Registered Reports

In Chapter 5, we talked a lot about open science and the issues in psychological research that it aims to counter. For example, you may remember about the file drawer problem, where findings that are not significant tend never to be published, so there is little understanding

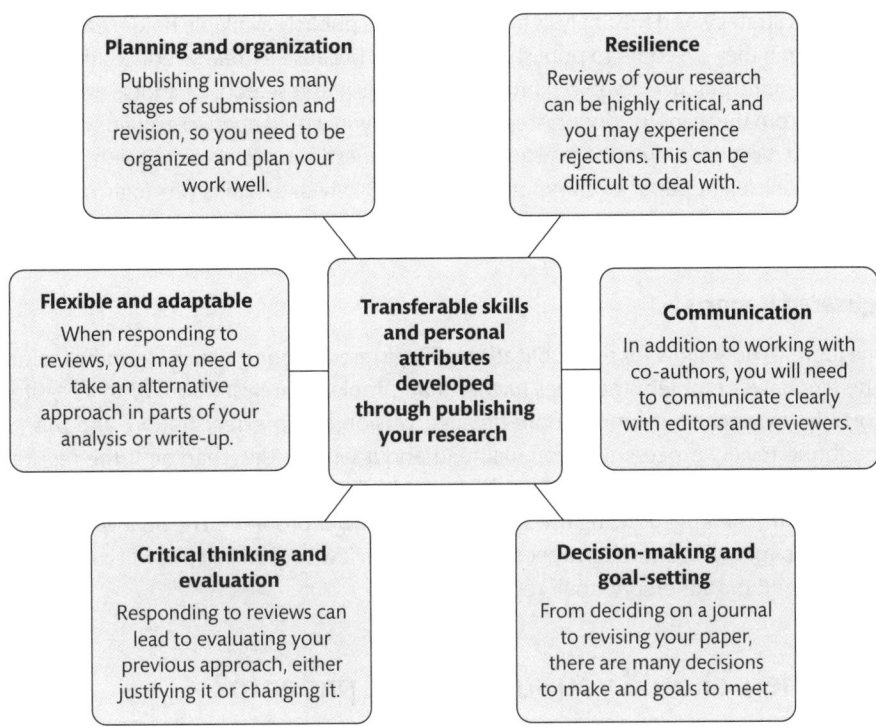

Figure 11.1 Transferable skills and personal attributes developed when publishing your research

of how often psychological research leads to null findings. You may also remember the issues of HARKing and *p*-hacking, whereby people either develop their hypotheses depending on their results or they repeatedly try different analysis strategies until they find a significant result. Open science practices aim to reduce all these problems by encouraging researchers to share their research designs, hypotheses, and analysis strategies before any data are collected. The logic here is that, if a study is well-designed and justified, then the findings should be publicly available, regardless of the findings. This is achieved through pre-registration and Registered Reports. This best practice also maps onto a researcher's responsibility to share their work appropriately, and to ensure that it can be used by others to either further research or to apply the findings in a more real-world and socially responsible manner.

Pre-registration of research studies

Pre-registering a research study involves submitting an overview of a study that you plan to run in advance of actually running it. These summaries are usually submitted to an online and publicly available repository (e.g. the Open Science Framework website[1]) and will include the hypotheses, the main aspects of the design, the variables to be collected, the sampling and

[1] osf.io

recruitment strategy, and the analysis plan. Having this publicly available holds researchers to account when they do come to publish their findings because it greatly reduces the chances of poor scientific practice creeping through into published research. Of course, it is possible to deviate from the plans in your pre-registration, but you would need to explain why this was needed (e.g. Why did you end up using a different questionnaire or recruitment strategy?). There is an excellent paper by Simmons et al. (2021), which explains pre-registration in far more detail in case you want to find out more.

Registered Reports

Some journals now allow for the publication of Registered Reports, which is another solution to the file drawer problem that goes further than simple pre-registration. With a registered report, the researchers submit a more detailed version of a pre-registration, and this goes through the review process that you will read about later in this chapter. If the registered report is accepted for publication, then the journal will publish the findings, even if they are not significant, thereby reducing the size of the file drawer problem. The final version of the completed paper will go through a second round of review, and part of this will consider how closely the authors adhered to their registered plan.

11.2 Where should you submit your paper to?

Your first decision is which journal you should submit your manuscript to. This is something to discuss with your supervisor because they will know the various journals well, so listen to their advice! It is important to bear in mind that researchers often have to submit their manuscript to a few journals before it is eventually published. This is because papers can be rejected, as you will find out later in this chapter. Usually, we start with the 'best' journal that is suitable and, if the paper is rejected, we go to the 'next best' and so on, until our work gets accepted for publication!

Which journal is most suitable for the topic of your research study?

The best indicator of a suitable journal is to look for ones that typically publish research in the area that you have worked in. An easy way to find this out is to look through the references list in your own paper. If the work that you have cited is frequently published in a particular journal, then that is probably one that should make it onto your shortlist of places you could submit to. You may also want to look at where your supervisor and other well-known researchers in the area have published. One point to bear in mind is that journals can differ a lot in the breadth of the work that they publish. Some are very broad and publish across a range of psychological research topics, whereas others are far more specialized and tend to only publish research that fits within a very specific area of interest. The more generalized journals can be perceived as 'better' because they attract a broader readership, whereas the more niche journals can have a narrower readership. But what determines the quality of a journal? How do we know which journals are 'good' and which are 'less good'?

Is there a standardized way to judge journal quality?

Judging a journal's quality is actually quite a controversial topic within psychological research. There are metrics that are intended to convey the 'quality' of a journal, but many researchers are sceptical about this. There are lots of ways that you can judge a journal and the papers that are published in it, such as the number of downloads or shares through social media. However, the main metric is the impact factor of a journal. These are relatively easy to find on most journal websites, or you can trace them through databases such as Web of Science. The impact factor of a journal is based on citation information, working on the assumption that, if the papers in a journal are cited frequently, then that must mean that the research, the paper, and the journal are of high quality. You can see how an impact factor is calculated in Figure 11.2, along with examples of a lower impact factor (fewer citations per paper published) and a higher impact factor (more citations per paper published).

While impact factors can be used to judge the quality of a journal, it is important to not rely on them too heavily because there are a few issues with impact factors. First, they assume that work being highly cited is a positive outcome, but what if a piece of research is particularly controversial and therefore highly cited by other researchers being highly critical of the work? Second, going back to there being more generalized and more specialized journals, this can influence a journal's impact factor, because a generalized journal has a wider readership and therefore the work is more likely to be read and cited. In contrast, a paper in a specialist journal may not attract the same level of attention and readership. Consequently, it is always good to bear in mind the target audience of a journal if using the impact factor to judge its quality. Third, there can be big differences in impact factors across different disciplines, or even within different areas of psychology. This can be a consequence of the impact factor only using citations from the previous two years. This means that research that takes longer, such as longitudinal research, may take longer to become highly cited. This is because longitudinal research takes a long time to complete, so it may not be published and citing a

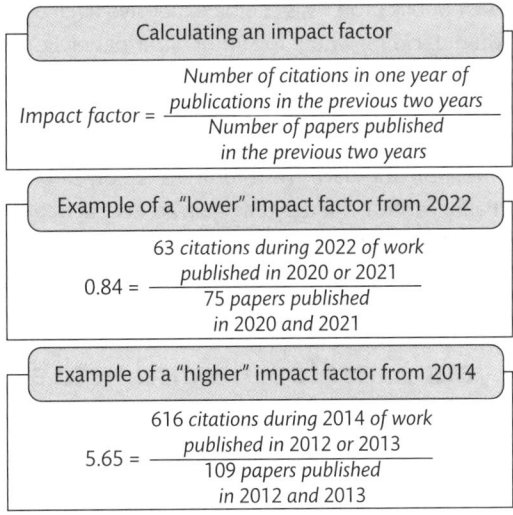

Figure 11.2 Calculating journal impact factors

highly relevant paper for a few years. If the citation in other publications is 'delayed' due to the type of research, those citations won't happen until after the impact factor for that year of publication has happened and so, effectively, won't count towards the impact factor. So, if you look through psychology journal impact factors, you may notice that developmental and educational journals sometimes have lower impact factors than cognitive and neuroscience journals. This difference is absolutely not a direct result of one area of psychological research being 'better' than the other, just a reflection on the length of time that different types of research can take. So, while impact factors can be a useful tool in thinking about journal quality, they should certainly not be the only deciding factor in where to submit to.

Do you pay to publish? Or does the reader pay to access your paper?

Publishers of journals are typically businesses and this means that they need to cover all of the expenses incurred through publishing (e.g. paying staff, website maintenance). There are two main ways that this is achieved. The more traditional route is through the reader paying to access a journal. Your university library will have subscribed to the key psychology journals, which means they will pay an annual fee so that all members of that university can freely access all the papers published by that journal. If your university does not subscribe to a journal, or if you are not a member of an academic institution, then there is usually also the option of paying to access an individual article. Assuming that you are a student at a university: before paying for any paper, do check whether your university has an interlibrary loan service because this will give you free access to any paper even if your library does not subscribe to that journal.

More recently, partly due to the move towards open science, there has been a large push towards published research papers being freely available to readers. This is known as 'open access' and means anyone can read that piece of research. This is particularly important in allowing research to be accessed by individuals or organizations outside academia, and can provide a way in which academic research can contribute to advancing social causes. However, the publisher still needs to cover their costs and, in this situation, it is typically the researcher who will cover the costs of publication. This can be expensive (well over £1,000), so discuss it with your supervisor when deciding where to submit your paper. Some academics will have funds available to pay for open access publication through their research grants, or some universities will make funds available to allow for research from their institution to be published in high-quality, open access journals. Just be careful, because there are now a large number of what are known as 'predatory journals'. These journals rapidly publish research papers with very little review and quality control, but they charge a great deal to publish in them. It can be difficult to distinguish between a predatory journal and a genuine journal that has open access, so do consult your supervisor if the possibility of needing to pay for publication ever comes up.

11.3 Preparing your paper for submission to a journal

When you wrote up your research project, your focus would have been on the educational aspects that you needed to meet. However, the requirements may be different when you submit your paper to a journal. Typically, journals will expect APA formatting, but this is not always the case. There may be specific requirements for the word length of the paper or the length of particular sections, and you should check whether the length includes the references or not. Some journals also allow supplemental materials to be submitted, which are not part of the paper but can add more detail, such as to the methods or results. Each journal will have a website that clearly sets out its requirements, and it is important that you follow this because a paper can be rejected just for not following the journal's specified format. Good attention to detail, planning, and critical thinking are essential at this stage, so please do take the time to check on the requirements and ensure that you follow them precisely.

Getting feedback on your paper

When preparing your paper, it is helpful to get as much feedback from experienced researchers as possible. They can identify possible issues that you can try to resolve before submitting the paper and either the editor or a reviewer picking up on them. Your supervisor is likely to give you good feedback on the paper, and they may also ask other academics in their lab, their department, or their wider research network to comment on it. While it can sometimes feel uncomfortable receiving feedback on your paper, this can be invaluable to give your paper the best chance of being published in a good journal.

Authorship decisions

It is incredibly unlikely that you will be the only author on the paper. Your supervisor will be a co-author and others may also be involved in transforming your student research project into a published piece of work. For example, if your study is combined with other studies, then the other researchers will join as co-authors. If you conducted your study in your supervisor's lab, used materials developed by other researchers in the lab, or worked closely with other researchers in the lab, then they may also be co-authors. The key point is that each author needs to have made a real contribution towards the paper, and some journals actually ask for this to be specified – for example, whether each author was involved in the design, preparation of materials, collection and analysis of data, and/or the preparation of the manuscript.

It is best to have an open and honest discussion about authorship and any other possible authors. The key discussions are likely to be around who will be first author and last author. First author is often seen as preferable because this will be the primary author. However, the last author can also be a prestigious role because this is often the most senior researcher who oversees the entire paper. You will also need to agree on who will be the corresponding author: the person who communicates with the journal and the editor through the review process, and the one who is flagged in the published paper for people to get in touch with if they have any questions. This is likely to be your supervisor, because the corresponding author is typically the more senior researcher and someone with more experience in publishing research.

Submitting your paper to a journal

Once your manuscript is ready to submit, there are some final tasks that you will need to do to allow you to submit. The corresponding author usually completes that actual submission, but they may ask for your help in preparing the additional items needed. For example, you may need to submit two versions of the paper, one with your names included and one that is anonymized. Some journals also ask you to submit the cover page, the abstract, and sometimes other parts of the manuscript as individual files. Finally, you need to submit a covering letter with your manuscript. This is a short letter to the editor, typically around a page long, in which you very briefly summarize the key findings of your research and why they are important, as well as confirming that your work received appropriate ethical approval and that it has not been published elsewhere, which would be considered academic dishonesty. Your supervisor will have written a few covering letters so they will be able to guide you in this process.

11.4 The review process

When you submit your paper to a journal, the process will be overseen by an editor. Often a journal has a few different editors, and they will all be well-established academics who work and frequently publish in the area of research that the journal specializes in. The editorial board of any journal will be shown on the journal's website. When you submit your paper, it will be allocated to a specific editor and they will oversee the whole review process. This is the person you will communicate with throughout the review process, and you can see a summary of the entire process in Figure 11.3.

The first stage of editorial review

When an editor first receives your paper, they will read it through with two questions in mind. First, does the research topic fit the remit of the journal? They may decide that it is not suitable for the journal and reject it on this basis. This does not necessarily reflect on the quality of your paper, so try not to be too disheartened if your paper is rejected for this reason. Resilience is a good skill to try to build, especially if you are considering going into academia as

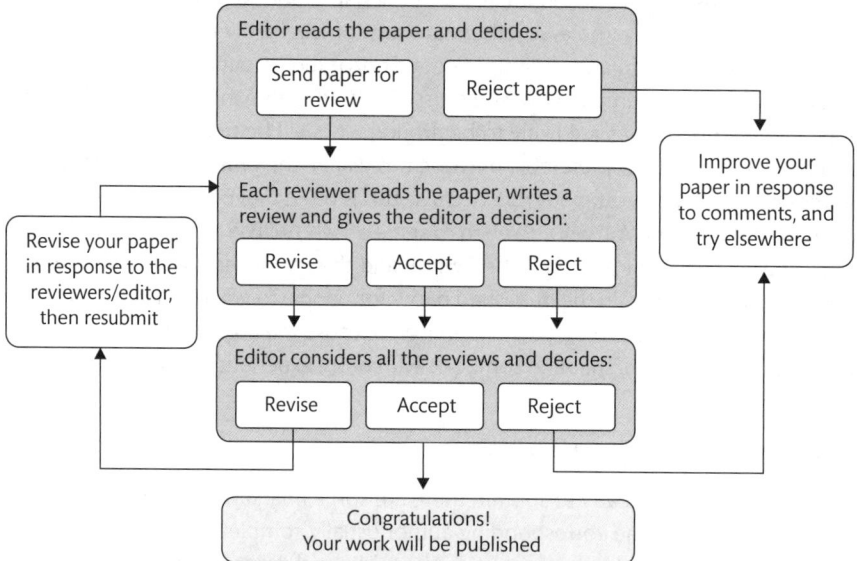

Figure 11.3 The process of publishing a research paper

a career, because we often have to deal with rejections and disappointing decisions. A large number of papers can be rejected at this stage and a rejection does not mean that your work will never be published. However, the editor may decide that your paper has some fundamental flaws that mean it is very unlikely to be accepted following a full review process. This outcome is more upsetting to receive, but the editor will usually give you a short explanation as to why they have rejected your paper. You can use this to improve your paper before submitting it to a different journal.

Papers are often submitted to a couple of different journals before finally being accepted for publication. So, while it may be difficult to receive the bad news of rejection, this does not mean that your paper will never be published, just that it will not be published in that particular journal. When the editor rejects a paper directly, this is sometimes called a 'desk reject'. However, if the editor decides that your paper fits the remit of the journal and is potentially of publishable quality, then they will send your paper out to review by two or three academics who have published research that is relevant to your subject.

The role of the reviewer is to critically evaluate your paper to determine whether it is of high enough quality for publication, and what revisions you would need to make to raise its standard to publishable quality. Depending on the journal you submit to, the review process may be 'blind' in that the reviewers' names are not revealed to the authors (although some reviewers will include their name in their review). This allows more junior reviewers to be honest in their review without worrying about upsetting a more senior researcher, who may later be reviewing their papers or may even be their boss! Some journals also insist that the papers are anonymized before going to review, so the reviewers do not know who the authors are. This ensures that well-known researchers do not have advantages in publishing over more junior researchers (i.e. the assumption that a paper from a well-known researcher is of higher quality than a paper by a more junior researcher). Even if the review process is fully anonymized, it is the role of the editor to ensure that the review process is fair.

The main reviews and editorial decision

Once a reviewer has agreed to review your paper, they will take the time to carefully read through it and to think critically about the novelty and relevance of your research question, the rigour of your design and analysis, and the implications of your interpretation of your findings. Each reviewer will write a review that is typically quite lengthy, often one or two pages long. This will summarize the factors that the reviewer sees as the particular strengths of your paper as well as its potential flaws and weaknesses.

With all this in mind, the reviewers will conclude with one of three possible decisions. 1: Accept the paper without revisions. This is exceptionally rare because it means that they feel your paper is ready for publication and needs no improvements, additions, or changes at all. 2: Revise and resubmit: This is a good outcome because it means that the reviewer believes that your paper is publishable, as long as you address the key points that they raise in their review. 3: Reject. This is the one we all hope to avoid because it means that the reviewer considers that your paper is not of publishable quality and that any changes you might make will not improve it enough to make it publishable. This may be due to a fundamental flaw in your design, which means that you would need to run the study again with an improved design for the work to be potentially publishable.

Once the editor has received sufficient reviews on your paper, usually two to four, they will read through it again, along with the reviews, and then make a final decision. This will typically be either a 'revise and resubmit' or a 'reject' decision because outright acceptances from an editor are exceptionally rare (other than perhaps when you submit to student journals, which tend to be a little nicer!). If the editor decides to reject your paper, they will usually give you the main reasons why. There might be a particularly fundamental flaw identified by one reviewer, or perhaps an issue that was raised by multiple reviewers. If this happens, then you can use this feedback to improve your paper before trying to publish it with a different journal. If you do receive an invitation to revise and resubmit your paper, then the editor will usually identify what they see as the key issues that you need to address in your revision in order to improve your paper to a publishable standard. At this stage, it is helpful to chat with your supervisor and any other co-authors to decide whether the revisions requested are achievable and, if so, whether to try to revise and resubmit the paper to the journal.

Responding to reviews and resubmitting your paper

If you are invited to revise and resubmit your paper, and if you choose to do this, then there is usually a deadline for the submission of your revision. In addition to revising your paper, you need to submit a letter to the editor in which you respond to all the reviewers' comments. This letter is very important and it can be a deciding factor as to whether the editor ultimately accepts your revised paper. In your letter, it is usually good to start with a summary of the key aspects you have addressed in your revision, and here you should pick up on any points that the editor has flagged. Remember that these are the issues that the editor felt were the most important based on the reviews and their own reading of your paper, so you need to include a clear account of how you considered them in your revision.

When responding to each reviewer, it is helpful to break down each review into individual points (maybe number them, if the reviewer has not already done so). In your response letter, it is helpful to include the reviewer's comment, and then to respond to it, explaining how you have revised your paper (or not) and where the changes can be found in the text. You can see an example of how this might look in Figure 11.4. While it is important to respond to each point raised, you do not necessarily have to do everything that the reviewer suggests. It is often good to follow their advice, but there may be some points where you disagree and feel that the suggested revisions would not be appropriate. This is when it is vital to discuss the reviews and your responses with your supervisor, because they will have been through this process before and will have a good feel for how best to address each point.

Quite often, the reviewers will make a good suggestion that will improve your paper, and here you would simply need to explain how you have integrated the revision, as in the response to Reviewer 1 in Figure 11.4. Sometimes, they will raise a point that may be relevant, but you may not want to make any substantial changes to your paper as a result of the comment. Here, it is very important to clearly justify and explain your decision not to make any major changes, while addressing aspects of it wherever possible, and you can sometimes add some supplementary analyses for the reviewers, like the response to Reviewer 3 in Figure 11.4. Occasionally, a reviewer may ask for a change that you disagree with. It may be that they have misunderstood something in your paper. In this situation, the appropriate revision would be to add clarity around the misunderstood issue to ensure that other readers do

Reviewer 1 comment: The Introduction clearly addresses the main aims of the study, but I wonder if the work of Smith and Cadbury might strengthen the justification for this alternative methodology.

Response to reviewer 1, comment d: We appreciate the reviewer's suggestion to consider the work of Smith and Cadbury, and have now integrated some of this work into our Introduction to further justify our choice of questionnaire (see pages 8-9).

Reviewer 2 comment: While some evaluative issues are raised in the Discussion, I was surprised that they did not consider the impact of personality. According to Jones and Lindt, this is essential and may render these findings null and void.

Response to reviewer 2, comment m: While we accept that there are likely to be a number of unmeasured confounding variables in our design, we feel that the work of Jones and Lindt is not directly applicable to our study, as their work was based on clinical samples, while our participants were non-clinical. Nevertheless, we concede that personality is a potential confound, and we briefly consider this in the Discussion (see page 26).

Reviewer 3 comment: While the analyses address the key research questions, I suspect that the parametric assumptions will have been violated. Therefore I believe the analyses are inappropriate.

Response to reviewer 3, comment e: We have evaluated all the parametric assumptions and all are met within our dataset. We have now included a paragraph in the Results to summarize these additional analyses (see page 19). Additionally, we have analysed the data using non-parametric approaches, and the findings are unchanged. While we felt that this would not enhance the paper, we have included the findings at the end of these reviews to reassure the reviewer.

Figure 11.4 Responding to reviewers' comments when revising and resubmitting a paper

not have a similar misunderstanding. If you do choose to not make changes in response to a reviewer, then you need to clearly explain and justify why, such as with Reviewer 2 in Figure 11.4. Your supervisor can help you frame your points, and ultimately this can help you to develop your critical thinking and communication skills (Box 11.1).

Remember that the review process is intended to improve your paper and, while reviews can feel harsh, they usually do lead to an improved version. It is not unusual to have a strong emotional response to reviews. You may initially feel angry or upset at some of the comments made, as when you receive a disappointing mark on an assessment! All academics have the same kind of emotional response to reviews, no matter how experienced they are in publishing papers and dealing with reviewers. Sometimes, it helps to put the reviews to one side for a couple of days, while the emotions calm a little, and then arrange to discuss them with your supervisor. You may even be reassured to see their own emotional response to the reviews. If you want to find out more about how academics can feel about this process, do an internet search for 'Reviewer Two', who has come to represent the grumpy and negative reviewer that we all hope not to encounter! If you do happen to get a 'Reviewer Two', please try to remember that we have all had this experience, and that their comments do not reflect on you as an individual or as a researcher. Your supervisor will have been through this many times and they will be able to help you discuss the best way to respond.

11.5 What happens after your paper is accepted for publication?

Once your paper is officially accepted for publication, there is still some more waiting and work to be done before you can celebrate publishing your work! The next step is receiving the proofs of your paper, where the journal will have converted your submitted document into the journal format. This is when you will see your work actually looking like a published paper. The proofs are usually sent to the corresponding author and, as we discussed earlier, this will probably be your supervisor although they may involve you in this process.

When you receive the proofs, you are likely to get a number of queries from the publisher, which will be issues or inconsistencies that they have identified while making the proofs. For example, you may have referenced Smith and Jones (2014) in the text of the paper but included Smith and Jones (2015) in your references list – which is the correct reference? You will need to respond to every author query when you return the proofs. You will also need to read through your proofs to check very carefully for any final errors or typos. Importantly, you will not be able to make any substantive changes to your paper, such as adding a paragraph or rewriting a sentence. This stage is purely for identifying any errors in your accepted paper before it is officially published.

There can sometimes be quite a long delay between the email from the editor saying that your paper is accepted for publication and your being asked to review the proofs. When this does happen, there is usually a very short turnaround for you to review and return the proofs. This is because the publishers usually have deadlines to meet for the publication of each journal issue. There can then be another delay before your paper is officially published, but more journals now have an 'in press' section on their website, where they have all the accepted and proofed papers that are waiting to be published. When this happens, your paper will have a year of publication, issue, volume, page numbers, and a digital object identifier (doi). You are now officially a published author – congratulations!

Sharing your research with others

Now that your work is published, there are just three things left to do. First, it is always good to follow the principles of open science, so you should make your raw data and any code you used for your analysis publicly available. Depending on where you publish, you may be able to do this alongside the online version of your paper at the publisher's website. Otherwise, you can use a site such as psyarxiv.com or your supervisor's research lab page. Second, publicize your paper so that people know it is published and available. X (previously Twitter) is a great place to do this because many academics use X and there is a strong academic community there. Include a link to the paper and a summary of the key methods and findings, add in some eye-catching figures and relevant hashtags, and you can easily share your findings with the wider academic community. If your research has the potential to be applied outside academia and to be used by others to have an impact in the real world, try to think about which audiences are most appropriate to share your work with. Third, but possibly most importantly, celebrate your fantastic achievement of publishing a paper! Publishing is not easy, and you can see some further hints and tips in Box 11.2. It takes a long time, much hard work, and a good dose of emotional resilience. Even established academics, who have been through the process a few times, can find it difficult. However, getting your work published is a fantastic achievement and definitely something to celebrate!

> **BOX 11.1 An example of how to recognize, reflect, and relate your skill development around communication**
>
> **Reflecting on your transferable skills and personal attributes**
> An example – communication
>
> **Recognize:** From the research you have conducted, what is the best example of when you have demonstrated this skill or attribute?
>
> I was asked to revise and resubmit the paper I submitted to a journal. Working on the revisions to the paper wasn't too bad, but writing the response letter to the reviewers was very different to anything I had done before. My supervisor helped me to develop appropriate ways to communicate the changes made to the paper in response to the reviews.
>
> **Reflect:** What are my strengths with regard to this skill or attribute? How can I further develop or improve them?
>
> I felt that I was good at explaining the changes I had made to the paper where I could understand and agree with the reviewer's comments. Here I was able to write clear and well-structured responses.
>
> **Relate:** Imagine you are being interviewed for your dream job or course. How would your skills in this area make you suitable for this position?
>
> I found it far more difficult to write the responses when I disagreed with the reviewer's suggestions, and to communicate this in a clear and considered way. My supervisor was very helpful in giving me hints and tips about how to communicate my response in a thoughtful way.

> **BOX 11.2 Hints and tips from psychology graduates and employers of psychology graduates**
>
> The student's perspective . . . reflecting on being flexible and adaptable
>
> In the process of publishing, I learnt to manage my time and do more research beyond the typical readings around my research topic. Since it doubled the responsibility on each member of the group to go beyond what they had written, it made us all confident in the end piece of published research and allowed us to write better for our own final year project.
>
> Oliver, psychology graduate
>
> The employer's perspective . . . reflecting on critical thinking
>
> Written communication skills are the most important part of the job. The ability to summarize and evaluate data, and explain statistical findings clearly is essential. Therefore, experience writing research reports, and possibly even publishing their work, looks very strong in a job application.
>
> Achara, educational psychologist

12 Using your research project to benefit your career and beyond

 In this chapter you will learn . . .

- about the importance of *recognizing*, *reflecting* on, and *relating* the skills you developed during your project to your next career step;
- how these skills can benefit your career and your personal development; and
- where to get advice for your career development.

This final chapter is about using your final year project to benefit yourself and others after you graduate from university. In the previous chapters, we focused on specific aspects of your project and specific skills that your project will help you develop. We tried to highlight that your project will help you develop highly specialized research skills as well as many more generic transferable skills. In this chapter, I (Danijela) encourage you to think about your project as a whole and what it can do for your career. In addition, we will go a step further and think about how these skills can benefit you (personal development) as well as others (social responsibility). For you to do this, you first need to be able to *recognize* and *reflect* on your skills (see Figure 12.1). This might not always be an easy thing to do, so in this chapter we will break down this process. We encourage you to read this chapter even if you are at the early stages of your project. This will help you become aware of the learning and skill development that is taking place during your final year project. This chapter will help you engage with the process, monitor, and *reflect* on your skill development, as well as helping you to make adjustments and improvements where needed.

12.1 Understanding the skills you have developed

As illustrated in Figure 12.1, when thinking about your skill development, it is helpful to envisage this as a process and break it down into three stages or steps: *recognizing* skills, *reflecting* on your skills, and *relating* or applying your skills. We call them the '3Rs'. Note that this process is not always linear. For example, you may find yourself in a situation (e.g. preparing for a job interview) where you need to map out (*relate*) your skills to the job requirements. But then you suddenly realize that – for some skills – you do not have much to say. At this point, it would be good for you to take a step back and *reflect* on those skills (i.e. to assess

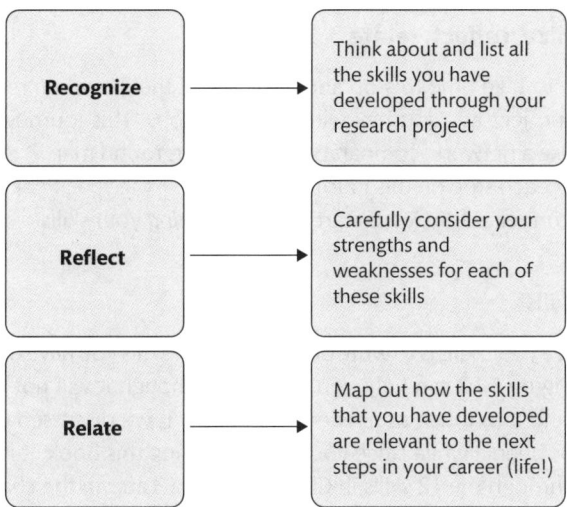

Figure 12.1 Applying the *3Rs* (recognizing, reflecting, and relating to your skills) at the end of your studies and when planning what to do after graduation

your strengths and weaknesses for them). Moreover, while engaging in this process, you may realize that a certain skill can be broken down into several components and that each of these requires separate assessment on your part. For example, communication skills encompass several modes of communication (e.g. written, spoken), and that when reflecting on those you may conclude that you are better at some but still need to develop others. We will embed the *3Rs* approach throughout this chapter and provide advice on how you can use it to monitor and assess your skill development.

Skills versus knowledge

Before you start *recognizing, reflecting* on, and *relating* your skills to a particular situation, it is important for you to be able to distinguish between the transferable skill development and the specialized theoretical knowledge that your project has equipped you with. For example, your project topic may be unrelated to your career plans. Consequently, you may think that your project can add very little to your career. But this could not be further from the truth! Even if your topic is not entirely (or at all!) relevant to the job or further study you are applying for, the transferable skills that you have developed throughout your project will be.

On the other hand, your project topic may be relevant to the job/further study you are applying for, and this is great news. But do be cautious not to overemphasize your project topic at the expense of your skill development: students sometimes do this in their job applications and personal statements, with the unintended consequence of underselling their skills. Transferable skills are as important (and sometimes even more so) as your project topic and the theoretical knowledge that you have gained. So, in both scenarios, you need to think carefully about how to highlight your skills and make them relevant to what you want to do. The *3Rs* approach can help you with that.

The *3Rs* – recognize, reflect, relate

We encourage you to take time to stop and think about the *3Rs* when reading this chapter. Think about your project as a journey with multiple stops. This journey is not necessarily straight but more like a network, comparable to an underground map. It is important for you to understand what each stop on this journey is about (e.g. the specific skills you developed) and how they are connected. So let us start with *recognizing* your skills.

Recognize your skills

One way to *recognize* your skills is to write down/list all the skills you have developed throughout your project. Figure 12.2 can help you with this, although it will not be a definitive list, so feel free to expand it as much as needed. In Chapter 1, we discussed each of these skills in detail, so, if it has been a while since you started reading this book, it might be helpful to go back and look through the 12 skills in Chapter 1 again. Later in the chapter we elaborate on each of these skills and discuss them in the light of career development, personal development, and social responsibility. For now, try to come up with examples of how you have developed each skill.

Next, you may want to see whether any of the skills are similar or co-dependent, and therefore can be linked in some way or even grouped. We recommend that you do some mapping of skills, like we have done in Figure 12.3. This will help you to think carefully about each skill, and what they really mean and involve. It will also encourage you to think flexibly about them, which might be handy in a job interview situation. For instance, you might be asked by the interviewer: "Tell me about your teamwork skills and provide an example of these." As shown

Recognize and come up with examples of where you have used and developed each of the twelve skills...

Figure 12.2 Recognizing the skills that you will have developed through your research project

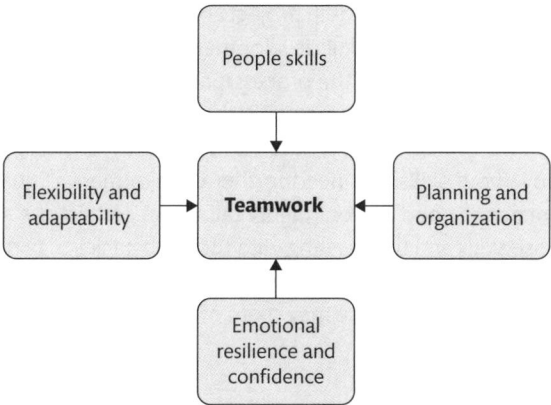

Figure 12.3 Mapping out how different skills are brought together

in Figure 12.3, teamwork skills actually comprise several skills and attributes that help you work effectively with others. For example, to be a good team player, you need to have good people skills. Good organizational skills are also necessary to help your team achieve certain goals. Being resilient is important too, because you are likely to be working with individuals with different personalities and abilities, and being flexible and adaptable will help with that. So, when answering this interview question, it is useful to think about the relationship between teamwork and other skills. This might help you realize that you're better at teamwork than you initially thought. You can do the same exercise with other skills.

Reflect on your skills

Next, carefully consider each skill shown in Figure 12.2 and decide how good you are at them. You can use Figure 12.4 to help you assess your skills. Are there any that you are especially good at and, if yes, how would you describe them? Are there any skills that you could be more confident with and, if yes, how do you plan to improve them? Make sure to support

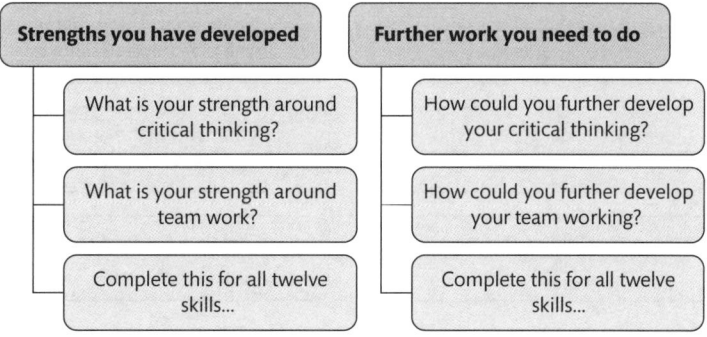

Figure 12.4 Reflecting on your own strengths and the areas where you could still develop your skills further

each skill with examples from your research project and beyond. One way to assess your skills is to think about the very process of skill development. For example, how did you succeed in developing certain skills? What was the process/path/timeline behind each skill development? Is there a key ingredient to this process? Perhaps it is your personality, or maybe specific circumstances or people whom you were surrounded by at the time. Can you use this knowledge to improve your skills that need further development? Equally, when assessing the skills that you are not so good at, you might realize that certain obstacles prevented you from developing those skills and that dealing with those obstacles may require a completely different skill. This thought process should help you answer interview questions more analytically, even those ones that at first glance may seem of little relevance to you.

Relate your skills

Now it is time to think about the relevance of all those skills that you possess, semi-possess, or do not possess. Engaging in the *recognition* and *reflection* of skills should help you have a clear idea of the skills you have and how good you are at them. You will need to relate them to the job that you are applying for, and you can see how you might be able to do this in Figure 12.5. Each job will require a specific set of skills, and you can find out about them in the person specification and job description documents. Job interviews typically involve questions that directly relate to the criteria listed in those two documents. For example, if being resilient is listed as an essential or desirable skill, you may get asked: "Tell me of a time when you had to deal with a problem at work or study and how you overcame that problem."

Note that being a perfect job candidate is not about being perfect at all the required skills. It also involves being able to self-assess your skills, with a clear understanding of how to improve them. Doing this will demonstrate that you are able to engage in critical self-reflection and self-evaluation, and to take the necessary steps to learn and improve your skills. When reading a job description, many of us will be worried if we do not meet every

Relate the skills that you have developed to the job/course that you are applying for...

Skills you have developed	Relevance to the next step in your career
Identify a technical skill you have developed	Identify where this is relevant in the job/course description
Identify a leadership skill you have developed	Identify where this is relevant in the job/course description
Complete this for all twelve skills...	Complete this for all twelve skills...

Figure 12.5 Think about the skills that are required in the job or course that you aim to do, and how you have developed these through your own research

single requirement, but try not to let that hold you back from applying for jobs. You do not need to meet every single aspect. Instead, try to reflect on how you can adapt your skills and how best to develop new ones. To enable you to practise this further, please see the student workbook in the online resources.

12.2 Skills developed through becoming a researcher

In this section, we will go back over the 12 key skills presented in Figure 12.2 and bring together the most important points from across the book for you to use as a springboard for whatever you do next. We want you to be able to apply our key points in the 'real world'. By the 'real world', we do not just mean in your career but also in your personal development and in the social responsibilities that you have as a person, citizen, employee, student, and researcher (see Figure 12.6). Both personal development and social responsibility are important for your career too. In fact, all three areas of development are highly connected and co-dependent. For example, you could become a mentor, giving you the opportunity to apply and develop your own skills in supporting and developing others. In the following sections, we will flag key times when you are likely to use a specific skill in your project and relate it to your career development, personal development, and social responsibility.

Communication skills in the real world

During your research project, you will have to communicate clearly with your supervisor, project group, study participants, and other research stakeholders. You will also have to deliver accurate information in a suitable manner. This involves being able to adapt information and your communication style to your audience. For example, presenting your research to your supervisor, project group, or department requires using scientific language and a lot

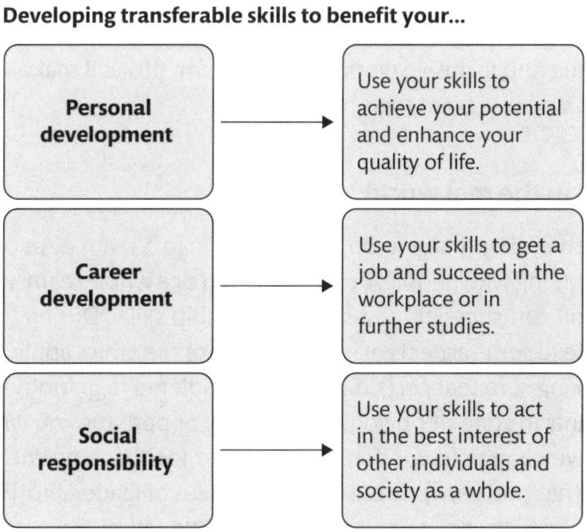

Figure 12.6 Using the skills you develop in different aspects of your life

of detail, whereas presenting your research to your participants and other non-academic audiences requires simplifying information and describing your study in lay terms. This is mirrored in work settings where you will be required to adapt your communication style to different audiences. Your project provides you with numerous opportunities to develop into an effective, versatile, and flexible communicator. These characteristics can also contribute to creating a more socially responsible workplace – for instance, by being a role model to others in how to communicate clearly, effectively, and respectfully.

People skills in the real world

Good communication skills depend highly on good people skills. Showing empathy, respect, and interest in what others say or do is crucial for successful communication. Communicating information in a kind, understanding, and supportive way is also useful in the world of work. This involves understanding the diverse characteristics and needs of people whom you interact with, and adapting your people skills to them. During your project, you will have many opportunities to practise this. For example, in Chapters 2 and 3, we discussed how to use your best people skills with your supervisor and your project group. Good personal skills will benefit you personally, too, by helping to improve your self-confidence, communication with others, and resolution of conflicts and issues. Your good people skills can also contribute to a more positive and compassionate work environment that supports your colleagues' motivation, commitment to work, and also well-being.

Teamwork skills in the real world

Sometimes, students find it difficult to appreciate group projects and they wish they could conduct their research entirely independently. This is not that surprising because it can be challenging working with people with different personalities and styles of working. However, group projects provide an amazing opportunity for developing teamwork skills. They are a great introduction to the world of employment, where even the most independent and lonely jobs still require working with others to a certain degree. Good teamworking can contribute to an inspiring and inclusive workplace. In return, this will make you feel like you are an appreciated and valuable team member.

Leadership skills in the real world

It is important to remember that you do not need to lead a team of people to demonstrate leadership skills. Working with people, be it one person or a whole team, will present you with situations where you can show at least some leadership skills. During your group research project, you might lead some aspects of it (e.g. aspects of the ethics application), or you might be proactive in making sure that certain tasks are completed (e.g. motivating others to keep recruiting participants in spite of obvious challenges), or perhaps you will provide feedback that leads to positive change (e.g. offering to provide feedback on the recruitment leaflet that your colleague has prepared). These are all examples of leadership. For you to be a good leader, you should strive to inspire and motivate people rather than control them. It is not simply about telling people what to do. Instead, show trustworthiness, positivity, ability to listen, and openness to feedback – and delegate fairly. This will help your personal development, as well as promoting diversity and inclusivity in your workplace.

Independence and autonomy skills in the real world

Employers typically want employees who do not need an inappropriate amount of hand-holding in their role and who have developed a certain level of independence and autonomy. The final year project is a large aspect of your degree and consists of lots of different parts. As such, it often requires you to work independently and take responsibility for your own actions – probably more so than any other module in a degree. For example, data collection typically requires a good level of independence, such as finding participants on your own and communicating with them. Independence and autonomy can empower you and give you confidence to be more active with decision-making, initiatives, problem-solving, tackling issues at work, and broader social issues.

Initiative and motivation skills in the real world

Taking initiative is different from being independent. Being independent is about being able to carry out and take responsibility for a task on one's own or with little assistance. Taking initiative is about being enthusiastic, proactive, and motivated to suggest and/or do things without being requested to do them. When carrying out your research project, you will be using a lot of initiative. After all, research is a creative process. Employers prefer candidates who are self-driven and bring innovation to the workplace by suggesting changes and new solutions. Initiative-taking skills can help promote social responsibility by creating and taking charge of initiatives that are beneficial for others – for example, people with good initiative skills often organize fundraisers and prosocial events.

Flexibility and adaptability skills in the real world

Managing change is an important life and work skill that normally requires high levels of flexibility and adaptability. During your research project, you will have many opportunities to apply and develop this skill. For instance, you might have to adjust your data collection strategy because a problem has occurred, or you might personally have to adapt to your fellow students' style of working because it is more beneficial to the outcome of the project. Flexibility and adaptability skills are very important in work settings too, and typically employers look for flexible individuals who are capable of change. They will help you to adapt more easily and to respond to situations, tasks, and people in a more inclusive manner.

Emotional resilience and confidence in the real world

Emotional resilience is an underlying attribute that is a key to many skills discussed in this book. Your project will present you with many challenges, and learning to deal with them (even if it seems like a failure at first) will help to build your resilience and give you the confidence to start your working career and life. However, it is normal to feel all kinds of negative emotions at the end of your degree, such as uncertainty and worry about the future and future choices. Even very experienced and confident people feel this way. It can be helpful to speak to others about this, because it is easy to look at others and assume that they do not have similar struggles. Try to reach out to your supervisor or personal tutor (or academic adviser), because all academics have experienced some level of self-doubt and apprehension so will likely have many kind words of support and encouragement. Do not forget to be kind to yourself, give yourself time, and seek opportunities to build your confidence and resilience. This will make you better equipped to face challenges as well as to focus more on others and their needs. In Box 12.1, you can see an example of how a student might reflect on the resilience skills that they used and developed while conducting their final year project.

Decision-making and goal-setting skills in the real world

Throughout your project, you will have to make many decisions from those relating to choosing a research topic/supervisor to writing up/presenting your research. A lot of these decisions can easily be clouded or enhanced by your emotions, so it is important to be able to step back from the issue at hand, do some research, and seek advice from others so that you can make informed decisions. Your goal setting for the issue or task at hand will be based on those decisions and the decision-making process behind it. It might be good for you to pay attention to this process: How did/do you make decisions? Is there anything that would help you feel less anxious about it, less rushed, and more confident? Should you change anything? This kind of brainstorming may also help you to be more prepared for job interviews and the world of employment, and to feel more at ease with making decisions in general. In addition, good decision-making skills will help you understand the impact of your decisions and their consequences on other individuals, communities, and wider society.

Critical thinking and evaluation skills in the real world

Doing research involves a lot of critical thinking. The process of completing a final year project is similar to the process of completing projects in other real-world situations, so developing and using critical thinking skills during your project will be helpful later. It is highly likely that you will need to use these skills in a workplace, where you can strive to engage in reflective discussions and constructive feedback to help address problems and improve work practices. By developing your reflective/critical thinking, you will be better able to participate in constructive discussions and debates, consider multiple perspectives, and be involved in informed decision-making that will benefit others.

Planning and organizational skills in the real world

This is a fundamental employability skill that underpins so many other skills discussed in this book. For instance, you cannot be a good team player, leader or problem-solver without having good planning and organizational skills. Your final year project will provide you with many opportunities to practise this skill (e.g. to plan and organize your tasks, time, schedule, deadlines, and so on). In general, being organized helps your personal life too! Planning and organizational skills will be critical to your being able to set clear goals, track progress towards them, and achieve them. This will not only benefit you, but also your colleagues, employers, and – potentially – the wider community too, because, when you take a strategic approach to tasks, this is likely to result not only in better outcomes but also a greater impact.

IT and technical skills in the real world

Your research project will require you to use a variety of IT and technical skills, such as using software for data collection (e.g. Qualtrics, Gorilla) and a statistical package for data analysis (e.g. SPSS, R). These skills are likely to serve you well in your future job because most jobs entail at least some use of IT/technical skills and some may be largely based on them (e.g. working as a data analyst, a popular career choice with psychology graduates). Good IT and technical skills will benefit you personally because they can increase your efficiency, interaction, collaboration, and support of others, and therefore contribute to social responsibility at your place of work and outside it.

12.3 Where to get advice for your career development

There are many avenues to receiving career advice in and outside your university. Within your university, your personal tutor and lecturers are always a good source of valuable career-related information. Typically, some personal tutor meetings will specifically focus on employability and careers, which means that you will have many opportunities to discuss these with your tutor. Many psychology departments have members of staff responsible for employability-related activities and/or an online channel for communicating employability and career-related information to their students. Your department is also likely to organize various career-focused events, such as inviting former graduates to talk about their career progression and experiences. You may also have opportunities to engage in your lecturers' research by becoming their research assistant. Such opportunities are usually advertised to students via email or some other means, and a formal application process may be in place. You can also consider approaching some of your lecturers directly and asking them if they need assistance with their research, particularly if you are interested in their area of research. If you decide to do this, make sure to explain why you are interested in their research, what you can offer (your skills and knowledge), and your availability.

Your final year project supervisor can help you understand and articulate the skills you are developing throughout your project so that you can showcase them in job applications and interviews. For example, in our department, final year project students are expected to attend employability-focused lectures that are specifically designed to address the skills they are developing during their projects, and how to use those skills in job applications and interviews. Students' project presentations are also focused on employability and designed as mock interview scenarios whereby students can talk about the skills they have developed and used for their project. You can read about this in more detail in our published paper (Serbic & Bourne, 2020).

Another key source of information is your university career service. Try to make good use of this service by regularly checking their website and posts, attending events they organize, and scheduling one-to-one appointments with them. These appointments can be used to ask questions about your career, potential internships, placements, etc. but also to check that your CV is properly structured and contains appropriate and necessary information. You may also be able to request a mock interview to help you prepare for an upcoming job interview. Also, your university career service is likely to offer ongoing career support after graduation for a period of time.

Outside university, there are of course many platforms that offer career advice. We suggest that you start with three key resources particularly relevant to psychology students:

- Advance HE Psychology Student Employability Guide[1] (online and e-book only). This includes lots of practical guidance and advice for putting together CVs and covering letters.
- The British Psychological Society careers page[2] (online and e-book only). Here you can find lots of information about psychology careers. Remember, though, that your skills will also be relevant in many other career paths.
- Prospects:[3] If you are considering jobs outside psychology, you may find it helpful to look at other pages to help you find suitable jobs, internships, or postgraduate courses.

12.4 Increasing your chances of success in employment

There is much that we could list here to help you increase your chances of finding a job, and there are some final extra hints and tips from some psychology graduates in Box 12.2 at the end of this chapter. But to keep things focused, we have condensed our advice to three top tips.

Our three top tips are as follows:

1. Look for the skills the employer flags in the job advertisement, as well as in the job description and person specification documents. Make sure to explicitly link your skills and experience to those: be as specific as possible and include examples.
2. Research the company you are applying to work with. In your job application and interview, show enthusiasm and knowledge about the job and company.
3. Remember professionalism and attention to detail. Pay careful attention to deadlines and instructions. Include the right amount and type of information, and make it easy for the interviewing panel to shortlist you and give you the job.

Transitioning from student life to employment

It is time to say goodbye!

A key aim of this book was to show you that your final year project can provide you with bountiful opportunities to develop several important skills. Hopefully, the book has been helpful in guiding you through the complex process of conducting your research project.

---

[1] https://www.advance-he.ac.uk/knowledge-hub/psychology-student-employability-guide
[2] https://www.bps.org.uk/find-your-career-psychology
[3] https://www.prospects.ac.uk/graduate-jobs

What you have learned about research and yourself will place you in a strong position for whatever it is that you choose to do next.

We hope that you feel ready to start the next chapter in your life, whether that is through further studies or by entering the world of employment. If, however, you feel that you are not there yet or perhaps feel uncertain about your next step, don't worry: it is normal and okay to feel this way. Make sure to always seek support and give yourself time.

Good luck!

Danijela and Victoria

BOX 12.1 An example of how to recognize, reflect, and relate your skill development around resilience

Reflecting on your transferable skills and personal attributes
An example – being resilient

Recognize: From the research you have conducted, what is the best example of when you have demonstrated this skill or attribute?

During my research project, I encountered several setbacks, personal and professional, which made me doubt myself and my ability to complete my project to a desired standard. I worried that my supervisor and my project group would perceive me as incompetent and lazy. However, after discussing this with my supervisor, I realized that setbacks are normal in life, and that the capability to adapt and address them is an important skill to learn. I also realized that seeking extensions for my deadlines and adjusting my project timeline did not mean I was failing anything or anyone, and this gave me the needed time to bounce back from the difficult situation and focus on producing good work.

Reflect: What are my strengths with regard to this skill or attribute? How can I further develop or improve with regard to them?

I am good at seeking advice from others when I encounter difficulties. I think this is very important when you experience struggle in life because it helps you re-evaluate your situation and reflect on it.

Relate: Imagine you are being interviewed for your dream job or course. How would your skills in this area make you suitable for this position?

I tend to be too hard on myself when things don't go as planned and I quickly start doubting myself. I'm getting better at recognizing that setbacks are unavoidable in life, and that the ability to learn and bounce back from them is important for our personal growth and striving in the workplace.

BOX 12.2 Hints and tips from psychology graduates

The student's perspective . . . reflecting on skills discussed across the whole book

> Your project should give you multiple STAR (situation, task, action, result) situations to talk about in interviews. I suggest actively making notes of the times you show the skills (teamwork, communication, leadership, etc). If you're not finding enough to write about, create the STAR situations. Put yourself forward. Take lead, show creativity, mediate situations between group members.
>
> Mei, psychology graduate

I advise you to speak about it (the research project) in your cover letters and showcase it in your interviews – your employer may not always know what a dissertation entails and what skills you developed. Describe the challenges, the skills you developed, the outcomes, and then tie it all together and say how these all are relevant in the specific job you applied to.

Elias, psychology graduate

Take the time out to research how the topic applies to what career you'd like to go in. Then speak to your supervisor about career pathways and then make sure you are working towards building those skills during the time of your project.

Elizabeth, psychology graduate

The employer's perspective . . . reflecting on skills discussed across the whole book

Ability to adapt language to patients with communication difficulties but also relatives and colleagues with limited knowledge of Psychology. Able to use jargon-free language without diminishing the complexity of problems described. Be concise, articulate clearly and logically complex ideas.

Jelena, clinical psychologist

A cover letter absolutely MUST show an understanding of the role they are applying for. Remember that it is not expected that you will fulfil all competencies for the role at the beginning. Saying "I think what I have done will help me in the job in these ways that are in line with the job description" is important but saying "and while I have not had any experience in that area, I have transferable skills from another area which I think will stand me in good stead to learn quickly. Coupled with my drive and enthusiasm for this area I don't think the lack of current experience would hold me back" is also very important.

Stefan, senior researcher

Be enthusiastic. No candidate is a perfect fit so showing you're able and willing to take on new skills is important.

Talia, director of human resources

References

AMSTAR (n.d.). *Assessing the Methodological Quality of Systematic Reviews*. https://amstar.ca/index.php

AMSTAR (2017). *Assessing the Methodological Quality of Systematic Reviews*. https://amstar.ca/Amstar_Checklist.php

Bourne, V., James, A.I., & Wilson-Smith, K. (2021). *Understanding Quantitative and Qualitative Research in Psychology: A Practical Guide to Methods, Statistics and Analysis*. Oxford University Press. https://global.oup.com/ukhe/product/understanding-quantitative-and-qualitative-research-in-psychology-9780198823049?cc=gb&lang=en&

Braun, V., & Clarke, V. (2006). Using thematic analysis in psychology. *Qualitative Research in Psychology*, 3(2): 77–101. https://www.tandfonline.com/doi/abs/10.1191/1478088706qp063oa

Braun, V., & Clarke, V. (2021a). *Thematic Analysis: A Practical Guide*. SAGE Publications Ltd. https://uk.sagepub.com/en-gb/eur/thematic-analysis/book248481

Braun, V., & Clarke, V. (2021b). To saturate or not to saturate? Questioning data saturation as a useful concept for thematic analysis and sample-size rationales. *Qualitative Research in Sport, Exercise and Health*, 13(2): 201–216. https://doi.org/10.1080/2159676X.2019.1704846

Braun, V., Clarke, V., Hayfield, N. et al. (2018). Thematic analysis. In P. Liamputtong (Ed.) *Handbook of Research Methods in Health Social Sciences* (pp. 843–860). Springer Singapore. . https://doi.org/10.1080/07448481.2021.2006199

British Psychological Society (BPS). (2021). *Code of Ethics and Conduct*. BPS. https://explore.bps.org.uk/content/report-guideline/bpsrep.2021.inf94

British Psychological Society (BPS). (2021). *Code of Human Research Ethics*. BPS. https://explore.bps.org.uk/content/report-guideline/bpsrep.2021.inf180

British Psychological Society (BPS). (2021). *Ethics Guidelines for Internet-Mediated Research*. BPS, https://explore.bps.org.uk/content/report-guideline/bpsrep.2021.rep155

Button, K.S., Chambers, C.D., Munafò, M.R. et al. (2019). Grassroots training for reproducible science: A consortium-based approach to the empirical dissertation. *Psychology Learning & Teaching*, 19(1).

Byrne, D. (2022). A worked example of Braun and Clarke's approach to reflexive thematic analysis. *Quality & Quantity*, 56(3): 1391–1412. https://doi.org/10.1007/s11135-021-01182-y

Campbell, M., McKenzie, J.E., Sowden, A. et al. (2020). Synthesis without meta-analysis (SWiM) in systematic reviews: reporting guideline. *BMJ* 368. https://www.bmj.com/content/368/bmj.l6890.abstract

Cochrane.org: The Cochrane Consumer Network: *Systematic reviews*. https://consumers.cochrane.org/cochrane-and-systematic-reviews

Cohen, J. (1992). A power primer. *Psychological Bulletin*, 112(1): 155–159.

CRD. (2009). *Systematic reviews: Centre for reviews and dissemination guidance for undertaking reviews in healthcare*. York, UK: Centre for Reviews and Dissemination, https://www.york.ac.uk/media/crd/Systematic_Reviews.pdf

Cuijpers, P., Noma, H., Karyotaki, E. et al. (2019). Effectiveness and acceptability of cognitive behavior therapy delivery formats in adults with depression: a network meta-analysis. *JAMA Psychiatry*, 76(7): 700–707. https://doi:10.1001/jamapsychiatry.2019.0268

Drinkwater, K.G., Dagnall, N., Walsh, S. et al. (2022). Self-ascribed paranormal ability: Reflexive thematic analysis. *Frontiers in Psychology*, 13, 845283. https://doi.org/10.3389/fpsyg.2022.845283

EPPI-Reviewer: systematic review software (n.d.) https://eppi.ioe.ac.uk/cms/Default.aspx?tabid=2914

Glaser, B., & Strauss, A. (2017). *Discovery of Grounded Theory: Strategies for Qualitative Research*. Routledge. https://doi.org/10.4324/9780203793206

Hewitt, P.L., Flett, G.L., Turnbull-Donovan, W. et al. (1991). The Multidimensional Perfectionism Scale: Reliability, validity, and psychometric properties in psychiatric samples. *Psychological Assessment: A Journal of Consulting and Clinical Psychology*, 3(3): 464–468.

Higgins, J.P.T., Thomas, J., Chandler, J. et al. (2024). *Cochrane Handbook for Systematic Reviews of Interventions*. https://www.training.cochrane.org/handbook

Hogan, K.F., Clarke, V., & Ward, T. (2022). The impact of masculine ideologies on heterosexual men's experiences of intimate partner violence: A qualitative exploration. *Journal of Aggression, Maltreatment & Trauma*, 33(1): 123–142. https://doi.org/10.1080/10926771.2022.2061881

REFERENCES

Howitt, D. (2019). *Introduction to Qualitative Research Methods in Psychology: Putting Theory Into Practice* (4th ed.). Pearson. https://thuvienso.hoasen.edu.vn/bitstream/handle/123456789/12840/Contents.pdf?sequence=1

Joanna Briggs Institute (JBI). (2020). *Critical appraisal tools*. https://jbi.global/critical-appraisal-tools

John, L.K., Loewenstein, G., & Prelec, G. (2012). Measuring the prevalence of questionable research practices with incentives for truth telling. *Psychological Science*, 23(5). https://doi.org/10.1177/0956797611430953

LeMoyne, T., & Buchanan, T. (2011). Does "hovering" matter? Helicopter parenting and its effect on well-being. *Sociological Spectrum*, 31(4): 399–418. https://doi.org/10.1080/02732173.2011.574038

Luo, C., Sanger, N., Singhal, N. et al. (2020). Addendum to 'A comparison of electronically-delivered and face to face cognitive behavioural therapies in depressive disorders: A systematic review and meta-analysis' [EClinicalMedicine 24 (2020) 100442]. https://www.thelancet.com/journals/eclinm/article/PIIS2589-5370(20)30324-2/fulltext

Moher, D., Liberati, A., Tetzlaff, J. et al. & PRISMA Group*, T. (2009). Preferred reporting items for systematic reviews and meta-analyses: The PRISMA statement. *Annals of Internal Medicine*, 151(4): 264–269. https://www.acpjournals.org/doi/full/10.7326/0003-4819-151-4-200908180-00135.

Nuzzo, R. (2015). How scientists fool themselves – and how they can stop. *Nature*, 526: 182–185. https://https://doi.org/10.1038/526182a

Open Science Collaboration (2015). Estimating the reproducibility of psychological science. *Science*, 349(6251). https://www.science.org/doi/10.1126/science.aac4716

Oud, M., de Winter, L., Vermeulen-Smit, E. et al. (2019). Effectiveness of CBT for children and adolescents with depression: A systematic review and meta-regression analysis. *European Psychiatry*, 57: 33–45. doi:10.1016/j.eurpsy.2018.12.008

Popay, J., Roberts, H., Sowden, A. et al. (2006). Guidance on the Conduct of Narrative Synthesis in Systematic Reviews. *A product from the ESRC Methods Programme Version*, 1(1), b92. https://citeseerx.ist.psu.edu/document?repid=rep1&type=pdf&doi=ed8b23836338f6fdea0cc55e161b0fc5805f9e27

Rosenthal, R. (1979). The file drawer problem and tolerance for null results. *Psychological Bulletin*, 86(3): 638–641. https://doi.org/10.1037/0033-2909.86.3.638

Serbic, D., & Bourne, V. (2020). Final Year Research Project as a Tool for Maximising Students' Employability Prospects. *Psychology Teaching Review*, 26(1): 90–95 https://eric.ed.gov/?id=EJ1257757

Serbic, D., Evangeli, M., Probyn, K., & Pincus, T. (2021). Health-related guilt in chronic primary pain: A systematic review of evidence. *British Journal of Health Psychology*, 27(1): 67–95. https://doi.org/10.1111/bjhp.12529

Serbic, D., Friedrich, C., & Murray, R. (2023). Psychological, social and academic functioning in university students with chronic pain: A systematic review. *Journal of American College Health*, 71(9): 2894–2908. https://doi.org/10.1080/07448481.2021.2006199

Simmons, J.P., Nelson, L.D., & Simonsohn, U. (2021). Pre-registration: Why and how. *Journal of Consumer Psychology*, 31(1): 151–162. https://doi.org/10.1002/jcpy.1208

Smith, J.A. (2017). Interpretative phenomenological analysis: Getting at lived experience. *Journal of Positive Psychology*, 12(3): 303–304. https://doi.org/10.1080/17439760.2016.1262622

Spielberger, C.D. (1983). *State-Trait Anxiety Inventory for Adults (STAI-AD)* [Database record]. APA PsycTests. https://doi.org/10.1037/t06496-000

Tong, A., Sainsbury, P., & Craig, J. (2007). Consolidated criteria for reporting qualitative research (COREQ): A 32-item checklist for interviews and focus groups. *International Journal for Quality in Health Care*, 19(6): 349–357 https://academic.oup.com/intqhc/article/19/6/349/1791966

Yarbro, J., & Ventura, M. (2019). *Skills for Today: What We Know About Teaching and Assessing Social Responsibility*. Pearson. https://www.pearson.com/content/dam/one-dot-com/one-dot-com/global/Files/efficacy-and-research/skills-for-today/4008-SFT-Social-Responsibility.pdf

Index

2*3*3* mixed design ANCOVA 54, 59, 61f
2*3 mixed design 58
3*2*3 mixed design 66

A

Abstract 79, 109, 135, 164, 169, 171, 176, 177f
academic achievement (fictional research) 87-8, 90, 91, 92, 94, 96, 107
academic dishonesty 188
acceptance for publication 192-3
acceptance without revisions 189
accuracy 159
adaptability *see* flexibility and adaptability
Advance HE Psychology Student Employability Guide 204
alpha level 101
American Psychological Association (APA) guidelines 74, 79, 81, 102, 109, 111, 137, 169, 177, 186
AMSTAR checklist 156-7, 157f
analysis
   qualitative research 130-3
   section 80
   tools 50
analytical workflows 50
ANCOVA 72, 75, 80
   2*3*3* mixed design 54, 59, 61f
   one-way 77
   three-way 63, 63f, 67
anonymity/anonymization 66, 71, 102, 103, 104, 127, 130, 137, 188, 189
ANOVA 54, 57, 60, 72, 74, 74f, 77, 80, 109
   two-way 78
ANVOVA 75
AsPredicted 49
assertiveness 5
assistant positions 3
assumptions analysis 74-5, 74f
attributes *see* skills and attributes
authenticity 7
authorship decisions 187
autonomy *see* independence and autonomy

B

back-ups 72
backward searching 149
balancing tasks 38
beta values 92, 93, 107, 108
bias 166
   experimenter 70
   minimization 142, 144, 145, 149, 156, 157, 160
   publication 45f, 46, 49
   researcher 103, 125
   risk of 155-6, 163
   social desirability 103
binary correlations 85
binary predictors 93, 96
binary variables 90
body language 6
Bonferroni corrected t tests 77
Boolean operators 151
box plot 73
branded templates 172
British Psychological Society (BPS) 16, 102, 115, 130, 204
   Code of Ethics and Conduct 39, 127
   Code of Human Research Ethics 127
   Guidance for Internet Mediated Research 129
bullet point lists 179

C

calculated estimate 73
career development 3-4, 196, 199f
   advice 203-4
categorical predictors 110
categorical variables 59, 88, 90
causation versus correlation 87-8
CBT effectiveness for depression (fictional review question) 145-6, 149, 153
Centre for Open Science 50
Centre for Review and Dissemination 151
challenging situations 13, 39-41
checklists 70, 127, 161f
chronic pain, university students with (fictional review question) 145-6, 148
chunking tasks 38
citation information 185
clinical, forensic or educational psychology 3
clinical trials 49
closing slides 172-3
co-authors 187
Cochrane Database of Systematic Reviews 142
Cochrane Handbook assessment tool 155
codebook thematic analysis 120-1
codes 117, 133
   generating 132t
   semantic 120
   see also data coding
Cohen's kappa 118
collaborative research 12, 13-14, 13f, 30, 41-2, 69-70, 102-3, 128
   see also teamwork skills
communication skills 4, 6
   experimental research 55f, 69, 71, 84b
   presenting research 169, 170f, 181b
   publishing research 183f, 193b
   qualitative research 115, 116f, 127, 128, 129, 138b
   real world 195, 199-200
concepts 148
Conclusion 137, 166
conduct, appropriate 39
conferences 171, 174, 179-80
   online 176
confidence 13, 59
confidentiality 39, 66, 71, 102, 104, 127, 130
confirmatory analysis 48
confounding variables 57, 61-3, 95
consistency 70, 83, 159
Consolidated Criteria for Reporting Qualitative Research (COREQ) 127
construct validity 99
constructivist approach 136
continuous predictors 96, 110
continuous variables 59, 85, 88, 90, 99
control predictors 96
control variables 95-6, 107

INDEX

controlling experimental design 83
correlational research 85-113
  advanced 86
  data analysis 104-9
    analysis strategy 104
    checking regression assumptions 105
    effect sizes 108-9
    individual predictors 106f, 107-8
    making sense of findings 105-8
    Model 1 analysis 96, 97f, 105-6, 106f, 107, 110
    Model 2 analysis 96, 97f, 107, 108, 108f, 110
    overall model analysis 106-7, 106f
    preparation for analysis 104-5
  ethics 102
  main aim of research design 86-7, 87f
  negative correlation 88
  no correlation 88
  positive correlations 89f
  reliability 97-9
  robust study design 97-101
  running study 102-4
    collaborative study 102-3
    data collection, coding and storage 103-4
    recruitment and data collection 103
  sample size 101
  simple correlation 86
  skills and attributes 85, 86f
  transferable skills through correlational methodology 112
  validity 97-9
  variables 88
  versus causation 87-8
  writing up study 109-11, 111f
    Abstract 109
    Discussion 111
    Introduction 109-10
    Methods 110
    Results 110-11
    Title 109
  see also regression
counterbalancing 61, 63-4, 65f
covariables 67, 72, 73, 75
credibility 48
critical self-reflection 198
critical thinking and evaluation skills 8, 51f, 52-3b, 115
  correlational research 85, 86f
  presenting research 169, 170f
publishing research 183f, 187, 193b
qualitative research 116f, 128
real world 202
systematic review 143f, 167b
Cronbach's alpha 98, 105, 125
current state of psychological research 44-53
  open science 44-6, 45f, 48-51, 52
    pre-registration 48-9
    rapid dissemination 50-1
    Registered Reports 49
    study design improvement and statistical power 49-50
    transferable skills development 51-2, 51f
    transparency, data sharing and analysis tools 50
  replication crisis 44-8
    publication bias or file drawer problem 46
    questionable research practices 46-7
    study design, poor and statistical power, low 47-8
    transparency, lack of 48

D

data, familiarization with 130
data analysis 136
  see also under correlational research; experimental research
data cleaning 73
data coding 71-2, 103-4, 130-1
  latent 120
  semantic 120
data collection 34, 49, 70, 71-2, 103-4, 128-9
  online 70, 103
data extraction 160, 161f
  plan 153, 165
  tables 160, 166
data orientation, experiential versus critical 119-20
data preparation for analysis 73
data saturation 124
data sharing 45f, 50
data sources 136
data storage 71-2, 103-4, 130
data synthesis plan 165
database searches 149
datasets, incomplete 70
de-duplicating records 158
deadlines 35-6
debriefing of participants 69, 103
deception, active and passive 66-7
decision-making and goal-setting skills 8, 19-20, 20b, 21b, 37, 37f, 42, 51f, 55f, 183f, 202
deductive approach 120-1
dependent variables (DVs) 56, 56f, 60, 67
descriptive statistics 73, 80-1, 81t
design
  improvement 49-50
  poor 47-8
  section 80, 110, 135
  three-way 57, 59-60, 62f, 68-9, 68f
  two-way 57, 58-9, 60f, 62f, 68, 68f
  types 55-7
  see also under experimental research; systematic reviews
desk reject 189
detail, attention to 187
Discussion section 81-2, 111, 136-7, 166, 169, 172, 177
dissemination barriers 48
distribution analysis 74
doctoral programmes 3
double hermeneutics 122

E

effect sizes 47-8, 49, 108-9
emotional affect 17
emotional response to reviews 191
empathy 6
employability 3
  increasing chances of success 204
  prospects 7
  skills 5, 25
EndNote 143, 158
enthusiasm 7, 17
epistemological assumptions 118-19, 136
EPPI-Reviewer 143, 152, 152f, 158
error minimization 156, 160
ethics 38-9, 66-7, 70-1, 104, 128, 129, 130, 136
  approval 17
  correlational research project 102
  procedures 103
  publishing research 188
  social responsibility component 4, 4f
  systematic review 157
evaluation skills *see* critical thinking and evaluation skills
exclusion criteria 40, 64, 67, 148-9, 151, 152, 158-9, 165
expectations management 32

experience 16
experimental independent
    variables 66
experimental research 54–84
  data analysis 72–8
    assumptions 74–5, 74f
    covariables 75
    data preparation 73
    main effects 75–6, 76f
    making sense of findings 73–8
    strategy development 72–3
    three-way interaction 78, 78f
    two-way interactions 76–8, 77f
  design 57–69
    2*3*3* mixed design 59, 61f
    2*3*3* mixed design
        ANCOVA 54
    2*3 mixed design 58
    3*2*3 mixed design 66
    confounding variables 61–3
    ethics 66–7
    factorial design 57, 59f, 60
    hypothesis development
        67–9, 68f
    main effects 68, 68f
    one-way design 57
    randomizing and
        counterbalancing 61,
        63–4, 65f
    recruitment strategy 61,
        64–5, 66
    reliability and validity 66
    robust study 60–6
    sample size 61, 65–6
    three-way ANCOVA 63,
        63f, 67
    three-way design 57, 59–60,
        62f, 68–9, 68f
    two-way design 57, 58–9, 60f,
        62f, 68, 68f
  experimental manipulation and
      types of design 55–7
  manipulation 55–7
  running study 69–72
    collaboration 69–70
    data collection, coding and
        storing 70, 71–2
    recruiting participants 71
  skills required 54
  transferable skills building
      through methodology 83
  variance 57
  writing up 79–82
    Abstract 79
    Discussion 81–2
    Introduction 79–80
    Methods 80
    Results 80–1
    Title 79

expertise, cross-disciplinary 49
exploratory analysis 48
eye contact 175

F

F tests 105, 109
face-to-face interviews 128
factor analysis 98
factorial design 57, 59f, 60
false null hypothesis 47
false-positive result 48
fatigue effects 56
feedback 118, 187, 190
file drawer problem 46, 182–3
findings 80
  making sense of 73–8, 163
first come, first served basis 22
first-generation students
    (fictional study) 90, 94, 96,
    106, 107, 108
flexibility and adaptability 5, 6, 8,
    10b, 23, 37f, 51f, 116f
  publishing research 183f, 193b
  real world 197, 201
font style and size 179
footnotes 75
formatting requirements 176
forward searching 149
framework analysis 121
frequency analysis 73, 105
future career plan 17
future research, practice and policy
    directions 166

G

G Power calculator 66, 101
Gantt charts 33–5, 35f, 36f, 38
General Data Protection Regulation
    (GDPR) 1, 130
generating codes 132t
generic skills 5
goal-setting skills see decision-
    making and goal-setting
    skills
good judgement 115
good listener 115
Google Forms 103
Gorilla 70, 203
gratitude 39
Greenhouse-Geisser correction 75
'grey' literature 148, 149
ground rules and expectations
    management 24–5
grounded theory 121, 122, 122f
group conflict 13
group work see collaborative
    research

H

HARKing (hypothesizing after the
    results are known) 40, 45,
    45f, 46–9, 68, 97, 104, 183f
helicopter parenting (fictional
    research) 90, 94, 96, 106,
    107, 108
hierarchical regression 88, 98f, 104,
    105, 106f, 107, 107f, 108f,
    110, 111, 111f
histograms 73
homoscedasticity 101, 101f
human factors 27
humility 39
hypothesis development 67–9, 68f

I

impact factors of journals
    185–6, 185f
improvement, opportunities for 9
inclusion criteria 40, 64, 148–9,
    151, 152, 158–9, 165
inclusivity 30
independence and autonomy 7,
    10b, 13–16, 15f, 25–6, 26f
  correlational research 85, 86f
  presenting research 170f
  qualitative research 115, 116f,
    137–8b
  real world 201
independent measures design
    56, 58
independent reviewer, second
    156, 160
independent screening 159
independent variables 55–7, 56f,
    59–60, 62f, 63, 66, 82
  experimental 66
  manipulated 67
  repeated measures 58
individual predictors 106f,
    107–8, 108f
individual projects 12–13, 13f, 41–2
inductive analysis 120, 122
information sources 165
informed consent 66–7, 102,
    103, 127
initial themes, generating 131–2
initiative and motivation 7, 26f,
    31b, 37f, 38, 42, 55f,
    69, 143f
  correlational research 85, 86f
  real world 201
  systematic review 167b
institutional barriers 48
interactions 6, 63
intercept values 92, 92f

interest, genuine 6
interlibrary loan service 186
internal consistency 98
interpersonal skills 129
interpretative analysis 118
　phenomenological 121-2, 122f
interrater agreement score 161
interrater reliability 118
Introduction 79-80, 109-10, 135, 164-5, 169, 172, 177, 177f
invisible health conditions stigma (fictional research) 14-15
IT and technical skills 9, 51f, 55f, 113b, 143f
　correlational research 85, 86f
　presenting research 170f
　real world 203

J
JASP 72
Joanna Briggs Institute checklist 155, 156f

K
Kappa statistic 161
keynote talks 172
Kolmogorov-Smirnov test 99

L
language 148
leadership skills 4, 7, 13, 26f, 37f, 69
　correlational research 85, 86f, 112b, 113b
　presenting research 170f
　real world 200-1
learning/workplace transition 1-10
　career paths 3-4
　skills and attributes 5-9, 5f
lecturer personal characteristics 18
legal issues 130
limitations 137
literature search strategy 149-51
　additional searches 149
　database searches 149
　key search terms 149-51, 150f
　search precision 151
log transformation 74
logos 172, 178

M
main effects analysis 63, 68, 68f, 73, 75-6, 76f
manipulation 66-7

Master's programme 3
Materials section 80
measurement error 57
Mendeley 143
mentoring 4
meta-analysis 49, 140, 153-4
methodological issues 27, 60, 83, 118
Methods section 80, 110, 135-6, 165-6, 165f, 169, 172, 173, 177, 177f
missing data 73, 105
mixed methods research 115
Model 1 96, 97f, 107, 110
Model 2 96, 97f, 107, 110
module coordinator 27
Moodle 41
motivation *see* initiative and motivation
multicollinearity 99
multicultural component of social responsibility 4, 4f
Multidimensional Perfectionism Scale (MPS) 87

N
narrative synthesis 140, 162-3
National Institute for Health and Care Excellence 142
negotiations, individual 22
null hypothesis 67
　false 47
NVivo 131

O
objectivity 118, 125
observational studies 155
obstacles, potential 40
one-tailed (directional) hypothesis 67, 72
one-way ANCOVA 77
one-way ANOVA 73
one-way design 57
online data collection 70, 103
online interviews 128
online research platforms 70
online talks 172
ontological assumptions 118, 136
open science 50, 73, 127, 130, 186, 192
　see also under current state of psychological research
Open Science Collaboration (2015) 44
Open Science Framework (OSF) 49, 50, 183

oral presentations 170, 171-5
　delivering 174-5
　preparing 172-4
organization skills *see* planning and organization skills
other-oriented perfectionism (fictional research) 87
outcome variables 88, 90, 91f, 92, 93, 95-6, 99, 108, 110
outliers 73, 99-100, 101, 105

P
p value 77, 88, 105, 107, 108
p-hacking 45, 45f, 46, 49, 183
paradigm 118, 124, 136
partial reporting of research 48
participant burden 102-3
participant debriefing 69, 103
participants, number of 80
participants section 80
passion for project 7, 17
payment to publish/reader payment to access paper 186
Pearson's correlation 88, 99
peer reviews 49, 148, 171
people skills 6, 13, 23, 26f, 31b, 115, 116f, 127
　experimental research 55f, 83, 83b, 84b
　presenting research 169, 170f, 181b
　real world 197, 200
perfectionism (fictional research) 87, 88, 90, 91, 123
personal attributes 5-6, 5f, 6, 7, 9, 30, 36, 51f, 181b, 200
　see also skills and attributes
personal challenges, dealing with 27
personal development 194, 196, 199, 199f
personal experience and interests influencing decisions 16-17
personal factors 17
personal growth 14
personality 36
PhD programme 3
phenomenological analysis 118, 121
philosophical approach 118-20, 121, 126, 134, 135
PICOS 146-7, 147f, 148, 149
pilot study 70
piloting extraction tables 160
Pint of Science 180
plan, feasible 32
planned analysis 48

planned contrasts 72, 75, 77
planning and organization skills 9, 21*b*, 37*f*, 42–3*b*, 51*f*, 53*b*, 55*f*, 197
  publishing research 183*f*, 187
  real world 202–3
  systematic review 142–4, 143*f*, 144
positivism 7, 118
post hoc contrasts 72, 75
poster presentations 170, 176–80, 177*f*, 178*f*
  colour schemes 177–8
  conferences 179–80
  content development 178–9
  formatting and structuring 176–8
postgraduate education 3, 16
power, low 45*f*
PowerPoint 173–4, 177
practical challenges 27
practice 174–5
  effects 56
pre-planning, in-depth understanding of 32–3
pre-prints 50–1
pre-registration 45*f*, 48–9, 50, 183–4
predatory journals 186
predictor variables 88, 90, 91, 91*f*, 92, 95–6, 99
preferences 36
Preferred Reporting Items for Systematic Reviews and Meta-analyses (PRISMA) guidelines 50, 157, 159–60, 159*f*, 163–4, 164*f*
preliminary literature search for review question suitability 146
presentation of research 168–81
  duration 174
  format 172
  keynote talks 172
  length 172
  manner of 174
  online talks 172
  oral presentations 170, 171–5
  poster presentations 170, 176–80
  quick-fire presentations 171
  research articles 169
  sharing research 180
  skills development 169, 170*f*
  standard presentations 171
  structuring 172
  symposiums 171–2
  workshops 171

prevention better than cure 40
previous research experience 16
privacy 129
  see also anonymity/anonymization; confidentiality
proactiveness 42
problem-solving 23, 42
Procedure section 80
project allocation 22–3
PROSPERO 49, 144–5, 153
protocols 50, 69, 71, 145, 165
PsyArXiv 50, 192
PsychINFO 149, 150*f*, 151, 158
psychological harm 66, 67, 102
psychological research, role of in society 4
publication bias 45*f*, 46, 49
publication type 148
publishing research 182–93
  acceptance for publication 192–3
  journal quality judgment, standardized 185–6
  journal suitability for study topic 184
  payment to publish/reader payment to access paper 186
  pre-registration 183–4
  Registered Reports 183, 184
  review process 188–92, 188*f*
    first stage of editorial review 188–9
    main reviews and editorial decision 189–90
    responding to reviews and resubmitting paper 190–2, 191*f*
  sharing research with others 192–3
  submission preparation 186–8
    authorship decisions 187
    feedback 187
    submission to journal 187–8
PubMed 149, 150*f*, 151
pure experiment 56–7

Q

qualitative research 114–38
  analysis 130–3
  collaborative study 128
  data coding 130–1
  data storage 130
  familiarization with data 130
  generating codes 132*t*
  initial themes, generation of 131–2

positioning within psychology 114–15
recruitment of participants and data collection 128–9
refining, defining and labelling themes 133
skills required 115
theme development and review 132–3
transferable skills 137
writing up 133–7
  Abstract 135
  Introduction 135
  key sections within report 134–7
  Methods 135–6
  reflexivity, embedding 134
  Results and Discussion 136–7
  start early 134
  Title 134–5
  see also reflective thematic analysis
qualitative systematic reviews 139–40
quality assessment 50, 154–5, 161–2, 165–6
Qualtrics 70, 103, 203
quantitative research 114, 115, 118, 121, 123, 123*f*, 125, 130, 136, 137
quantitative synthesis 153
quantitative systematic review 139–40
quasi-experimental design 56–7
question development 145–7
question/answer session 175, 179
questionable research practices 46–7
questionnaires 97–8, 99, 102, 110
questions, open-ended 123
quotations 136–7

R

R 72, 104, 203
r coefficient 108
R squared statistic 92–3, 94, 96, 105, 106, 109
r statistic 88, 108
r values 99
random allocation 56, 64
random variance 60–1, 63–4, 65*f*, 69–70, 72, 82
randomized controlled trials (RCTs) 146, 153, 155
rank order choices 22

rapid dissemination of research 50-1
rapid reviews 140
Rayyan 143, 152
re-running searches 151
real world 194-206
  career development advice 203-4
  communication skills 199-200
  critical thinking and evaluation 202
  decision-making and goal-setting 202
  employment success, increasing chances of 204
  flexibility and adaptability 201
  independence and autonomy 201
  initiative and motivation 201
  IT and technical skills 203
  leadership skills 200-1
  people skills 200
  planning and organization skills 202-3
  resilience and confidence 201-2, 205b
  skills acquired 194-9
  skills versus knowledge 195
  teamwork skills 200
  three Rs (recognize, reflect, relate) 194-5, 195f, 196-9, 205b
  transitioning from student life to employment 204-5
recognize see three Rs (recognize, reflect, relate)
records 143, 158
  de-duplicating 158
recruitment of participants 40, 61, 64-5, 66, 69, 71, 103, 128-9
References 169, 177
referencing manager 144, 158
refining, defining and labelling themes 133
reflect see three Rs (recognize, reflect, relate)
reflective thematic analysis 114, 115-27
  comparisons with other qualitative approaches 121-2
  comparisons with other thematic approaches 120-1
  definition 116-17
  design 123-7
  ethics 127
  example questions to prompt self-reflection 126
  key characteristics 115-22, 116f

philosophical and theoretical approaches 118-20, 126
reflexivity 117-18, 125-6
reliability and validity 125
robustness 125-7
sample size and type 124-5
stages 129f
subjectivity 125-6
suitable research question 123-4
theme generation versus theme extraction 117, 117f
transparency 126-7
reflexivity, embedding 134
Registered Reports 49, 183, 184
registration fee 171
regression 86, 88-97
  assumptions of 99-101
  basics 91-2
  correlation to regression 90
  hierarchical 85, 88, 94-7, 97f, 98f, 104-5, 106f, 107, 107f, 108f, 110-11, 111f
  key steps 92-3
  linear 91
  logistic 90
  multiple 91f, 93, 95f
  purpose 90-1
  residual values 100f
  simultaneous 91f, 93, 95f
  slope 91, 92, 92f
  types of 90, 93-4, 94f
  variance, different sources of 93f
rejection 189-90
relate see three Rs (recognize, reflect, relate)
reliability 44, 66, 67, 82, 97-9, 120-1, 125, 160
  inter-rater 118
repeated measures design 58
repeated measures independent variable 58
replicability 48
replication crisis see under current state of psychological research
research articles 169
research assistant projects 12, 13f, 14
research process overview 2f
research topic 22
researcher bias 103, 125
residuals 100, 100f, 101f
  negative 100
  positive 100
resilience 5, 8, 13, 23, 26f, 40-1, 43b, 143f, 193
  publishing research 183f
  qualitative research 115, 116f
  real world 197, 201-2, 205b

respect 6
responsibilities, other 36
resubmitting paper 190-2, 191f
Results section 80-1, 110-11, 136-7, 165f, 166, 169, 172, 173, 177
review implications 166
review process see under publishing research
review question 149
review of themes 133
revise and resubmit 189-90, 191f
rewarding yourself 38
rigidity 154
rigour 125, 140
robustness 60-6, 97-101, 125-7, 155-7, 163
running study see under correlational research; experimental research

S
sample size 13, 49-50, 61, 65-6, 101, 103, 110, 124-5
sample type 124-5
sampling
  convenience 124
  non-probability 124
  purposive 124
scatterplot 99
Science Festivals 180
scope 146
scoping reviews 140
Scopus 149, 150f, 151, 158
screening of studies plan 165
search
  additional 149
  precision 151
  re-running 151
  strategy 158
  terms 149-51, 150f
second independent reviewer 156, 160
selection criteria 147-9
selection of studies plan 165
selective analysis 45
selective reporting of positive results 45
self-assessment 38
self-deception 47
self-evaluation 198
self-management see time and self-management
self-oriented perfectionism (fictional research) 87, 89f, 90, 92-4, 96, 98-9, 106-9
self-reflection 38

INDEX

self-reflective log 9, 30, 41
semantic coding of data 120
sensibility 115
sensitive questions/information 17, 70, 102, 103, 115, 127, 128, 129
sharing research with others 180, 192–3
skills and attributes 5–9, 5f, 6, 30, 36
   communication skills 6
   correlational research project 85
   critical thinking and evaluation skills 8
   decision-making and goal-setting skills 8
   development 23f
   experimental research project 54
   flexibility and adaptability skills 8
   independence and autonomy skills 7
   initiative and motivation skills 7
   IT and technical skills 9
   leadership skills 7
   people skills 6
   planning and organization skills 9
   qualitative research 115
   resilience and confidence skills 8
   systematic review 142–4
   teamwork skills 6–7
   see also transferable skills
skills versus knowledge 195
slides, closing 172–3
social desirability bias 103
social media information 172–3, 178, 180, 185
social responsibility 4, 4f, 39, 180, 194, 196, 199, 199f
   civic component 4, 4f
   environmental component 4, 4f
   ethics component 4, 4f
   multicultural component 4, 4f
   skills 24, 25, 30
socially prescribed perfectionism (fictional research) 87, 88, 89f, 94, 96, 99, 106, 107, 108, 109
soft skills 5
sphericity 74, 75, 77
Spielberger State-Trait Anxiety Inventory (STAI) 96
SPSS 72, 75, 76f, 104, 203
square root transformation 74
stakeholders, consideration of 38–9

standardized beta 108
standardized residuals 99, 101
statistical package 104, 110
statistical pooling 154
statistical power 47–50
strategy development analysis 72–3
strengths 5, 7, 9, 18, 26–7
student representative 4
student-directed research 14, 15f
student-supervisor relationship 22–31
   different supervision styles, working with 27–30, 28f
   Dr Hands-off 28f, 29, 30
   Dr Over-enthusiastic 28–9, 28f
   ground rules and expectations management 24–5
   group projects 30
   human factors 27
   independence 25–6, 26f
   methodological or technical issues 27
   personal challenges, dealing with 27
   practical challenges 27
   Prof Control freak 28f, 29
   project allocation 22–3
   respect, mutual 24
   strengths and weakness 26–7, 30
   understanding 23–4
study procedure 136
study screening and selection 152–3, 152f, 158–60
subgroup comparisons 162–3
subjectivity 116, 117–18, 125–6
submission preparation *see under* publishing research
subsections 135, 171
Summary section 166
supervision styles, different, working with 27–30, 28f
supervisor-directed research 14, 15f
supervisors 16
support 102
surveys 102
symposiums 171–2
synthesis strategy 153–4, 162–3
   making sense of findings 163
   meta-analysis 153–4
   narrative synthesis 153, 154, 162–3
systematic reviews 49, 139–67
   compared to other types of reviews 140
   conducting 141f, 143f, 158–62
   data extraction 160, 161f
   literature searches 158

   quality assessment of included studies 161–2
   study screening and selection 158–60
   design 144–57
   checking necessity of review 144
   data extraction plan 153
   ethics 157
   literature search strategy 149–51
   PICOS 146–7, 147f
   preliminary literature search for review question suitability 146
   quality assessment of included studies 154–5
   question development 145–7
   review protocol and pre-registration 145
   robustness 155–7
   selection criteria 147–9
   study screening and selection strategy 152–3, 152f
   synthesis strategy 153–4
   key stages 141f
   meta-analysis, with and without 140
   mixed 139–40
   necessity for 141–2
   planning and designing 141f
   planning and organizational skills 142–4
   qualitative 139–40
   quantitative 139–40
   register 144
   skills required 142–4
   synthesizing data 141f, 162–3
   teamwork skills 144
   transferable skills 167
   writing up 141f, 163–6
      Abstract 164
      Discussion 166
      Introduction 164–5
      Methods 165–6, 165f
      PRISMA statement/checklist 163–4, 164f
      Results 165f, 166
      structure and sections 164–6
      Title 164

T

t tests 77, 107
tables 137
target audience 185
team science 49
Teams 172

INDEX

teamwork skills 4, 6–7, 13, 23, 26*f*, 37*f*, 42, 51*f*
  correlational research 85, 86*f*
  qualitative research 128, 138*b*
  real world 197, 200
  systematic review 143*f*, 144, 167*b*
technical issues 27
technical skills *see* IT and technical skills
telephone interviews 128
templates, branded 172
testing of participants 69
thematic analysis *see* reflexive thematic analysis
thematic map/diagram 137
themes 117, 133
  development and review 132–3
theoretical approach 118–20, 121, 126, 134, 135
third reviewer 161
three Rs (recognize, reflect, relate) 2, 3*f*, 9, 10*b*, 18–19, 20*b*, 52, 52–3*b*, 55*f*
  correlational research 112*b*
  experimental research 83*b*
  presenting research 181*b*
  publishing research 193*b*
  qualitative research 116*f*, 137–8*b*
  real world 196–9, 205*b*
  recognize 196–7
  reflect 18, 20*b*, 31*b*, 197–8
  relate 198–9
  systematic review 143*f*, 167*b*
  time and self-management 36–7, 40, 41*f*, 42–3*f*
  working with a supervisor 23*f*, 26, 31*b*
three-way ANCOVA 63, 63*f*, 67
three-way design 57, 59–60, 62*f*, 68–9, 68*f*
three-way interactions 73, 78, 78*f*, 81*t*
time and self-management 32–43, 142, 148
  balancing tasks 38
  challenges, dealing with 39–41
  chunking tasks 38
  effective time and tasks management 35–8
  ethical research setting 38–9
  Gantt charts 33–5, 35*f*, 36*f*, 38
  in-depth understanding of project pre-planning 32–3

individual or group work 41–2
key skills 37*f*
motivation strategy 38
prevention better than cure 40
resilience 40–1
rewarding yourself 38
skills 144
stakeholders, consideration for 38–9
three Rs (recognize, reflect, relate) 36–7, 40, 41*f*, 42–3*f*
time limits 148
timelines 33–5, 34*f*
timelines and Gantt charts 33–5, 34*f*
title 79, 109, 134–5, 164
  slide 172
training 16
trait anxiety (fictional research) 96, 105, 107, 108
transferable skills 5, 5*f*, 9, 12, 18–19, 19*f*
  correlational methodology 112
  methodology 83
  presenting research 181*b*
  qualitative research 137
  real world 195, 196*f*
  systematic review 167
  working with a supervisor 20, 23, 29
transitioning from student life to employment 204–5
transparency 45, 45*f*, 48, 50, 126–7, 136, 140, 166
  see also open science
Transparency and Openness Promotion (TOP) guidelines 50
truncation 151
trustworthiness 7, 115, 125, 128
two-tailed (not directional) hypothesis 67, 72
two-way ANOVA 78
two-way design 57, 58–9, 60*f*, 62*f*, 68, 68*f*
two-way interactions 73, 76–8, 77*f*, 80–1, 81*f*
Type I error 48, 77
Type II error 47–8

U

unique identifying code 71
university career service 203–4
unstandardized beta value 92, 108

V

validity 66, 67, 97–9, 125, 160
  external 99
  internal 99
variability 57, 58*f*, 70
variables, types of 90
variance 57, 58, 75, 90, 96
  cake 93, 105
  experimental 61
  homogeneity 74–5
  sources of 93*f*
voluntary positions 3–4
vulnerable participants 6

W

ways of developing research projects 12–21
  academic strengths and interests influencing decisions 18
  group projects 12, 13–14, 13*f*
  independence and supervision 14–16, 15*f*
  individual projects 12–13, 13*f*
  key factors influencing decision-making 19–20
  personal experience and interests influencing decisions 16–17
  previous research experience 16
  research assistant projects 12, 13*f*, 14
  transferable skills 12, 18–19, 19*f*, 20
weaknesses 5, 7, 26–7
Web of Science 149, 150*f*, 151, 185
wildcards 151
withdrawal, right to 66
working style 36
workshops 171
writing up *see under* correlational research; experimental research; qualitative research; systematic reviews

X

X (previously Twitter) 192

Y

YouTube 180

Z

Zoom 172